Created and Directed by Hans Höfer

INSIGHT GUIDES
CHICAGO

Edited by Tim Harper
Principal Photography by Chuck Berman
Managing Editor: Martha Ellen Zenfell

Editorial Director: Brian Bell

HOUGHTON MIFFLIN COMPANY

APA PUBLICATIONS

CHICago

First Edition (Revised)
© 1995 APA PUBLICATIONS (HK) LTD
All Rights Reserved
Printed in Singapore by Höfer Press Pte Ltd

Distributed in the United States by:	Distributed in Canada by:	Distributed in the UK & Ireland by:	Worldwide distribution enquiries:
Houghton Mifflin Company	**Thomas Allen & Son**	**GeoCenter International UK Ltd**	**Höfer Communications Pte Ltd**
222 Berkeley Street	390 Steelcase Road East	The Viables Center, Harrow Way	38 Joo Koon Road
Boston, Massachusetts 02116-3764	Markham, Ontario L3R 1G2	Basingstoke, Hampshire RG22 4BJ	Singapore 2262
ISBN: 0-395-66318-0	ISBN: 0-395-66318-0	ISBN: 9-62421-133-7	ISBN: 9-62421-133-7

ABOUT THIS BOOK

Chicago has always been a city of very strong impressions. It is a classic American city, yet it remains distinctive among US metropolitan centers. *Insight Guide: Chicago* examines not only its physical and cultural aspects but also the many historical, social and economic factors that have made Chicago the unique place it is.

Chicago is also a writers' town. The broad shoulders that assembled this book span a wide variety of journalistic talent, from lifelong natives and devoted transplants to informed outsiders looking in. The thread linking these writers and photographers is their fascination with Chicago, both its good and bad sides, and an unyielding interest in the city's effect on the human condition.

The Big City

Project editor **Tim Harper** grew up 150 miles to the south, in Peoria, Illinois. To him Chicago was always the exciting, pulsing big city – of museums and shopping and baseball games in his early years and, later, of smoky clubs and ethnic restaurants and, yes, baseball games. Today, as a journalist and lawyer based in London, he still occasionally wears his "No Lights in Wrigley Field" T-shirt, a reminder of the ill-fated 1980s campaign to keep the Cubs from hosting night games. Harper did much of the work on this book during trips from London to the Midwest as he and his wife, Nancy Bobrowitz, ferried their two children to visits with grandparents in Brookfield, Wisconsin, and Peoria.

Martha Ellen Zenfell, editor-in-chief of Apa Publications' US Insight titles, monitored and guided the project from her base in Apa's London office. A native of the American South, Zenfell picked up many of the tricks of the travel-writing trade while working on European guides.

Chuck Berman, the principal photographer, is a veteran *Chicago Tribune* lensman known for his sharp attention to detail and his talent for composing feature photos with just the right touch of whimsy. His wife, **Barbara Brotman**, a *Tribune* writer, put together the chapters on the Magnificent Mile and the Black Sox baseball scandal. They live with their two children on the North Side.

Manuel Galvan, a *Chicago Tribune* executive and member of the John Dillinger Died for You Society, was this book's expert on Al Capone and other mobsters. Galvan, who became intimate with the city as he moved up through the ranks as a reporter, editor and member of the editorial board, also wrote the insider's look at nightlife and dining out in Chicago.

Tom Hardy, who analyzed Chicago's ever-windy political scene, is the political editor of the *Chicago Tribune*. As a South Sider – just like the Daleys and so many other Chicago mayors – he has grown up amid the rough and tumble of Chicago politics, yet is still able to appreciate just how the Chicago political scene is sometimes unusual, occasionally funny and always remarkable. His wife, **Pam Hardy**, assembled the information-packed "Travel Tips" section, and keeps the book up to date.

Tom McNamee, a native South Sider, now lives in Evanston, a leafy northern suburb, with his journalist wife Deborah Wood and their three children. He adapted his essay on Chicago history from his work as a reporter for the *Chicago Sun-Times*. McNamee, who

Harper

Zenfell

Berman

Brotman

Galvan

also wrote the section on the North Side, is co-host of a popular Saturday-morning talk show on Chicago radio, and co-author of *Streetwise Chicago*, a guide to every street in Chicago and how it got its name.

Don Hayner, McNamee's co-host on the radio program and co-author of *Streetwise in Chicago*, is another *Sun-Times* reporter. As a lifelong resident of Beverly, a quintessential South Side neighborhood, his story on the South Side underscores the divisions between the different sides of town, both in terms of geography and attitude. He and his wife Dawn, his toughest editor, have two sons.

Joseph Epstein, whose witty and perceptive essay, "A Hustlin' Town," looks at the people of Chicago, is the editor of *American Scholar* magazine. A lifelong Chicagoan who now lives in suburban Evanston, he is the author of several books, including the recent collection of essays *A Line Out for a Walk*.

Carol Jouzaitis, who once aspired to be a Chicago police officer but instead became a business reporter at the *Tribune*, profiled the city's financial district and its lakefront – her own personal work-ground and playground. Now covering higher education, she lives near Wrigley Field and sneaks off to as many afternoon games as she can.

Food and Travel

Stuart Silverman and his wife **Sondra Rosenberg**, freelance writers who often work together, shared a number of assignments for this book, including descriptions of the Loop, the West Side, Chicago shopping centers and the famous suburb Oak Park. Silverman emigrated from the East Coast as a college lecturer, but in recent years has combined food and travel writing with poetry and literary criticism. Rosenberg, a native of Austria, is a professor of humanities at Harold Washington College in Chicago. She also writes and broadcasts on the arts and travel.

Eileen Norris, who did double duty by looking at the rise and fall of the Playboy empire along with the rise and rise of the Oprah Winfrey empire, was born in Chicago and grew up on the South Side. She is a former *Chicago Tribune* reporter whose work has appeared in many major American magazines since she left to freelance in 1982.

Janet Neiman, who recounted some of Chicago's best-loved scandals and described its history of grass-roots liberal activism, is a Chicago freelance journalist who grew up in suburban Evanston and earned a graduate degree in urban studies from Loyola University. She writes for many local and national publications.

Lisa Goff, an editor for *Crain's Chicago Business*, relied on her considerable experience in writing about urban design to recap Chicago's famed architecture. She also wrote extensively on local real estate, economic development, retailing and politics during her years in Chicago. She is now based in New York City.

Fernando Jones is an up-and-coming bluesman and bluesologist. In the former role, he plays the guitar and harmonica with various groups around Chicago, including his own. In the latter role, his contributions to the "Chicago Blues" section of this book grew out of his self-published memoir, *I Was There When The Blues Was Red Hot*.

The text was proof-read and indexed by **Elizabeth Boleman-Herring,** and marshaled through a variety of Macintosh computers by **Jill Anderson**.

McNamee   *Hayner*   *Norris*   *Neiman*   *Goff*

CONTENTS

History

Features

Places

Maps

TRAVEL TIPS

THE CITY OF BROAD SHOULDERS

Chicago is a city of strength – of bold visions, deep emotions, pungent flavors and decisive actions. Small wonder it was immortalized as "the city of broad shoulders," that it boasts three of the world's five tallest buildings and that its traditional food specialties include various forms of protein-rich red meat.

Many people like to characterize Chicago as the most American of all the big cities in the United States. With little of the pretension of New York and even less of the glamour of Los Angeles, Chicago is a city that was born of and still fits its geography. From flat prairies and swampland, Chicago in a remarkably short time became a world trade center, but has never been regarded as particularly cosmopolitan. Its financial markets and commercial enterprises influence economies all over the globe, but Chicago hardly considers itself "international" in the manner of European capitals and even smaller US cities such as San Francisco and New Orleans.

Chicago is a big, brassy, blowzy town where people, including strangers, tell each other what's on their minds. And in no uncertain terms. Chicago is known for its tough guys, for the machine-gun mobsters of the past and for the hardball politicians and manic financial traders of recent years. Today, politics and sports – not necessarily in that order – are the main topics of conversation in most Chicago social circles. But visitors need not try to initiate discussions about either political situations or sporting events – or anything else – that doesn't have some direct bearing on Chicago. A better conversational tack is to examine how events in Chicago may affect the outside world. Unlike other cities, Chicago doesn't depend on or need the outside world; everything a person could want, from a great education to a great pizza, is homegrown in the heart of the Midwest.

Even Chicago's remarkable literary history, where the lines between journalism and literature are blurred as perhaps nowhere else, is of a robust, take-no-prisoners style. And the music that came from the South Side, now known the world over as the Chicago blues, is driven by the hard edge and fast pace of a note-bending electric guitar.

Chicago is a town that outsiders, especially other Americans, often take for granted. It's not until they begin to learn of its complexities, of its many offerings to those of all interests and tastes, that visitors start to appreciate just how special Chicago is – and how much Chicagoans already appreciate it.

Preceding pages: Downtown clock; tuned-in fan; Loop skyline; reflected glory; rising moon; brassy bird. **Left**, the Chicago River. **Following pages:** Chagall's *The America Windows*, Art Institute.

Jacques Marquette.

Two French explorers with very different reasons for being in the New World are given the credit for being the first Europeans to set eyes on what is now Chicago. Louis Jolliet was searching for gold. Father Jacques Marquette was out saving souls. Splashing about in the marshlands together in 1673, they formed Chicago's prototypical dynamic duo: the man of plunder and the man of prayer, the getter and the giver. They represented two strains of men who one day would build this contradictory city, who would nail it together in a greedy man's haste, jack it up out of a prehistoric muck and reshape it like soft putty after it had endured cholera, fire and financial collapse.

Meatpackers and merchants: Jolliet was the forefather who begat meatpacker barons and merchant princes and condominium kings. Marquette was the forefather who begat social workers and community organizers and spirited advocates for the street-curb poor. At worst, they worked at cross purposes, the men on the make trampling all. At best, they joined in common cause, cash and compassion working together. A pretty park, for example, can soothe men's souls – and increase a real estate agent's profits. These are the types who built Chicago, transforming marshland into Big Shoulders.

Chicago is, above all, an American city, a mid-continental Uncle Sam of gold coasts and slums, of babbling tongues, of punch clocks and blues and verve. It owes that verve to generations of strong backs, to its precious few visionaries and to a few scoundrels, too. Lovely on its lakefront, shabby on its back streets, like a rusting Chevy in the alley, Chicago is a cauldron bubbling with contrasts, like the nation itself. It both nurtures and corrupts. Chicago, America's City. Incorporated March 4, 1837.

Twelve thousand years ago, Lake Chicago, a larger version of today's Lake Michigan, covered much of what is now the Midwest. As the great glacial lake receded, it left

behind vast, waving prairies and a shoreline swamp. America's native people – the Indians who were Chicago's first immigrants – embraced the swampland. They called it Checagou or Checaguar – or something close. It meant "wild onion" or "skunk," apparently a reference to the smell of rotting marshland onions that permeated the entire area. The name implied – and still implies – great strength.

From the beginnings of human inhabita-

tion, the swamp was a place of action, a dealing and swapping ground. The Pottawattomies, traveling by canoe, traded furs and skins there. The swamp linked North America's two great waterways: the Mississippi to the southwest – via the Des Plaines and Illinois rivers – and the Great Lakes to the north and east. During spring rains, shallow-bottomed Indian canoes traversed the swamp, traveling about eight miles from the Des Plaines River to Lake Michigan for trading powwows.

Jolliet saw the big town coming. Paddling along, coasting past 10-foot-high prairie

Left, Marquette. **Right**, Pottawattomie chief.

grasses, he predicted to Marquette: "Here some day will be found one of the world's great cities." And a later explorer, Robert Cavalier, Sieur de La Salle, saw it, too. "This will be the gate of an empire," he said. "The typical man who will grow up here must be enterprising. Each day, as he rises, he will exclaim, 'I act, I move, I push.'"

America became a land where bustling, sophisticated cities and towns dotted the East Coast. Those cities' paved streets were lined with shops selling imported goods. People read newspapers every day and went to the doctor when they were sick or to the lawyer when they had a legal problem. Fami-

lies attended church together on Sunday.

Only a few hundred miles to the west, however, were farmers and trappers and hunters who literally lived off the land and might go weeks without seeing a neighbor. Many believed that the country was getting too crowded if they could see the smoke from the next farm. For what few supplies and little companionship they needed, these self-sufficient frontiersmen depended on the small, scattered settlements and trading posts. There they would swap their vegetables or skins culled from the local animals for food and luxury items that they didn't

grow or make for themselves at home.

Chicago was one such gathering place, growing from trading post to settlement to village to city largely because of a geographical location that allowed easy transport in all directions. Many of those who came to Chicago in the early days were not farmers or frontiersmen themselves. Some were misfits drawn by the prospect of fewer social and legal constraints in what was at that time the "Wild West." Many were dreamers who believed the West was going to grow dramatically, and then went west themselves to realize those prophecies. They came to Chicago to be big fish in a little pond, and then to make the pond bigger.

The fort: It was a black man who led the way. Jean Baptiste Point DuSable, the tall French-speaking son of a Quebec merchant and a black slave, established a trading post in 1779 on the north bank of the Chicago River at what is now Michigan Avenue. He erected Chicago's first permanent house. Later, he sold the house to another trader, John Kinzie.

Meanwhile, the white man's government began to force out the red man – in the name of progress, of course. General "Mad Anthony" Wayne in 1795 overran the Indians and forced the Pottawattomie tribe to cede huge tracts of Midwestern land, including "six miles square at the mouth of the Chickago River." It was prime real estate even then, a speculator's dream as swamps and forestland turned almost overnight into commercial property. The Indians, who had no concept of "owning" the land, were pushed out as white men sold each other pieces of paper they called "titles." The white man thus entitled himself to control and own the land.

Blue-coated US soldiers arrived from Detroit. In 1803, they built Fort Dearborn at what is now Lower Wacker and Michigan. Ordered to evacuate Fort Dearborn during the War of 1812 against the British, settlers and soldiers fleeing the fort were ambushed by Indians allied with the British. Fifty-two men, women and children from the fort were slain in what is now known as the Fort Dearborn Massacre. But the pioneering deluge was checked only briefly. The soldiers returned, Fort Dearborn was rebuilt, and 5,000 Pottawattomies were booted out for good. Scattered like bungalow dwellers in the path of a coming expressway, some Indians were relocated or drifted to government reservations, often hundreds of miles away; others tried to eke out a living on the edge of the white world, doing menial labor. A few Indian families and small groups became poor wanderers, seeking but never finding a place where they could carry on their traditional way of life. No matter what the Indians tried, however, Pottawattomie children and grandchildren became more and more absorbed into the white world. In effect, after

less a town than a real estate lottery. A chunk of Lake Street property bought for $300 in 1833 – the year Chicago was incorporated as a village – was sold one year later for $60,000.

New wagons rolled in daily. Settlers from the East swelled the population from 50 in 1830 to 4,170 in 1837. Buoyed by immigrants from Ireland and Germany, within 30 years the population had topped 40,000. Traders and merchants came. So did saloon keepers and prostitutes. As with Jolliet, the lure was money. An early mayor, newspaper publisher "Long John" Wentworth, recalled in the 1880s: "We had people from almost

the Fort Dearborn Massacre the traditional Pottawattomie tribe ceased to function as it had for generations.

Boom town: Things happened fast after that. In 1825, the Erie Canal was opened, creating a new water route between Chicago and the East to transport furs, grain, lumber and livestock. The Illinois Legislature plotted a course for the Illinois-Michigan Canal that would connect Lake Michigan and the Mississippi. Federal dollars paid for dredging a harbor. Chicago boomed, though it was

Left, DuSable. **Right**, Fort Dearborn, 1803.

every clime, and almost every opinion. We had Jews and Christians, Protestants, Catholics and infidels. Among Protestants there were Calvinists and Armenians. Nearly every language was represented. Some people had seen much of the world, and some very little."

Everything was new. Anything was possible. Audacious men blustered like the prairie winds. On March 4, 1837, in Vandalia, the southern Illinois community that was later replaced by Springfield as the state capital, the Legislature approved a charter that formally recognized Chicago, previously a village, as a city. The tallest building was two stories. Nobody had a basement. Nobody had gas. Nobody had a paved street.

In New York, the *Chicago American* reported that day, picketers were protesting against the price of bread. In Washington, contributions were being accepted for the construction of the Washington National Monument. Out in the brand-new city of Chicago, meanwhile, local businessmen were advertising 4,000 pounds of log chains, bushels of garden seed, Brandreth Vegetable Pills ("known to benefit persons of a bilious or costive habit of body") and even encouraging migration to smaller Midwestern

town. He was part Jolliet and part Marquette, part money man and part civic man, a getter and a giver. In the course of piling up his fortune, he built the city's first drawbridge and first railroad – now called the Chicago & North Western.

Aspirations and action: Chicago's early history is replete with the doings of men with huge egos and boundless ambition. They left personal imprints (and sometimes skid marks) on an impressionable city. When "Long John" Wentworth, elected mayor in 1857, tired of the dogfights and sex shows in the red-light district, he personally led a posse of 30 cops and hundreds of citizens on

towns ("Albion – One of the Healthiest Spots in Western America").

Two months later, in an election marred by brawls, a former New York state legislator named William B. Ogden defeated the early settler, John Kinzie, to become Chicago's first mayor. Ogden first stomped into town in the 1830s, steaming mad because a relative had purchased, sight unseen, a muddy tract along State Street for $100,000. Ogden wanted to dump the land and get on home. But after selling a third of the land for $100,000, he changed his mind. He stuck around. He got rich. Ogden was made for this

a clean-up crusade. They demolished every disreputable house.

When Chicagoans tired of slopping around in the mud, a sanitation engineer named Ellis Sylvester Chesbrough proposed raising the level of the entire city. Sidewalks were promptly boosted up, turning ground floors into basements. George Pullman, the railroad man, then used armies of workmen to jack up the buildings themselves. And when Chicagoans tired of contracting cholera and dysentery from foul shoreline drinking water, city workers dug a two-mile tunnel out into the lake to tap clean water. For good measure, Chicago amazed the world in 1900 by making the Chicago River run backward. That feat, aimed at using fresh lake water to flush away the polluted, disease-carrying riverflow, was an engineering marvel of locks and channels that is still often studied today.

Chicago was leaving the provinces behind and emerging as America's crossroads. By 1856, Chicago was the hub of 10 railroad trunk lines. Raw materials brought by wagon, barge, ship and train were turned into products to build and feed the country – lumber from nearby forests, iron ore from Minnesota, livestock and produce from

in evidence not only on Chicago hotels and department stores but in branches scattered across America's retail landscape, included Marshall Field, William Wieboldt, Potter Palmer, Samuel Carson and John Pirie. And, if the soul of Marquette was sometimes conspicuously absent, if the rascals sold spoiled beef and defective weapons to the Union Army, if the political booster boys seemed all too forgiving of City Hall corruption and 400 brothels – well, hell, to quote a future alderman, "Hinky Dink" Kenna: "Chicago ain't no sissy town."

Up in flames: Then came the fire. The Great Chicago Fire of 1871 started, according to

some of the richest farmland in the world. Chicago led the world in the transportation of cattle, grain and lumber. Grain elevators, jabbing the skyline, were the Sears Towers of the day.

As surely as one clever manufacturer knew how to turn out a product, someone else knew how to sell it. The mail-order giants Sears, Roebuck & Co. and Montgomery Ward & Co. were born in Chicago. Legendary merchants, whose names are still

Left, displaced Indians, *circa* 1907. **Right**, the new Chicagoans, *circa* 1907.

the legend, on October 8 in Mrs O'Leary's barn, now the site of the Chicago Fire Department Training Academy. O'Leary's cow got the rap; it kicked a lantern, they said. The fire spread fast, an eyewitness describing it as "a vast ocean of flames, sweeping in mile-long billows and breakers over the doomed city." Three hundred people were killed; 100,000 were left homeless; 18,000 buildings were destroyed. Chicago's first city was in ashes.

So they built a second: this time a sturdier town of fireproof brick. Two days after the fire, W.D. Kerfoot, a spunky real estate agent, posted a sign on a shack: "All gone but wife, children and energy." Money was there to be made. No time to mourn. Chicago warn't no sissy town.

A civic ripening emerged out of the great fire's ashes. Architects, sensing unlimited opportunity, flocked to Chicago. They endowed the city with a touch of New World class, a skyline of state-of-the-art office buildings. Many of the post-fire classics, particularly those in the range of 14 to 18 stories high along South Dearborn Street, remain the relatively earthbound bulwarks of the steel-frame construction process that led to today's skyscrapers. Because it was

and-glass modernism, nailed it down. Helmut Jahn, iconoclastic creator of the rolling Xerox building and the hotly disputed State of Illinois Center, helped ensure its strength today.

Cultural birth: By 1890, Chicago was struggling out of an era of cut-throat Social Darwinism into an age of social reform. In the City Council, the avaricious "Gray Wolves," the bribery-wizened councilmen who picked over the bones of every public spending project for kickbacks ranging from jobs for relatives to cash for themselves, still divvied up the boodle. But more civic-minded Chicagoans demanded social jus-

continuing to grow so quickly as an industrial and commercial center, downtown Chicago needed big buildings, and ambitious architects with powerful new designs were given free reign to build toward the clouds. Three world masters led the charge: John Root, designer of the graceful Rookery and Monadnock buildings; Louis Sullivan, designer of the efficient Auditorium and Carson Pirie Scott buildings; and Sullivan's peerless protégé, Frank Lloyd Wright. Brilliant innovators, they established Chicago's tradition of architectural leadership. Mies van der Rohe, the father of unadorned steel-

tice, a bit of high culture, and such public amenities as spacious parks and an uncluttered lakefront. The 1890s saw the establishment of the Art Institute, stocked with Dutch Masters' paintings; the University of Chicago, founded with Rockefeller money on Marshall Field real estate; the Museum of Science and Industry, and the Columbian Exposition of 1893, a fabulously successful world's fair that introduced the Ferris wheel and the "shake" dancer Little Egypt. Her "exotic" bumps and grinds were undoubtedly modest by today's standards, but Little Egypt's act nonetheless drew condemnation from moralizing newspaper editors and clergymen who warned that she was instilling evil lust in the hearts and minds of her many male fans.

The Chicago Symphony Orchestra made its debut, although the conductor, Theodore Thomas, recruited from the New York Philharmonic, dared not offer many symphonies at first. Chicago's musical taste was too undeveloped; "light music" had to suffice as culture. Asked why he bothered to settle in Chicago at all, he explained: "I would go to hell if they would give me a permanent orchestra." Thomas was one of those rare men of scope and vision who made Chicago

There was the architect Daniel H. Burnham, who enshrined the principle of a pristine lakefront in his famous city plan of 1909. No other plan has so influenced Chicago's growth. The Burnham Plan of 1909 resulted in the creation of a string of lakefront parks and beaches, including Jackson Park and Washington Park; the acquisition of a green belt of forest preserves on the city's periphery; the construction of Chicago's main post office, and the siting of the Eisenhower Expressway. Still, there was no pleasing everybody. An important councilman, Council Gray Wolf, growled: "The lakefront ain't no place for a park."

what it is today. There were also others.

There was A. Montgomery Ward, a stoical money man in the Jolliet mold who revealed the heart of a Marquette when he launched his 13-year court battle to save Grant Park from public buildings. City Hall, the press and the business community ganged up on the merchant, calling him an "obstructionist." But Ward legally established the principle that Chicago's entire lakefront should be preserved "forever open, clear and free."

Left, the Opera House after the fire, 1871. **Right**, Burnham's 1909 Plan for Chicago.

In many ways, Chicago's renowned social consciousness was a reaction against the city's legendary greed. In this town of extremes, with its unofficial "Where's mine?" motto, it made sense for the backlash against rampant capitalism to be a particularly selfless, far-reaching brand of humanitarianism.

Civic conscience: Social reform by 1890 was, in part, a survival tactic. Chicago seethed with labor unrest, and the city became an incubator for a national organized labor movement, then in its infancy. The class warfare, fueled by the loose alliance of young unions that were committed to better working and living conditions for all laborers, spooked Prairie Avenue's Millionaires' Row. In the 1880s and 1890s, a nationwide campaign for the eight-hour day and the minimum wage triggered bloody confrontations. Thirteen men were killed in Chicago during one summer week. The National Guard was called out to quell a workers' riot outside Pullman's railcar plant. Seven policemen were killed in the Haymarket Riot of 1886. No one saw who threw the bomb, but four anarchists went to the gallows.

Pressures for social reform came from other quarters. From an emerging profes-tending to the needs of immigrants at Blue Island and Halsted, became a model for the nation. Through the efforts of committed staff and concerned volunteers, it fought for an end to child labor, for factory inspections and a minimum wage. Jane Addams was some kind of crazy lady, according to the mavens of La Salle Street, Chicago's Wall Street – but, they had to admit, she was effective. Addams and her followers at Hull House and other settlement houses established throughout Chicago provided fresh clean milk for babies, taught immigrants English and set up day care centers for the children of working mothers. They provided

sional class stepped rebellious giants – social worker Jane Addams, attorney Clarence Darrow and muckraking journalist Upton Sinclair. Addams, a proper young woman from Rockford, walked among the shabby sweatshops and immigrant tenements on the city's Near West Side and decided to devote her life to helping the people there. Chicago's population had reached 1 million by 1890, including hundreds of thousands of Irish, Italian and Eastern European immigrants living in squalor within a whiff of the stockyards.

Addams' Hull House, a settlement house a range of care and comfort that became a model for inner-city social welfare programs, from prescribing balanced diets for young families to describing how to open a bank account, enroll children in school or apply for a better job. These early social workers helped instill a sense of self-esteem and hope in an exploited, downtrodden class of menial laborers.

Others have followed in Addams' footsteps. In the 1950s and 1960s, Saul Alinsky, the patriarch of militant community organizers, fought City Hall with his Back of the Yards Council and the Woodlawn Organization. In the 1980s and into the 1990s, Douglas Dobmeyer, president of the Chicago Coalition of the Homeless, led ragged demonstrations outside the yuppie high-rises that have displaced the Skid Row poor.

Upton Sinclair was crazier still. In *The Jungle*, his muckraking exposé of the stockyards, he wrote of "the secret rooms where the spoiled meats went to be doctored." He told of workmen whose feet were eaten away by acids in the fertilizer rooms. And he repeated dark tales of other workers who had fallen into steaming vats, and gone out to the world as pure beef lard. Federal investigators checked out the allegations. All of these

hearing from friends and relatives, earlier immigrants, about how easy it was to get a high-paying job, and about how wealthy Chicago was. What the immigrants didn't find out until they arrived was how hard they had to work, often in disgusting conditions; how much daily living cost, and how quickly those seemingly high wages disappeared; and how Chicago's vast wealth was accumulated and hoarded by a relative few who profited from the backbreaking labor of the new arrivals.

The Back of the Yards was a ghetto. Its "inmates" never escaped from the stink of animal manure, slaughterhouses and render-

things are pretty much true, they said.

But there was much more to the stockyards than the horrible sanitary and working conditions. There were the living conditions, often no less unsanitary. Families, many of them immigrants from Europe, were crowded into narrow wooden rowhouses in the neighborhood known as the Back of the Yards. Many of the workers were rural Europeans who spoke little or no English. Many were unfamiliar with living in America after

Left, back of the Union Stock Yard houses. **Right**, Union Stock Yard, 1866.

ing plants. In hopes of raising enough money to escape, or merely to meet the rents charged for their substandard housing, often owned by the companies using the stockyards, men and women worked long hours, sometimes at two jobs. They often kept their children out of school in order to put them to work, too, so that the whole family might have enough money to move to a new neighborhood and find better jobs. These were the people, whose children worked long hours and didn't have the ways or means to keep their babies healthy, whom social reformers tried to help.

After World War I, an influx of blacks from the Southern states provided a new source of cheap labor to be exploited by the stockyards. Almost overnight, much of Chicago's South Side became predominantly black neighborhoods.

In its peak year of 1924, the Union Stock Yard, a square mile of land down by Canaryville, employed over 30,000 workers and received more than 18.6 million head of cattle and calves, sheep and hogs. But in 1971 the big yard closed. Omaha and Iowa could cut a pork roast cheaper.

Sinclair was in the vanguard of the Chicago literary movement in the years before tunes ensconced themselves on the North Shore, crooked politicians and bootleggers plundered the city. The handful of social reformers were too focused on caring for deprived individuals to worry about the corruption of an entire political system, and they would probably have been no match for men with machine guns and briefcases anyway. In truth, most of the population didn't care about the corruption and booze smuggling – after all, anyone who made the right connections could always be assured of an easy job during the day and a hard drink at night. So the bootleggers dueled it out and more than 400 gangsters were killed over five years,

the Great Depression. Other notables included Carl Sandburg, the poet who wrote so eloquently of the city; Theodore Dreiser, chronicler of big-city sins and small-town waifs, and Ben Hecht, the ex-newsman who told Broadway a secret: Chicago loves its rogues as much as its squares – sometimes more. Writing a bit later were James T. Farrell, Nelson Algren, Richard Wright and Saul Bellow.

Machine guns, politics: After World War I, Chicago's focus of power shifted from industrialists to politicans. While heirs to Chicago's great retailing and meatpacking for-

including seven in the 1929 St Valentine's Day Massacre.

Bestriding the city during the Prohibition years – from 1920 to 1933 when a constitutional amendment outlawed alcoholic beverages of any sort throughout the United States – was that colossus of crime, Al Capone. Like many Chicagoans, he was an immigrant, born in Naples in 1899.

A one-time speakeasy bouncer who graduated to running houses of prostitution, Capone built a vast bootlegging empire that included importing real whisky from Canada and operating his own beer breweries right in the middle of Chicago. To keep his operations going, he made the bribery of officials at every level, from City Hall to cops on the beat, an everyday fact of life that still plagues Chicago.

Capone, whose business card identified him as a "Second-hand Furniture Dealer," was short and pot-bellied and not particularly physically imposing. But Capone was nicknamed Scarface for the parallel reminders of a knifing on his cheek, and he was a crudely brilliant and cunningly brutal organizer who ruled through a combination of fear and rewards, stick and carrot. Those who did what he wanted could get rich quickly.

year: $105 million in 1927, when he was 28 years old.

Chicago in general boomed during the Roaring Twenties. Fortunes were made in the rising stock market. More big buildings went up. Flappers danced on speakeasy tables. Legal nightlife sparkled with dozens of vaudeville houses and legitimate theaters that featured both local groups and touring professional troupes. Most people tolerated crime as a part of everyday life, as long as it wasn't one of their relatives or friends who was cut down in the latest careless crossfire among rival hoodlums.

Capone was finally brought down by a

 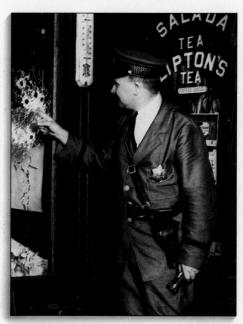

Those who refused requests could get dead even more quickly.

He often made his points in a most dramatic way, sending out carloads of gunmen with nonmusical violin cases or interrupting a black-tie banquet to kill a fellow diner, a disloyal lieutenant, with repeated blows to the back of the head with a baseball bat. Capone is listed in the *Guinness Book of Records* for the highest gross income ever accumulated by a private citizen in a single

Left, Al "Scarface" Capone, 1931 mug shot. **Right**, officers survey gangland carnage.

group of federal agents, led by Eliot Ness and known as the Untouchables for their refusal to take bribes. Unable to pin murder or even bootlegging directly on the crafty Capone, Ness and his men instead went after the gangster for failing to pay taxes on his millions in illicit gain. Capone was convicted and went to prison. He died in 1947, quietly, in bed, of syphilis.

But Capone didn't invent political corruption in Chicago. Back in 1837, on the very day Chicago voted to become a city, wagonloads of non-resident Irish canal diggers, technically ineligible to vote, were lugged to the convention hall to cast their ballots. Consider just two stealing mayors. When Fred A. Busse died, he left behind a safe-deposit box full of stock in a company that sold the city its manhole covers. And when Prohibition-era Mayor William Thompson died, he left behind safe-deposit boxes containing $1,578,000 in cash, stocks, bonds and certificates. No one knows exactly how the mayor got so rich, or where that money came from. However, Al Capone always liked Thompson, to the point of keeping Big Bill's picture on his office wall.

Tony Cermak, the mayor who died stopping a bullet meant for President Franklin D.

Roosevelt, dreamed up the political machine. Running as a Democrat against Thompson in the mayoral campaign of 1931, Cermak pieced together the first "balanced" party ticket – a Pole here, a German there, an Irishman here and there – and swept the white ethnic voting bloc. Only the blacks, still loyal to the party of Lincoln and Emancipation, backed Thompson. No surprise there: Chicago always has been a divided town – black here, white there, blood-red too often in between.

During the Civil War (1861–65), Irish canal diggers cheered Confederate victories.

To celebrate, they poured out of Archer Avenue saloons and chased down blacks. In 1919, a black boy drifted into a white swimming area and was drowned when a white man on shore hit him with a stone. The ensuing riots left 37 more dead. "The slums take their revenge," Carl Sandburg wrote. It would be fire the next time. In 1968, Dr Martin Luther King Jr was shot in Memphis and America's cities exploded. Chicago's West Side burned.

In the 1930s, the Great Depression hit hard. In Chicago, out-of-work men and women marched in protest down State Street. Businessmen cried. One of the richest, Sam Insull, who made a billion dollars from his power and light companies, lost it all and fled to London, where he died penniless. And yet, weak-kneed Chicago toddled along still. The city threw another world's fair in 1933, a Century of Progress, and gave the world another sexy sensation, Sally Rand. Like Little Egypt at the Columbian Exposition 40 years earlier, Sally Rand was an exotic dancer whose titillating act drew mobs of men and made her notorious. Unlike Little Egypt, however, Sally Rand went on stage nude except for large stage props, usually fans but sometimes feather boas or even a large ball, that she maneuvered enticingly to provide provocative glimpses of bare flesh while avoiding "total revelation."

Their Daley bread: World War II jerked the nation out of its doldrums. Chicago worked, all out – grunted, groaned and sweated. What with all the bustle, nobody paid much notice when, in 1942, a team of physicists at the University of Chicago – an historically prestigious institution that claims more Nobel Prize winners than any other university in the world – built the first nuclear reactor. The scientists, working under the direction of Italian-American physicist Enrico Fermi in a grim basement beneath the university athletic stadium, toiled in secret through the early part of World War II. They rarely spoke of the practical applications of their work. In 1942, their "atomic pile," as they called it, created the first controlled nuclear chain reaction, and with it the technology for both nuclear power and the bomb.

By the 1950s, Chicago was more than 100

years old. It had moved through eras of settlement, furious growth, depression and war. One last period remained: the Era of Daley. Richard J. Daley. "Da Boss." He ruled Chicago for 21 years. Daley was a man far more complicated than any Jolliet or Marquette caricature. He was a getter, yes, but he sought power, not money. He was a giver, yes, but he sometimes gave you what you didn't want. He loved the city and showed his love in a way all his own – take it or leave it. Like the city's skyscrapers, Mayor Daley was a monument on the landscape, and, despite his excesses, his legacy has proven as durable as reinforced concrete.

He bulldozed whole communities, always against their wills, for expressways and plazas and universities. He plowed old ghettos and built segregating walls of high-rise public housing. Daley ran expressways toward the Loop, the downtown area circumscribed by the city's elevated trains. The business center thrived. But, by that time, the Loop's once-glittering nightlife was history. Daley played kingmaker to a president, withholding the 1960 Chicago vote to see how the election was going and then delivering the winning margin to John F. Kennedy. In 1968, at the height of the Vietnam conflict, Daley's cops beat up anti-war protesters outside the Conrad Hilton Hotel during the Democratic National Convention. "The whole world is watching," demonstrators chanted. Chicago hasn't had a big political convention since.

Back to the future: So what of Chicago today? A city that stands as a monument to those who first passed through – Jolliet and Marquette, the getter and the giver. More Gold Coast. More ghetto. More growth. More decay. Post-industrial Chicago is shuffling along, learning to compete again in a service-oriented economy. Businesses and people have followed the expressways into the suburbs, trading bad schools and racial strife for green lawns and safer streets. Steel mills are rusting and stock yards closed.

But where there is doubt, there is hope.

Left, Sally Rand has a ball. **Right,** Nobel laureate Saul Bellow. **Following pages:** Dearborn and Randolph Streets, 1909.

Chicago theater, all but dormant since the heyday of the 1920s, struts again. Old Loop railyards are new office buildings. Midway, once an aviation ghost town, roars again. New immigrant groups from the Far East, the Asian subcontinent, the Caribbean and elsewhere give old neighborhoods new life. School drop-out rates soar, but innovative schools churn out top-class scholars. The old political machine is losing people and power, and the long-oppressed black minority is coming into its own.

A black man, the late Harold Washington, became mayor and built his own version of the Chicago machine in the 1980s, paving

the way for the 1990s streamlined political framework of "Richie" Daley, the son of Da Boss, who won the mayor's office and claimed what many stalwarts believed was his birthright. Saul Bellow, Chicago's Nobel laureate in literature, often commented on Chicago's history: "Cycles of prosperity and desolation... risings and fallings, so much death, rebirth, metamorphosis, so many tribal migrations."

Chicago is still a town of genius and guts and verve. And it still ain't a sissy town. Jolliet just might love it. Marquette might like it, too.

DECISIVE DATES

BC: Lake Chicago, which covered much of what is now the American Midwest, receded with the glaciers, leaving swamps separating the vast prairies and what is now Lake Michigan.

Pre-1800: Native Americans, the Pottawattomie Indians, used the swampland linking the Great Lakes and the Mississippi River as a trading area. They called it "Checagou" in reference to the stink of rotting wild onions.

1673: Jolliet, a gold-seeking explorer, and Marquette, a Jesuit priest, canoed together into the marshland that would become Chicago.

1779: Jean Baptiste Point DuSable, son of a black slave and a Quebec merchant, established a trading post on the north bank of the Chicago River, located at what is now Michigan Avenue.

1795: General "Mad Anthony" Wayne led troops that overran the Indians and forced them to give up tribal lands, including much of what is now downtown Chicago.

1803: Federal soldiers built Fort Dearborn at the location known today as Lower Wacker and Michigan Avenue.

1812: In an Indian insurrection, 52 men, women and children at the fort were slain in what came to be called the Fort Dearborn Massacre. Troop reinforcements soon put down the uprising and also rebuilt the fort.

1825: The Erie Canal opened, creating a new water route for shipping between Chicago and the East Coast.

1831: First bridge was erected over the Chicago River, linking the North and South sides of town.

1833: During the population and property boom, a downtown plot that had sold for $300 in the previous year was resold for $60,000.

1837: With a population that had grown to 4,170 from a mere 50 only seven years before, Chicago was incorporated as a city. William B. Ogden won the election as Chicago's first mayor.

1848: A group of businessmen formed the Chicago Board of Trade, the world's oldest and largest futures exchange, and launched Chicago as the world center for commodities trading.

1871: The Great Chicago Fire, reputedly begun in Mrs O'Leary's barn when her cow kicked over a lantern, killed 300, left 100,000 homeless and destroyed 18,000 buildings.

1886: Years of discontent among workers, including a riot outside the Pullman plant, culminated in the bombing deaths of seven policemen in the Haymarket Riot. Four anarchists were hanged for the bombing.

1889: Frank Lloyd Wright, the architect, built his much-admired Home and Studio on Chicago Avenue in suburban Oak Park.

1889: Jane Addams, a volunteer social worker, founded Hull House and began the welfare movement that was based on "settlement houses" serving poor communities.

1890: Chicago's population, heavily bolstered by European immigration, passed one million.

1892: The University of Chicago was founded.

1893: The Columbian Exposition was a world's fair that drew the nation's attention, gave Chicago its "Windy City" nickname because of pre-fair boasting, introduced the Ferris wheel and made the exotic dancer Little Egypt both famous and infamous.

1900: Engineers completed a massive project using a series of locks and channels to make the Chicago River reverse its flow so that river waste would no longer run into Lake Michigan.

1905: Wright revealed plans for his architectural masterpiece, Unity Temple, which opened four years later, also in suburban Oak Park.

1906: Upton Sinclair, a crusading journalist, caused a national uproar with his book *The Jungle*, an exposé of unsanitary conditions and cruel labor policies in the stockyards.

1909: Daniel H. Burnham, the architect, unveiled a city plan that called for preservation of the lakefront for public recreation and culture.

1919: After the drowning of a black boy on a public beach, race riots left 38 dead.

1919: The Chicago White Sox, favored to win baseball's World Series, lost. Eight players, including star slugger Joe Jackson, were subsequently banned from the sport for accepting bribes from gamblers to lose.

1920: The Michigan Avenue Bridge opened.

1924: The Union Stock Yard, employing more than 30,000 workers, received more than 18.6 million head of cattle, calves, sheep and hogs.

1929: The seven gangsters killed in the St Valentine's Day Massacre were among more than 400 mobsters eliminated during a five-year period.

1929: The Wall Street stock market crash sent Chicago plummeting into the Great Depression.

1931: Tony Cermak put together the first ethnically "balanced" ticket and laid the groundwork for Chicago's Democratic political machine.

1931: Crime boss Al "Scarface" Capone, after amassing gangland earnings of more than $100 million a year, was convicted of federal income tax evasion and sentenced to eight years in prison.

1933: Despite the Depression, Chicago staged the Century of Progress world's fair, introducing another sexy sensation, fan dancer Sally Rand.

1934: John Dillinger, the bank robber, was gunned down outside the Biograph Theatre by federal agents tipped off by the Lady in Red, the gangster's moll.

1942: As part of the Manhattan Project, a group of physicists achieved the first nuclear chain reaction, providing the technology for nuclear bombs and power.

1947: Capone died of syphilis.

1951: Nelson Algren, winner of the first National Book Award for fiction the previous year for his novel *The Man With the Golden Arm*, published the acclaimed prose poem *Chicago: City on the Make.*

1952: Hugh Hefner, circulation director of *Children's Activities* magazine, borrowed $1,600 to start a new publication called *Playboy.*

1955: Richard J. Daley, a.k.a. "Hizzoner" and "Da Boss," was elected mayor.

1960: Mayor Daley's "late" returns swung the presidential election away from Richard Nixon to John F. Kennedy.

1960: Saul Alinsky, a community organizer, formed the Woodlawn Organization, a grass-roots group that became a focal point for the Chicago civil rights movement.

1966: The Rev. Martin Luther King Jr founded the

Left, "Shoeless" Joe Jackson, 1919. **Right**, Mayor Richard J. Daley, 1975.

Chicago Freedom Movement, which spawned Operation Breadbasket and PUSH, the groups that gave the Rev. Jesse Jackson his national platform.

1968: Divisions in US society over the Vietnam War burst into street violence in what investigators, criticizing Daley and the Chicago police, later called a "police riot" against young demonstrators at the Democratic National Convention.

1969: The Chicago Seven conspiracy trial, which brought demonstrators from the Democratic Convention to court, riveted the nation's attention, along with the "Days of Rage" campaign by militant antiwar factions.

1971: Undercut by competition from smaller Midwestern cities, the Union Stock Yard closed.

1972: The Chicago Mercantile Exchange, begun in 1919 as a tiny butter and egg market, pioneered the financial futures markets.

1974: The world's tallest office building, the 110-story Sears Tower, was opened downtown.

1976: Chicagoan Saul Bellow won the Nobel Prize for Literature.

1976: After 21 tumultuous years, Mayor Daley died in office.

1979: Jane Byrne, having waged a strong "anti-machine" campaign, won the mayoral race against Michael Bilandic, Daley's successor, who was blamed for his inability to clear the streets during the winter's blizzards.

1987: Harold Washington, Chicago's first black mayor, died after four years in office.

1989: Despite decades of opposition, the Chicago Tribune Co., owners of the Cubs, installed lights at Wrigley Field and the baseball team played its first night games at home.

1989: Richard M. Daley, the son of Richard J. Daley, defeated Washington's successor, Eugene Sawyer, as well as several other candidates in a special mayoral election.

1989: Jesse Jackson removed his Rainbow Coalition headquarters and his presidential aspirations to a new home in Washington, DC.

1991: Mayor Daley, re-elected, vowed to fight crime and ease tension as the white population decreased while blacks and Hispanics increased.

1992: Carol Mosely Braun was the first black woman elected to the U.S. Senate.

1993: The Chicago Bulls won the NBA Basketball Championship for the third year in a row.

In Chicago, the Windy City, the prevailing political breezes come from the fifth-floor City Hall office of the mayor. Blowing through the glass and limestone office canyons of LaSalle Street and the Loop, up along the lakefront and into the neighborhoods, they shape and define Chicago's political character in the mayor's likeness – whoever happens to be the mayor at that particular moment.

Chicago's political winds can, depending on the given mayor, flatten the 50-member City Council like a field of wheat lying in the path of a Midwestern summer storm, or puff up the ambitions of a would-be foe like the spinnaker of a yacht plying Lake Michigan before a zephyr.

Presidents, governors, congressmen and every political wanna-be from the smallest on up have been well advised not to sally far into precincts from Rogers Park to Beverly without first lofting a finger toward City Hall to gauge wind velocity and direction, lest they end up turned as inside-out as an umbrella on State Street in April.

This city of 1.5 million registered voters – a solid three-fourths of them inclined to vote Democratic in major elections – has perhaps the most famous (or infamous depending on one's point of view) reputation for politics of any major US city. And mayors have always been at the center.

Daley duties: Richard J. Daley was the mayor most closely identified with the city. Elected to a record six terms, he died in office after serving 21 consecutive years and pulling the levers of the nation's last partisan political machine.

He also served as Cook County Democratic Party chairman – the only mayor ever to hold both posts at the same time – and handpicked candidates for office. Thus he saw to it that the Machine, fueled by some 40,000 city jobs he controlled and 20,000 more he influenced, churned out sure-bet

Democratic pluralities every time. With an accountant's precision, Daley kept tabs on party loyalty and used jobs as a means of rewarding friends and punishing enemies. During Daley's regime, the local political lexicon became salted with terms such as "clout" and "Boss." Cynical slogans such as "Vote early and vote often," became popular clichés for how the Machine succeeded, but the mayor's favorite maxim was "Good politics makes good government." Pithy

advice along the lines of "Don't make no waves, don't back no losers," succinctly stated the Machine philosophy.

Daley's accomplishments, however, were not simply raw political power. In the tradition of Chicago's most successful mayors, he was a master builder and the business community loved him. "The City that Works" was coined under Daley as the local motto that Chicago mayors have clung to ever since.

After Daley died in 1976, there were five mayors in 12 years. But the Daley name remained linked with the office in voters'

Left, "Hizzoner Da Mare." **Right**, William B. Ogden, the first mayor.

minds, so much so that his son, Richard M. Daley – also known as Richard II or simply Richie – was elected mayor in 1989.

Punchy quotes: Until landmark federal court rulings curtailed the use of partisan patronage hiring, politics was as avidly participatory in Chicago as playing 16-inch softball, and it continues to rank with Chicago's professional sports franchises as a top spectator activity.

People identify Chicago more with gangsterism than with deep-dish pizza, and so too are they more apt to remember its punch-in-the-nose style of politics than its renowned symphony. It is difficult to know

exactly which piece of the legacy is most responsible for Chicago's hurly-burly political reputation.

As for punches in the nose, Chicago politics was typified earlier this century when William Hale Thompson, a three-term mayor, boasted that he would like to sock the King of England in the snoot. While Thompson's comment was reviled by most of the civilized world, Chicagoans laughed it off as a stunt to attract Irish voters and reaffirm the city's "leave us alone" world view. Thompson, who consorted with Al Capone and died with $1.4 million stuffed

into safety-deposit boxes, was one in a long line of the larger-than-life characters that Chicagoans are accustomed to having for their mayors.

Another memorable comment came from alderman and saloon keeper Mathias "Paddy" Bauler when Daley was first elected in 1955: "Chicago ain't ready for reform." In 1968, when his police and the military clashed with Yippies and other Vietnam War protesters outside the Democratic National Convention, Daley came up with one of his classic malapropisms, declaring that the National Guard had been called out "to preserve disorder."

The graveyard vote: It is said that Democratic nominee Hubert H. Humphrey lost the election to Republican Richard Nixon that autumn largely because of the convention, as emblematic a Chicago political event as Daley's having "stolen" the presidency for Democrat John F. Kennedy. Illinois was a key state in the 1960 Nixon-Kennedy race, and Daley reputedly withheld Chicago's returns – possibly padding them out with ballots cast in the names of deceased party supporters – until the last moment, when the city miraculously supplied just enough of a margin for Kennedy to carry the state and eventually the nation.

Chicago's tough reputation got tougher during the 1969 "Chicago Seven" conspiracy trial, a legal circus that led to overturned convictions for abuse of the judicial system, and as a result of the "Days of Rage" rampage by a militant faction of Students for a Democratic Society, who took their Weathermen name from the Bob Dylan lyrics – appropriate for Chicago – about not needing a weatherman to tell which way the wind blows.

Nicknames: But Chicago's link with seamy politics was nothing new in the 1960s. For the whole of the previous century, the city reigned as the nation's smoke-filled-backroom capital, playing host to 24 Democratic and Republican national conventions – still more than any other US city. The first was a raucous 1860 Republican Party affair in the historic Wigwam, a temporary structure located near the Chicago River and Lake Street, where dark horse presidential candidate and Illinois native son Abraham Lincoln was nominated.

In a city with several nicknames, it's fitting that Chicago's colorful political characters had colorful nicknames of their own. Daley, of course, was "Da Mare," a linguistic bow to his own syntax, fractured as a result of growing up a sheet metal worker's son in a Back of the Yards neighborhood. The strapping Mayor Thompson was "Big Bill." Six-foot, six-inch, 300-pound Mayor "Long John" Wentworth was one of two newspaper publisher-mayors who served before the turn of the century, the other being Joseph Medill of the *Tribune*. The imperi-

Vrdolyak was a latter-day political sharpster who became the City Council kingpin after Daley's death but surrendered his Democratic Party chairmanship for disastrous mayoral candidacies, one as a third-party candidate and the other as the Republican nominee, when Chicago politics began to hinge rather importantly on black-white racial issues in the mid-1980s.

Populist "Walkin' Dan" Walker as a Chicago attorney authored the national report that depicted the 1968 convention fiasco as a police riot. Daley's lasting enmity helped Walker win the governor's office in 1972 after defeating the mayor's handpicked can-

ous, mercurial Jane Byrne, swept into office as Chicago's first woman mayor by voters fed up with Michael Bilandic's inept handling of an epic 1979 blizzard, was known as "Lady Jane."

Alderman "Bathhouse John" Coughlin and Michael "Hinky Dink" Kenna were flamboyant lords of the Levee, the downtown vice district, who controlled City Council politics and "boodle," or graft, from the 1890s until Prohibition. "Fast Eddie"

Left, Abraham Lincoln, 1860. **Right**, National Guard jeeps, 1968 Democratic Convention.

didate in the Democratic primary. "Big Jim" Thompson, another six-and-a-half-footer, was the federal prosecutor who put some of Daley's closest protégés in jail in the early 1970s, and went on to become Illinois' longest-serving governor.

Lifetime jobs: A handful of governors and US senators from Chicago managed to gain fame – and sometimes infamy – in the shadow of the mayor's office. Otto Kerner, a son-in-law to the late Mayor Anton Cermak, was a popular governor later convicted of corruption by Thompson. Adlai Stevenson II was an ex-governor who lost two successive presidential elections as the Democratic nominee, despite Daley's support. When Daley viewed Stevenson's son and namesake as a potential rival, he helped get Adlai III elected to the US Senate and safely out of town, 700 miles away in Washington, DC.

The mayoralty is viewed by most Chicago politicos as second only to the presidency. But just one Chicagoan – Edward Dunne, elected governor in 1912 – has risen to higher office. While many, particularly the city's early mayors, might have seen City Hall as a beginner's step to the White House, the fifth-floor office has now come to be viewed as a "career cul-de-sac."

Jesse's push: Without question the city's most famous non-elected politician has been Jesse Louis Jackson, unsuccessful but highly visible in his campaigns for the Democratic presidential nomination. The peripatetic civil rights activist played an integral role in the establishment of the political dynamics presently at work in Chicago.

Jackson marched with Martin Luther King Jr through Chicago's segregated white neighborhoods in the mid-1960s, and was a prominent minority voice in denouncing Daley's infamous "Shoot to kill" order in the wake of rioting touched off by King's 1968 assassination. In the 1970s and '80s, Jackson

Besides, the job carries a relatively low life expectancy: four of Chicago's 41 mayors have died in office, two by assassination. Carter Harrison I, widely viewed as the city's first modern professional politician-mayor, was slain at his home by a disgruntled patronage job seeker. Cermak was in his first term in 1933 when he was felled by a bullet intended for President-elect Franklin Roosevelt. Daley died in 1976 after he was stricken by a heart attack, the same fate that befell Harold Washington, Chicago's first black mayor, in 1987 as he was just beginning a second term.

used his South Side operation PUSH (People United to Save Humanity) as a revival meeting-cum-political rally venue to mobilize black voters outside the Democratic Machine. He directed voter registration drives and boycotts that helped build a monolithic black electoral movement, supporting Washington and other black candidates – including Jesse Jackson.

Anathema to the white Democratic Party establishment in Illinois and distrusted by black Machine regulars, not to mention some of his own allies in the independent movement, for his "me-first style," Jackson packed up his aspirations for national office and Rainbow Coalition operations in 1989, after 25 years in Chicago, and moved to Washington, DC.

A split city: What Jackson left behind is an overwhelmingly Democratic city; in 1989, for example, the Republican mayoral candidate, "Fast Eddie" Vrdolyak, was slowed to a crawl with barely 3 percent of the vote. But Chicago also remains a city in which the Democratic Party continues to be fractured by race.

White ethnic and black Democrats typically offset each other – there are 19 predominately white wards on the Northwest

ethnically diverse populace. For a time in Chicago, Republicans were about as good at it as Democrats.

But the Republican Party lost its domination of the City Council in 1931 when Anton Cermak, a businesslike professional politician, defeated "Big Bill" Thompson, the party's last mayor. Cermak melded, for the first time, white ethnic immigrants and black voters who had previously been Republicans – Lincoln's party. And of no little significance was the fact that the Czech-born Cermak put an end to Irish domination of the Democratic Party melting pot.

Bridgeport bossism: With his untimely

and Southwest sides and 19 predominantly black wards on the South and West sides. Sometimes, close elections are swung by "lakefront liberals," a nettlesome but inconsequential group during the late Mayor Daley's mayoralty, and Hispanics, the city's fastest growing minority.

Since 1837, when William Butler Ogden became the city's first mayor, the key to winning elections in Chicago has been knitting together a majority coalition from an

death, however, Cermak's new version of the Machine fell into the hands of Irish politicians yet again, specifically those from influential Bridgeport. Born and reared in this Back of the Yards enclave of packing houses, saloons, shops and bungalows were the next four mayors: Edward Kelly, Martin Kennelly, Richard Daley and Michael A. Bilandic. In succession, they occupied the mayor's office from 1933 until 1979.

Jane Byrne's upset of the taciturn and unlucky Bilandic did not end Machine domination or accelerate its demise. The coughing and sputtering, however, had started

<u>Left</u>, thumbs up from Jesse Jackson, 1984. <u>Right</u>, the Chicago 7, plus Jerry Rubin's girlfriend.

even before Daley's death. The real end of the old Machine came four years later when Byrne and young Richard M. Daley split the white vote, allowing Harold Washington to win the Democratic nomination.

Washington's winning coalition was built on a strong black turnout and a sufficient showing among Hispanics and the lakefront's "limousine liberals" to capture 52 percent of the vote.

Given Harold Washington's enormous popularity in the community, no black politician, either independent or erstwhile Machine loyalist, dared oppose him. His returns were essentially the same in 1987 in a primary rematch with Byrne.

Democratic primary. Legions of discontented blacks boycotted Sawyer's candidacy, despite the support of Jesse Jackson. Timothy Evans, who had been Washington's floor leader in the City Council, challenged Daley in the general election with a third-party candidacy. With a $7 million campaign treasury and the swing vote solidly in his column, Daley prevailed.

By every indication, however, the city's demographics may be shifting too rapidly – more blacks, and especially more Hispanics – for Mayor Daley to match his father's two decades in office. However, Daley began his tenure by shunning the trappings of bossism

Daley redux: Seven months after his re-election, however, the Mayor's office claimed another victim, and Washington was dead. The city reverberated with shock, and the prospect of a bitter succession battle. Washington's base was split and it was the black political community's turn for a double-barreled shot at the mayoralty in a special 1989 election.

The soft-spoken Eugene Sawyer, Washington's immediate successor and a man who had risen through the Machine ranks, was defeated by Richard the Second in the

that his father took on so eagerly. He won high marks for fairness, and quickly consolidated Hispanic and liberal support beyond that which Washington enjoyed. As a result, Daley, by then known to Chicagoans simply as "Richie," was re-elected in early 1991.

The question that remains blowing in the wind is whether Chicago can approach the year 2000 without the political bluster that has made its reputation for the past century.

Left, heir and mayor apparent, Richard M. Daley, 1990. Right, Mirage Tavern, site of the *Sun-Times* sting, 1977.

SCHOOLED IN SCANDAL

"I too wish to defend my city from people who keep saying it is crooked," author Nelson Algren once wrote. "In what other city can you be so sure a judge will keep his word for $500?"

Scandal is a fact of life in Chicago. Politics, Chicago's favorite pastime, has bred a local strain of unscrupulousness, born of audacity and disrespect for both the public and public office. At the same time, Chicago has a bumptious journalistic community with a long tradition of irreverence toward authority in general and politicians in particular. The result is both more wrongdoing, and more reporting of that wrongdoing, than perhaps anywhere else.

Any "greatest hits" of Chicago scandals and "stings" must include Operation Greylord, the Federal Bureau of Investigation probe into court corruption. Between 1979 and 1983, FBI agents masquerading as defendants, lawyers, prosecutors and even a judge uncovered widespread bribery, extortion and fraud in the courts. The sting led to the convictions of 14 judges and 75 prominent attorneys and court staffers.

The FBI then looked at influence over judges by downtown politicians with ties to organized crime. Operation Koffee Klatsch exploded in late 1989 after federal agents planted electronics bugs and hidden cameras in Counsellor's Row, a popular restaurant across from City Hall.

Corruption is hardly a new phenomenon in Chicago, of course. In the late 1880s, aldermen "Bathhouse" John Coughlin and Michael "Hinky Dink" Kenna offered protection from police interference to vice dealers in exchange for votes. One historian claims that during the 1890s, at least 56 of the 68 aldermen accepted bribes for their votes.

The era of the modern Chicago scandal was probably ushered in by the 1960 Sommerdale Police Scandal, when an arrested thief (the "Babbling Burglar") revealed he was in league with the police in the city's Sommerdale district. Eight policemen were arrested, and the scandal rattled the Democratic political machine.

Political scandal doesn't stop at the city limits, either. A favorite local yarn concerns the 1970 Paul Powell shoebox scandal. A plain cardboard shoebox containing about $800,000 in unaccounted-for cash was found in the hotel-room closet of recently-deceased Democratic secretary of state, Paul Powell.

The cash apparently represented part of the kickbacks Powell took from contractors working on state building projects. A church began annual services on the anniversary of Powell's death to recall the lack of honesty among officials. The collection was taken in shoeboxes.

In the 1977 Mirage Tavern sting, the *Chicago Sun-Times* set up a bar manned by undercover reporters. They discovered that for modest sums – $50, $100 or $200 – building, plumbing, electrical, food, liquor and fire inspectors would overlook violations such as exposed wiring and maggot-infested food. The reporters were able to bribe all but one of the official inspectors they met. Two weeks after the story broke, the same inspectors were again seeking bribes – except that they had raised their prices. Eventually, one-third of all the city's electrical inspectors were convicted.

In 1985, Operation Incubator stung the administration of the late Mayor Harold Washington. An undercover FBI "mole," himself a convicted felon, posed as a representative of a company seeking city contracts. The mole reportedly bribed several city officials, including the city's former deputy revenue director. Several officials and aldermen were convicted, and the public was widely entertained by televised videotapes of one former mayoral aide dickering over the exact amount of his bribe.

A commercial scandal hit the hallowed halls of the Chicago Board of Trade and the Chicago Mercantile Exchange in 1988. Federal undercover agents, wired for sound, went into the trading pits and returned with evidence of fraud: floor traders were trading for themselves at more favorable prices than they traded for their customers. Several traders in each pit admitted guilt and cooperated with the investigation, which focused on the trading of Swiss francs, Japanese yen, treasury bonds and soybeans.

Chicago was once expected to become the greatest city in America, and hence in the world. It never happened. But for a time it must have seemed a near thing.

Commerce was thriving. Millionaires – in the days before tax write-offs – unbuttoned their pocketbooks for civic halls, museums and monuments of great splendor. Skyscrapers, the first the world had known, pierced the low-lying prairie clouds. Visionary architects such as Louis Sullivan and Frank Lloyd Wright constructed elaborate buildings. H.L. Mencken said that everything interesting in American writing seemed to be coming out of Chicago. With its wonderful central location – in the heart of the Heartland – Chicago seemed certain to grow, to gain, to flourish.

What went wrong? Different people, historians among them, give different reasons: that Chicago lost its hopes of pre-eminence when its businessmen refused to bestir themselves to wrest the automobile industry from Detroit; that air travel deflated the city's aspirations, because with the advent of commercial flights people no longer needed to stop in Chicago en route coast to coast; that the opening of the St Lawrence Seaway, which was supposed to make Chicago a great international port, turned out a failure; that Chicago never really recovered from the Depression, or made up for the loss of the stockyards, or was able to live down its reputation as a crime-syndicate town – and so on and so forth.

Faded rivalry: Other people, other opinions; other historians, other causes. Whatever the opinions, whichever the causes, no one really feels any longer that Chicago is the country's greatest city. Yet the epithet "second city" no longer seems quite accurate. In Chicago nowadays, people feel no more intense a distaste for New Yorkers than the majority of their countrymen outside

New York appear to feel. The old inter-city, one-on-one rivalry between Chicago and New York, which Chicagoans always felt more vividly than New Yorkers, seems to have all but disappeared.

Ah, New York, New York – if you can make it there, the song goes, you can make it anywhere. Of Chicago, the exact reverse used to be said: If you can't make it here, you can't make it anywhere. The sentiment was meant to stand as a tribute to the wide voca-

tional opportunities Chicago then provided. It was probably never very true – to those who work without family money or other nets to catch them, every big city presents the possibility of a dangerous fall – and it may be even less true now. For many who choose to live in Chicago, one of the city's special delights is precisely that it is *not* New York. Judged by its vibrancy, tumult, concentration of talent and sheer excitement, New York is far and away America's greatest city – in fact, the country's only world city. Yet Chicago, for reasons that visitors often find difficult to grasp, nonetheless remains, for

Preceding pages: marching Shriners; voter registration; a chip off the old block. <u>Left</u>, fair and freckled. <u>Right</u>, a sweet Chicago smile.

many of those who have lived in it, America's best city.

The city is at its worst, however, when it sets out to imitate New York. It cannot be done, and it is a grave, when not altogether comic, mistake to even try. From "haute cuisine" restaurants to high society social events, pretensions somehow do not work in this town, though that doesn't stop people from trying.

A hustlin' town: Among modern writers, Nelson Algren probably has impressed on the national consciousness the strongest notion of what Chicago is. For Algren, Chicago was above all a hustler's town. "Right from

go it was a broker's town and the brokers run it yet," he wrote in a lengthy 1951 prose-poem entitled *Chicago: City on the Make*. Much of the poetry in his prose-poem is of a hopeless sort, yet every once in a while Algren hits a note that resounds with true feeling, as when he remarks that loving Chicago is "like loving a woman with a broken nose, you may well find lovelier lovelies. But never a lovely so real."

To end the litany of clichés about Chicago, one can scarcely do better than consult a volume entitled *Chicago* by Studs Terkel. Self-advertised man of the people, Terkel,

with his Uher tape recorder, has become Chicago's recording angel, and hence himself something of a cliché. Slim though Terkel's *Chicago* is, thick and fast fly the clichés that make up its substance. From the Pottawattomies to the Haymarket Riot to the bag lady in Uptown, the history of Chicago, in Terkel's view, is that of big guys screwing little guys, with occasional heroes such as Saul Alinsky popping in for cameo appearances; with plenty of villains such as the general run of businessmen, politicians and, currently, the prosperous young; and with just enough room for a feisty little guy with a cigar and a tape recorder to make a nice living. But then Chicago has always been a hustler's town.

By now, surely America's major-league hustlers must be elsewhere; taking important meetings in Los Angeles, doing power lunches in New York, cutting serious deals in Washington. The notion of Chicago as a powerful organized-crime town no longer seems quite convincing, either. Even in the post-Capone 1940s, the so-called Syndicate was still the behind-the-scenes explanation for everything that went on in the city; it was said to have taken its tribute for every jukebox, case of soda pop, carton of cigarettes and, if rumor were to be believed, nearly every other thing bought and sold in the city.

The Boys themselves were fierce characters, with nicknames (always printed in the press within quotation marks) like "Teets," or "The Camel" or "Big Tuna." Now they mostly seem to be either dead or old bulls gone weak in the knees. Their successors, though doubtless quite as vicious, are younger men with pot bellies and ambitious hairdos who live with their families in gaudily decorated ranch houses in the western suburbs. Chicago no longer seems the mainline crime-boss town it once was.

Perverse pride: Chicagoans generally have taken an old pride in their city's corruption. Not so long ago, when one needed special consideration of one kind or another, somebody always knew somebody who knew somebody else who could fix it, from a broken curb to a black-market baby adoption. In those days, the phrase "everything's on the up and up" was pressed into frequent service, probably because it was difficult to believe many things actually were on the up and up.

The suspicion that things aren't what they seem – aren't quite "on the up and up" – has long seemed one of the qualities that mark people raised in Chicago. In its gentler, and hence more pleasing aspect, it comes across as a humorous dubiety. It also qualifies as part of what is known as the big-city view. In Chicago it doesn't have the hard edge of nastiness that it can take on in New York. This is the Chicago skepticism that takes little or nothing at face value, that gets nervous when a "yes" answer comes a little too

minicams come roaring out onto the streets like fire engines. The editorialists work themselves up into high moral dudgeon. And almost none of it really matters. Black or white, a Chicago politician remains a Chicago politician; and Chicago remains a city that stands in refutation of Lord Acton's maxim by demonstrating, again and again, that only a small amount of power can corrupt absolutely.

Lake tastes: Lake Michigan is the only interesting natural feature in the city, and the Chicago writer Isaac Rosenfeld used to refer to "the lake culture," by which he meant chiefly Hyde Park and the Near North Side

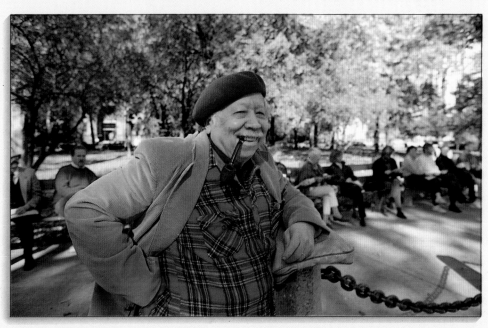

quickly, and that checks to see if the wallet is still in place after all large public functions at which a clergyman has been asked to give a benediction.

Chicagoans seem notable among Americans for being deeply suspicious of the next fellow's motives and then being delighted at having these suspicions confirmed. This applies particularly to public life. A large public scandal in Chicago seems to get the salivary glands working like nothing else. The

Left, a day out in the park. **Right**, a sidewalk philosopher.

with, despite the many differences between the two neighborhoods, their common interest in art, liberal politics and what their denizens take to be good taste. A lake culture persists, although now somewhat shriveled in Hyde Park and somewhat expanded beyond Lincoln Park. Life in Chicago, to adapt the local weatherman's phrase, is somewhat cooler near the lake. Yet the lake culture, though Chicago would be a barbarous place without it, is far from characteristic of the entire city.

Of course it is always the lake that people from out of town see and remember and remark upon. And why not? If they come to Chicago "holding," to use the old race track term to describe horse players who had money in their pockets, they might stay at the Drake Hotel, shop amid the glitz of Water Tower Place, dine at some slow-food joint such as the Everest Room, listen to a sumptuous opera at the Lyric, watch Sir Georg Solti do his snug little Central European bow at Orchestra Hall. All of which is fine, splendid even. "Enjoy," as the waitresses love to say at the many Italian restaurants around 26th and Oakley.

Between the Campbell Soup factory and the Fine Arts Building, the Black P-Stone galows, squat factory buildings and shops, and punctuated only by the occasional grandeur of a Catholic church built decades ago. True, there is a magnificent skyline with, to quote Louis Sullivan, its "proud and soaring" qualities, but one generally doesn't live in a skyline.

A city divided: The neighborhood has always been and remains Chicago's chief unit of social organization. Not many people really grew up in Chicago at all; instead they grew up in Austin, or South Shore, or Englewood or Albany Park or Ravenswood or Pullman or Gage Park. To this day there are North Siders who have never been south

Nation gang and the plummy announcers for WFMT, Chicago provides plenty in the way of extremes. Yet representative Chicago is not found in the extremes between the proud and the profane. It is less likely to be found in a four-bedroom, five-bath condominium in the John Hancock Center than in Jefferson Park (with bachelor Uncle Sven installed in the basement apartment), not in the lockup at 26th and California but on bingo night at Saint Dominic's Parish.

Chicago's solidity may derive from its flatness, an unrelieved stretch of prairie now covered principally by apartments and bun-

of the Museum of Science and Industry, and South Siders who have never been north of the Lincoln Park Zoo, and who are perfectly content to be so circumscribed in their local peregrinations.

Growing up in a Chicago neighborhood, the chances are great that one grew up among one's own, among one's fellow Swedes or Poles or Irish or Germans or Jews or blacks or Chinese or Ukrainians or Greeks or (more recently) Koreans or East Indians. As social units go, the neighborhood is long on familiarity and (in most instances) security. It is not strong on imagination; that is to say, growing up in a Chicago neighborhood, it is a bit difficult to imagine life outside the neighborhood. The reigning spirit of the neighborhood is conservative and traditional. Yet it is Chicago's organization around its neighborhoods that gave (and for the most part still gives) the city its feeling of solidity, solidity of a kind not so available elsewhere in the country.

As for physical solidity, Chicagoans, as a general type, tend to be beefier than people in New York (where anxiety peels away pounds) or San Francisco (where elegance is obligatory). Perhaps this is due to the peasant origins of so many of Chicago's early immigrants from Europe. Perhaps it is due to the Chicago diet, which tends to feature such fine and life-threatening items as pizza, ribs and every permutation played on beef. (Much fuss is made over hot dogs in Chicago, but the great, the archetypal Chicago sandwich is the Italian beef and sausage combo. There is no way to eat it without being reminded of one's prehistoric origins; upon finishing it one can almost hear the arteries leading to one's heart creaking to a close; and, unless one's taste buds have been ruined by the food served in spurious French restaurants, it happens to be delicious.)

Somehow, to be overweight – or even homely – in Chicago doesn't seem to be such a bad thing. In New York, if you are homely you had better be smart; in Los Angeles, the capital of cosmetic surgery, homeliness means unhappiness. But in Chicago it's all right to be the way you are.

A city that conveys so emphatic a feeling of solidity tends to induce in its citizens an habitual squinty-eyed realism. Gabble about the rich ethnic diversity of Chicago, for example, is all right coming from politicians, whom no one takes seriously anyhow, but anyone who has grown up in Chicago knows that the Italians don't trust the Jews, who don't think much of the Germans, who tend to be contemptuous of the Irish, who don't care much for the Poles, who could live nicely without the Greeks, who feel the East Indians are a pain, and who themselves wish the city's Spanish-speaking population

Left, slices for four, please. **Right,** campus cheer.

would get their damn kids under some kind of control. Ethnic diversity doesn't get much richer than that.

Still toddlin': The wonder of Chicago is that, despite its endemic corruption, its historic group animosities, its horrifying crime, the city keeps chugging along. Major hospitals and numerous schools and universities dot the cityscape. The Chicago Symphony, the Art Institute and the University of Chicago remain internationally renowned; the Lyric Opera is rapidly entering world-class, if it is not there already. On the debit side, the city is today without a great locally owned department store. Northwestern University

has never lived up to its potential to be one of America's elite academic institutions. The Chicago Public Library had been allowed to fall into disarray (although a new main library has now opened), which did not say much for the city's interest in any culture that was lacking in opportunities for snobbish and glitzy display.

The variety of activity in the city remains impressive. It is comforting to think that while the ensemble called The Music of the Baroque gathers in one Chicago-area church for a concert, the members of the group known as Gamblers Anonymous gather in another for a meeting. It is reassuring to know that one can eat reasonably and well at Stefani's on Fullerton, walk a few blocks east to an enormous used bookstore on Lincoln Avenue, then go off from there to a basketball game, or a blues bar or a production of a Greek play at the Court Theatre in Hyde Park.

Another wonder is Chicago talent, which keeps cropping up in odd and expected places. The Gilbert and Sullivan Society, for instance, performs elegant operettas in the battered auditorium of Saint Ignatius Church. Amid the ramshackle buildings of East Howard Street just off an alley, one

giving the letter "a" a harsh sound or reverting from time to time to "dems" and "doses" in the manner of the late Mayor Daley. This way of speaking, this characteristic Chicago voice, combines cynicism with love of life, knowingness with occasional sentimentality. To those that speak it, nothing in the way of corruption comes as news: the language itself has already been "corrupted."

The Chicago voice is a big city voice, and the people who speak with it tend to be old shoe, which is to say familiar and comfortable, for they know that pretensions will take you just so far and that life is a struggle that everyone loses in the end, so you may as well

comes upon a shop called Fritz Reuter and Sons, Master Violin Maker, Restorations and Appraisals. Or on 25th Avenue in Melrose Park, on a street doubtless zoned light industrial, a Chinese chef of unsurpassed quality named Ben Moy runs a restaurant frequented by many of the city's best-known artists and intellectuals. Such is Chicago – the figurative width of the place – that its wealth of cultural resources cannot be adequately covered by a single analysis or a single visit.

No surprises: There is a way that Chicagoans speak, and it has nothing to do with

relax and make the best of things. To a serious Chicagoan, life is inexhaustibly interesting, full of secret splendors and, when you come to consider the alternative, a damn fine thing. And Chicago is a good place to view life, a city where the sensible working assumption is that everyone and everything is a fake, except those people and things that one discovers are not, of which Chicago, being the kind of city that it is, has a great deal more than its share.

<u>Left</u>, feathered friends. <u>Right</u>, Jane Addams, left, and fellow campaigner Mary McDowell, 1917.

ROOTING OUT PROBLEMS

Despite its reputation as one of the most segregated cities in the United States, Chicago has a long tradition of grass roots movements strong enough to send ripples of liberalism through American society.

That Chicago should have such a tradition of liberal-minded social activism isn't really surprising. For one thing, the University of Chicago, founded in 1892, flourished from its inception as a center for urban sociology. Many of the most important studies of American urban life have come out of this university in Hyde Park. Its scholars historically have been aligned with social, labor and political reform movements.

Community action has been necessary in a city where politicians and employers have always had a vested interest in maintaining the status quo. This environment has encouraged both the rise of radical groups and a tradition of ground-level action aimed at improving social and labor conditions.

As far back as the 1880s, for instance, social worker Jane Addams thrust Chicago to the forefront of the Settlement House movement that sought to improve living conditions, community spirit, education and employment opportunities among immigrants and the urban poor. Addams' Hull House, which began in a mansion-turned-neighborhood center on South Halsted Street, included such features as a day nursery, adult education classes and even an employment bureau for the impoverished.

In contemporary Chicago, community organizer Saul Alinsky came to symbolize grass roots action. Alinsky, who hailed from the University of Chicago's sociology department and worked in the labor movement, helped establish several community organizations bent on social change through self-determination.

In his first effort, Alinsky helped found the Back of the Yards Council, a community group located in the area south of the old Union Stock Yard, where he saw a need for a local coalition to help unemployed workers fight for city services and tackle local crime. The council, now an institution in the neighborhood, still actively addresses public policy issues affecting Back of the Yards residents.

Alinsky is perhaps best known for his role, through his Industrial Areas Foundation, in founding The Woodlawn Organization (TWO), a community-based group organized in 1960 to empower the residents of the deteriorating Woodlawn community south of Hyde Park.

TWO became an important focal point for Chicago's civil rights movement. Its first efforts addressed education, beginning with pickets and leading to school boycotts that raised public awareness of the problems in ghetto schools. TWO also helped bring a branch of the City College into the community. The group battled slum landlords and white retailers who had been swindling their mostly black Woodlawn customers, and obtained federal funds to fight urban blight. While TWO has generally been a positive force in the community, its influence suffered from its dealings with street gangs. During the 1960s, for instance, the group was scandalized by reports that federal housing funds obtained by TWO had been funneled to a radical black street gang in exchange for protection from crime.

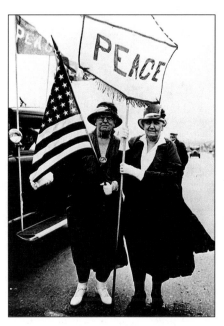

Nevertheless, Chicago's grass roots movement was important in the civil rights arena. When the Rev. Martin Luther King Jr expanded his crusade from the South to the northern US in the mid-1960s, he aligned his cause with the local Coordinating Council of Community Organizations (CCCO), a coalition already actively demonstrating against segregation.

In essence, King's Southern Christian Leadership Conference merged with the CCCO when, in 1966, King created the Chicago Freedom Movement with the aim of promoting improved housing, better education and more jobs. The Rev. Jesse Jackson was placed in charge of the movement's Operation Breadbasket, which boycotted stores and products in order to pressure employers to create jobs. From that base, Jackson went on to become one of America's most prominent and influential black political figures.

Chicago's premier columnist is Mike Royko, who writes five times a week for the *Chicago Tribune*. He trades in small words, short sentences and acerbic wit. He talks tough and aims at fat targets. He is the man who gave the city its unofficial motto: "Where's mine?"

Royko is something of a civic treasure in Chicago, celebrated among newspaper readers for his uncommon wealth of common sense. Royko fans, especially wide-eyed young men from the suburbs, sometimes drop by his favorite tavern, the Billy Goat on Hubbard Street, just to watch him drink.

But for all his skill, Royko is something less than a complete original. To the contrary, he writes in a Chicago literary voice that has been evolving for some 100 years, a voice that can be traced directly to earlier notable Chicago newsmen and writers and the penny newspapers of the 1890s.

Touch of gold: Before Royko there was the writer Nelson Algren, best known for his novel *The Man With the Golden Arm*, for which he won the first National Book Award for fiction in 1950; the prose-poem *Chicago: City on the Make*; and an excellent collection of short stories, *The Neo Wilderness*. Algren's most famous words of advice easily could have been written by Royko: "Never play cards with a guy named Doc. Never eat at a place called Mom's. And never sleep with someone whose problems are greater than your own."

Before Algren there was that master of the short story, Ring Lardner, who developed his style as a Chicago sportswriter. Lardner, the model for Abe North in F. Scott Fitzgerald's *Tender is the Night*, is best remembered for his two collections of baseball stories, *You Know Me Al* and *Alibi Ike*.

And before Lardner there was the syndicated Chicago newspaper columnist Finley Peter Dunne, whose literary alter ego, Mar-

tin J. Dooley, an Irish immigrant saloonkeeper of droll wit, entertained readers across the nation. Dooley had a knack for slicing through pretense, much in the manner of Royko's own alter ego, Slats Grobnik. It was Dooley who first said, "Trust iv'rybody, but cut the cards."

Like Royko, these earlier Chicago writers wrote for regular Joes, with bluntness and humor, in the language of the common man. Lardner, in particular, is credited by H.L.

Mencken with "reducing the American language to print." While East Coast writers in the years before World War I still adhered dutifully to every rule of proper syntax and grammar, Lardner was banging out dialogue such as: "I didn't used to eat no lunch in the playing season except when I knowed I was not going to work."

Vividness: From about 1890 to 1925, Chicago was a national hub of literary bustle, prompting critics to proclaim a "Chicago Renaissance." Mencken, writing in 1917, declared Chicago "the literary capital of the United States" and insisted that all the great

Preceding pages: Hugh Hefner and multiplying bunnies, 1966. **Left**, Tribune Tower entrance. **Right**, Mike Royko.

American writers of his day had lived at least for a time in Chicago.

"Chicago has drawn them in from their remote wheat towns and far-flung railroad junctions, and it has given them an impulse that New York simply cannot match – an impulse toward independence, toward honesty, toward a peculiar vividness and na-ivete," he wrote. "New York, when it lures such a recruit eastward, makes a compliant conformist of him, and so ruins him out of hand. But Chicago, however short the time it has him, leaves him irrevocably his own man, with pride sufficient to carry through a decisive trail of his talents. Witness (Sherwood) Anderson, (Theodore) Dreiser, (Edgar Lee) Masters, (Carl) Sandburg and (George) Ade."

Some historians say Chicago's reputation as a writer's town is rooted in the newspaper circulation wars of a century ago, when the morning papers dropped their prices from two cents to a penny. With the price cut, newspapers found their way into the hands of more average Chicagoans than ever before.

Blooming times: Many of the major papers, such as the *Daily News* and the *Inter-Ocean*, attempted to cater to their expanded readership by adopting a more democratic editorial tone. Even the staid *Tribune* made adjustments, such as giving news coverage for the first time to the plebeian sport of boxing and coming out in favor of the shocking new fad of bloomers.

The papers courted journalists who could write in an entertaining and personal style, almost always employing elements of spoken American English. One such pioneer, Eugene Field, wrote both journalism and poetry in his "Sharps and Flats" column for the *Daily News*. He used contractions, slang and offensive words like "ain't" in his poetry. His most enduring works are his children's poems "Little Boy Blue" and "Wynken, Blinken and Nod."

George Ade was another pioneer. He came to Chicago from Indiana in 1890, got a job alongside Field at the *Daily News*, and within three years was a star columnist. In his own words, he showed a "criminal preference for the Midwest vernacular."

But Chicago newspapers did more for literature than play a role in getting plain speech down on paper. In an age before writers' conferences and creative writing fellowships, the papers offered aspiring writers a sort of hardball literary apprenticeship. Dreiser, Sandburg, Field, Edna Ferber and Ben Hecht were among those who put in time on Chicago newspapers, happy for the paycheck and camaraderie.

Until the day it folded in 1978, the *Daily News* remained Chicago's most literate newspaper, conscientiously nurturing such talents as Field, Ade, Sandburg, Hecht and Royko, even when it meant allowing them to freelance a bit on company time. Henry

Justin Smith, editor of the *News* during the first third of the century, referred to his stable of writers as "budding Balzacs" and cut them a good deal of slack.

Sandburg covered the 1919 Chicago race riots for the *Daily News* and wrote a book about the tragedy. He later won three Pulitzer Prizes – two for poetry and one for his biography of Abraham Lincoln – and wrote the poem that would become a Chicago cliché: "Hog Butcher for the World, Tool Maker, Stacker of Wheat, Player with Railroads and the Nation's Freight Handler, Stormy, Husky, Brawling, City of the Big

Shoulders." Today, the stockyards are gone and the big shoulders wear Brooks Brothers, but the poem is still quoted and the old image still sticks.

Creative nonfiction: Smith hired Sandburg as much for his poetry as his journalism, so he assigned him the easy task of reviewing "picture plays" for the *News* and left him free to write poetry the rest of the day. Smith prized good writing above all else, possibly even facts. He once hired a reporter who had faked a story about a local resident living to a prodigious age, explaining, "Accuracy can be taught, imagination cannot."

Hecht worked at the *Daily News* alongside

Sandburg. It was Hecht, in fact, who got Sandburg the job. Hecht was an outstanding reporter and columnist, but notoriously lazy about doing his legwork. When a deadline loomed, he sometimes made up material. On one occasion he and a *News* photographer cajoled a police captain into posing for a picture aboard a police boat, gun in hand. To explain the picture in the paper, Hecht concocted the totally unsubstantiated headline: "Police Pursue River Bandits."

It made for bad journalism, but good

Left, Nelson Algren. Right, Carl Sandburg.

times. Hecht immortalized the Chicago school of high-jinks journalism in his smash play *The Front Page*, which later became a movie that has been remade again and again.

Outside the city's newsrooms, Chicago's literary scene in the 1910s and '20s was anchored by the poet and editor Harriet Monroe. The magazine she founded, *Poetry*, was the official organ of the American Modernist movement and the first to publish T.S. Eliot, Marianne Moore, William Carlos Williams and Ezra Pound.

Literary obsessions: During the next three decades, while the nation struggled through the Great Depression and another world war, Chicago produced four more nationally important writers, all of a proletarian bent: Algren, Richard Wright, Jack Conroy and James T. Farrell. They shared a fascination with Marxism politics and an obsessive interest in the underdog.

Wright, who moved up to Chicago from Mississippi in the 1920s, worked as a postal clerk by day and wrote by night. His best works, including the novel *Native Son*, which was set in Chicago, were strongly influenced by Dreiser's naturalistic fiction.

Conroy, a writer and editor in Chicago for some 40 years, is best remembered today for his 1933 proletarian novel *The Disinherited*. As editor of several leftist literary journals in the 1930s and '40s, he also published the early work of Wright and Algren. Of Algren, Conroy once said: "The gates of his soul opened on the hell side."

Farrell, a second-generation South Side Irishman, wrote more than 50 books and dozens of short stories. His brutally realistic trilogy of books about Studs Lonigan, an aimless youth growing up in Chicago from the early 1900s to the Depression, holds up well today.

Homeless Papa: Conspicuously absent from this rundown of major Chicago writers is the big daddy of them all, Ernest Hemingway, who grew up in suburban Oak Park. Hemingway skipped town after high school and never looked back. He belonged to Paris and Cuba and the world, but never really to Chicago.

"It's hard to imagine Faulkner not writing about Oxford, Mississippi, or Steinbeck leaving the Salinas Valley out of his fiction," observes Michael Reynolds, a Hemingway biographer. "It is almost axiomatic that American authors write about their home towns, yet Hemingway did not." His heroes were all homeless men, wasting few words and traveling light.

It is equally axiomatic that almost all Chicago writers eventually leave town, though seldom with Hemingway's haste. Dunne, Lardner, Dreiser, Sandburg, Hecht, Wright, Farrell and Algren are among those who moved on, lured away by the energy of New York and the big money of Hollywood.

In Algren's case, it was also a matter of named after two well-known columnists and broadcasters, Irv Kupcinet and Paul Harvey. Those streets, however, are not residential.

Chicago remains a writer's town, if no longer a literary titan. Among the critically acclaimed writers making their homes in Chicago in the 1990s are Pulitzer Prize winner Gwendolyn Brooks, National Book Award recipient Larry Heinemann, Cyrus Colter, Harry Mark Petrakis, Charles Dickinson, Bill Granger, Sara Paretsky, Richard Stern, Stuart Kaminsky and Stuart Dybek. And David Mamet developed his craft as a playwright in Chicago; it's doubtful that anyone has ever captured the pro-

hurt feelings. In his introduction to *The Neo Wilderness*, Algren groused that his books could be found in translation "in the libraries of all the large cities of Europe," but not "in the library of the city about which they were written."

Streets seen: Shortly after Algren's death, an alderman proposed to honor him by changing the name of West Evergreen Street to West Algren Street. But folks on the street objected, so the alderman abandoned the plan. The living sometimes vote in Chicago, while the dead usually don't. On the other hand, stretches of two downtown streets are fane, hustling attitude of Chicago in crisper dialogue than his real estate salesmen in *Glengarry Glen Ross*.

Over the past quarter-century, however, Chicago has been able to boast of only one *bona fide* literary superstar: Saul Bellow, who in 1976 won the Nobel Prize for literature. Before his recent move to Boston, he was constantly being asked why he did not leave the city. It's not just a matter of "roots," he said on several occasions. "It's more like a lot of old wires."

Above, the film *The Front Page*, 1974 version.

A FADED PLAYBOY

The year was 1952 and Hugh Hefner was earning $120 a week as circulation director of a magazine called *Children's Activities*. In the evening he lived out his fantasy of starting a men's magazine full of bare breasts.

"Hef" borrowed $1,000 from his parents, hocked his furniture for $400 and talked a Chicago bank into lending him $200 to get his fledgling *Stag Party* magazine off the kitchen table of his Hyde Park apartment and into the hands of the newly liberated male.

After objections from *Stag*, a hunting magazine, Hef changed the magazine's title to *Playboy*. A friend and artist designed the now famous rabbit-head trademark in a few minutes. Hef wisely paid $500 for never-before-seen nude pictures of Marilyn Monroe for the launch (or die) issue. With that, the Playboy party officially began in November of 1953.

No one anticipated the success of *Playboy* magazine. It was as if the nation had been waiting for something so out of the mainstream. Within three years, the magazine's circulation hit 500,000 and Hef bought mansions in Los Angeles and Chicago. His Chicago residence, at 1340 N. State Parkway, was a 72-room Victorian mansion with many bars, including one that had an underwater window for viewing the indoor pool.

He sank another $5 million into a DC-9, the *Big Bunny*. He opened Playboy Clubs around the country, generally enjoying his life as the pipe-smoking, pajama-clad guy who really had it made. However, Hef's lifestyle didn't sit well with his wife and the mother of his two children. In 1959, after 10 years of marriage, they were divorced.

The Playboy party lasted for about 30 years, but then it turned into a pumpkin as the public lost interest and the Playboy philosophy became passé. In 1986, Chicago-based Playboy Enterprises Inc. lost $62 million. The magazine's circulation, which peaked at 7.2 million in 1972, plummeted to 3.6 million.

A man of some wisdom, Hef appointed his daughter, Christie Hefner, as chairperson and chief executive officer of the company. She cleaned house in a major way, firing 100 executives and shutting down most of the Playboy Clubs. She even sold daddy's Chicago mansion and his airplane.

Today, Christie has moved her staff into a new headquarters at 680 N. Lake Shore Drive, a modern corporate spread bearing little resemblance to the hedonistic trappings of the past, except for a reception-area bronze sculpture of a Playboy bunny head by artist Richard Hunt.

The current building, formerly the American Furniture Mart, features a coolly modern atrium, which includes skylights, steel catwalks and translucent fiberglass panels – architecture that is hardly in keeping with a den of iniquity.

In 1989, 63-year-old Hef finally settled down and married a former centerfold, 26-year-old Kimberley Conrad. He declined a bachelor party, saying he'd "been at one for 30 years." They had a baby and called themselves an "old-fashioned" couple after they agreed that he would not be in the delivery room.

Even though Hef still controls about 67 percent of Playboy stock and is reportedly writing his autobiography, Christie is clearly wearing the trousers in the family, trying to reposition Playboy Enterprises to be a more profitable organization.

While the magazine is still the mainstay of the corporation, the firm has been having some success licensing products bearing the Playboy, Playmate and bunny-head trademarks. In fact, 80 licensees and 45 countries sell leisure apparel and trinkets, bringing in revenues to the company of about $260 million a year.

Otherwise, *Playboy*'s major excursions into the American consciousness these days come from its explicit photographs. Joan Collins, Jessica Hahn and LaToya Jackson have all stripped for the magazine in recent years. Christie Hefner has convinced her dad that Playboy, both the company and its magazine, must evolve in order to prosper in the future. But it's still not clear exactly what changes can be made to a naughty, libertine philosophy that is no longer either as naughty nor as libertine as it was in the 1950s and '60s.

THE CHICAGO BLUES

The long blond-wood bar of the neighborhood tavern was propping up only a few people. Three older black guys in short-sleeved shirts and snappy straw hats trash-talked and cackled back and forth as they sipped their beer, while a younger, thinner black guy in an identical hat looked around coolly as he nursed a fruit juice. A fat white man wearing a plaid shirt and a paisley tie grinned at the three old black guys as he worked on a whisky.

A newcomer, a Hispanic wearing baggy trousers and several earrings, made straight for the older black guys. After a few minutes of chatting and laughing, the whole group gradually migrated to the far end of the room. Two of the men nonchalantly slung guitars over their shoulders, while another settled behind a drum kit. Another adjusted a mike and yet another blew a few tentative notes on his harmonica.

Their music hit the ground running: the heavy beat, the surging bass, the overlay of harp and, leading it all, the whine and squeal of the lead guitar. They grinned at each other. It didn't matter that there were only half a dozen people in the bar. Within minutes, however, the place was jammed with people: more old black guys, nodding their heads in time, and a bunch of young whites who were shouting along, clapping and boogying on their stools. Some started dancing in front of the band, pausing between songs to shake hands with the musicians or offer some words of approval.

It was 3:30 on a Wednesday afternoon in a residential neighborhood. Welcome to the blues, Chicago style.

Blue notes: The Chicago blues hold a secure niche in both the annals of American music and today's popular entertainment, as much a part of the town as Dixieland jazz is to New Orleans. It is a loud, showy, rocking type of music that takes traditional blues

themes, chords and bent notes, and then juices them up with amplification. Musicologists could go on and on about the characteristic 12-bar, three-chord schematics and "the dominant seventh," with split quarter tones.

To music scholars, blues music does not refer to "blue" themes in lyrics, but to the "blue" notes that have been played natural or flatted, often deliberately out of tune. It's a style that has been described as getting music

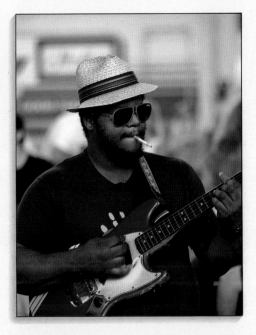

out of the cracks between the keys on the piano. To non-experts, the overriding musical feature of the Chicago blues is that the music is guitar-driven.

It would be difficult to overstate the influence of the Chicago blues and Chicago bluesmen on today's popular music, particularly mainstream rock 'n' roll. Anyone who listens to a set of live blues anywhere in Chicago is sure to mark it as the roots of rock. "Musicians treat the blues like gospel; it's a kind of honesty meter, a measure of belief," according to Paris-based music critic Mike Zwerin. "'He can't even play the blues,' is to

<u>Preceding pages</u>: rockin' all night long. <u>Left</u>, KoKo Taylor, Chicago's Queen of the Blues. <u>Right</u>, backyard barbecue blues.

say he's hopeless… Chicago remains the point of reference – a mecca."

African roots: Everyone has a personal interpretation and feel for the blues, as with any other art form. But to appreciate the development of Chicago blues, it is important to understand the people who created it. The genesis of the blues can be traced back to Africa, where tribes developed strong oral traditions of passing down their lessons and legends. In some African cultures, one sign of masculinity was the falsetto singing that has become such a part of modern blues, rhythm and blues, soul and rock music.

The Africans who became slaves in the only way of keeping in touch with their African traditions, and sometimes the only way of tracking down family members lost when sold into slavery.

As African rhythms melded with European styles of harmony, the field hollers led to the Negro spirituals and hymns that looked toward happiness some day, but probably not in this lifetime. The early blues, often referred to as the "downhome" or "country" blues, came out of the Mississippi delta, and featured songs that were typically more personal than spiritual. They were songs about loving and leaving, about loyalty and betrayal, about desire and tempta-

America brought their traditions with them, and hung onto vestiges of those traditions despite the cultural influences that led them to speak the language, wear the clothes and use the manners forced on them by white owners. The blues grew out of the "field hollers" of slave times, when the workers bending over cotton or other crops would communicate with each other in long slow chants and songs. Many owners refused to let their slaves talk to each other, but didn't mind them singing while they worked. For many, the holler messages passed from field to field, from plantation to plantation, were tion. They were sung for friends at home, for cellmates in prison or for tips on the street.

Accompanied at first by finger-snapping, stomping, "hambone" thigh-slapping and other crude forms of percussion, the downhome blues ultimately became associated with the acoustic guitar, particularly the homemade "bottleneck" style. Some black freemen became wandering minstrels, taking the field hollers and early blues on the road to entertain slave and master alike.

Moving north: In the post-slavery industrial era, the expanding mills and factories of the North brought many blacks up the Mississippi Valley to Chicago. The migration varied between a trickle and a steady stream for much of the first half of this century, but after World War II it became a positive flood as young blacks, often with their families, sought out the bright lights and higher-paying jobs.

Using the government aid for returning servicemen, many came to Chicago to be educated and to become professionals. Thousands took up the jobs – generally menial, but relatively high paying – offered by the ever-growing stockyards. Chicago's two large black-dominated neighborhoods developed because the migrants from the South one of the first American artists to take the blues to Europe, where it was embraced by sophisticated audiences. Chicago performers often bracket dates in small clubs in their home neighborhoods with tours of big halls in Europe, and a handful of Chicago blues expatriates, notably Paris-based guitarist Luther Allison, have resettled in Europe to take advantage of the enthusiastic audiences. In Chicago, visiting Europeans often seek out the blues bars and clubs, and the annual Chicago Blues Fest has become a focus for many foreign tourists.

Electrifying: Though still popular after World War II, the rural, relatively simple

typically got off the trains at one of two stops. If they got off at the 63rd Street station, they usually settled right there on the South Side; if they got off at the 12th Street station, they generally ended up on the West Side. The Southern musicians, naturally, followed their audience.

One of the men who acted as a bridge between the delta and the city, from Mississippi to Chicago, from downhome to urban blues, was Big Bill Broonzy. He was also

Left, Junior Wells, the "godfather" of the blues scene. **Right**, Ruth Brown, wide and wailin'.

downhome blues – typically one man with one guitar, mourning the love he done lost – eventually gave way to a faster, more raucous, often joyful music. When the electric guitar came along in the 1950s, it was embraced wholeheartedly in the black clubs and living rooms and back yards, and Chicago blues was born.

The man with the guitar not only had an amplifier, but he also had an electric bass player, a drummer, a harmonica player, a saxophone player and perhaps even a lady – sometimes slim and sultry, sometimes wide and wailin' – to sing the blues. The resulting

Chicago blues, however, retained and intensified many of the features experts use to characterize downhome blues: vocal moans and drones, for example, along with "constant repetition of melodic figures, harmonica tremeloes, a heavy sound and rough intensity," according to noted blues author Charles Keil.

The delta bluesmen who defined and refined the new style in the 1950s included J.B. Lenoir, Jimmy Reed, Little Walter, Howlin' Wolf, Sonny Boy Williamson, John Lee Hooker and Muddy Waters, who became the single performer most identified with the earthy, vibrant, driving style of Chicago

Many of the themes and lyrics have become more sophisticated, of course, and humor has become one of the strongest undercurrents in the Chicago blues, as when the singer complains about a straying spouse or a meddling mother-in-law. A modern bluesman – or woman – may complain about a lover who cheats, but may also threaten to kick that lover's ass. Willie Dixon sang many of his own songs, but his true legacy will be the hundreds of blues songs he wrote for other artists, often tailoring the themes, lyrics and rhythms to a performer's individual style. To Dixon, who said, "The wisdom of the blues is the true facts of life,"

blues. Waters' songs, such as *Hoochie Coochie Man*, *Got My Mojo Workin'* and *I'm Ready* epitomize the rollicking sexual boastfulness that often replaced the theme of sorrow and helplessness so common in the downhome blues. In *Tiger in Your Tank*, Waters sang:

I can raise your hood.
I can clean your coils.
Check the transmissions,
And give you the oils.
I don't care what the people think,
I want to put a tiger,
You know, in your tank.

everything that did and could happen was fair game for a blues song.

Chess game: One of the cornerstones of the development of the Chicago blues in the 1950s and '60s was Chess Records, the recording company operated by Leonard Chess, his brother Phil and Leonard's son Marshall. Many of the leading talents in blues cut records with the Chess family. Muddy Waters was with them for years with no contract beyond a handshake. Willie Dixon, who as well as writing songs was an accomplished upright bass player, was a Chess stalwart who often used his basement to audition new talent for the Chess family.

Today, more than 20 years after guiding light Leonard Chess died and the studio was closed, the debate continues in Chicago over the role of the Chess family. Were they whites who exploited black talent? Would the Chicago blues have become so popular if they hadn't given so many unheard artists a chance to record?

One thing not in doubt is that many of the architects of modern rock 'n' roll made formative pilgrimages to the tiny Chess studio on South Michigan Avenue. Prominent rock singers and guitarists, particularly the leaders of the 1960s "English invasion" such

Dixon's *Little Red Rooster*, for example, it sold 20,000 copies, a big hit for a local blues record. When the Rolling Stones re-recorded the song in a nearly identical manner, it sold more than 500,000 copies. Tom Marker, a longtime Chicago blues disc jockey, recalled that the English rockers, especially the Stones, were "just crazy" about the blues. "Those guys were big fans of the Chicago sound when they were getting their blues thing together themselves," he said. "They were just trying to copy the stuff. Sometimes they would copy the song lick for lick." The black bluesmen made the music, and the white rockers made it famous.

as the Rolling Stones, paid personal homage to Chess's blues artists. For a time, Marshall Chess managed the Rolling Stones, who took their name from a Muddy Waters song. They and other modern rock stars not only re-recorded many Chicago blues songs to create international hits, but often borrowed or stole outright individual guitarists' distinctive riffs.

When Howlin' Wolf recorded Willie

Left, bassist and songwriter Willie Dixon and Muddy Waters. **Right**, Marshall Chess with classic vinyl.

Many blues performers literally sang for their supper and not much more. Even name performers often lived on a shoestring – and still do. For example, Koko Taylor, known in Chicago as the Queen of the Blues, needed the receipts of a benefit thrown by friends and fellow performers to pay the bills after she and several band members were injured in a 1988 auto accident. "Musicians all over Chicago are working hard, but they're working for almost nothing," Taylor told the *Chicago Tribune*.

"You sing the blues, die and they have a benefit to bury you. That's the pattern," added Valerie Wellington, another leading lady blues singer in Chicago. That's why Wellington and a number of other performers formed the Chicago Blues Artists Coalition, a sort of blues-rights organization that aims to help performers learn how to handle their own business and financial affairs. The group is also providing self-help counseling and drug-awareness programs. "In this business, it's very easy to get caught up in things of that nature," Wellington said.

Blues survivors: Not all blues artists end up down and out, of course. The Chicago blues have made a lot of money for some artists who have reclaimed the traditions from the

But there's a second rank that includes many fans' favorites, including patriarchs such as Sunnyland Slim and Jimmy Walker. Two popular tradition-minded blues guitarists who seem to be playing somewhere in Chicago almost every day are Lefty Dizz, who used to tutor Jimi Hendrix on blues licks, and Muddy Waters Jr, who is actually no relation to "the old man" but has declared himself an unofficial adopted son and continues the raunchy tradition with lyrics such as, "If you wouldn't have kicked the door down, you wouldn't have caught me in bed with your wife."

For visiting blues fans who seek out the

white-dominated world of rock. Though not from Chicago, the influence of the Chicago style is heard in many of the tunes of artists B.B. King and Robert Cray. The Chess recording studio is gone, and so are some of the classic South Side blues clubs such as Theresa's, but the Chicago blues scene remains as lively in the 1990s as ever. Following the death of Muddy Waters, guitarist Buddy Guy and singer-harpist Junior Wells share the unofficial title of greatest living Chicago bluesmen. Buddy Guy, for instance, is the man Eric Clapton nominates as the world's greatest guitarist.

music, an added benefit is the musicians, even the headliners, who typically mingle with the crowd before and after shows. They are often happy to have a chat and maybe a drink; more than any other music, the Chicago blues remain of and for everyday people, with all the highs and lows and worries of everyday life. As Purvis Spann, the old Chicago blues disc jockey, used to say, "If you don't like the blues, you got a hole in your soul."

Left, Aretha Franklin testifies for *The Blues Brothers*. **Right**, John Lee Hooker.

BLUES JOINTS

In the city that created a blues style in its own image, one of the best places to hear the music is on downtown street corners, where individual performers and sometimes whole bands set up to play for donations from passersby. On a Sunday morning, the Maxwell Street market often features a variety of street blues performers, both individuals and entire bands.

There are a number of popular blues clubs on the North Side of Chicago, in neighborhoods that feel safer and more familiar to both visitors and the Chicago middle-class and young professional types who favor the music. The best North Side and downtown clubs include Blue Chicago, B.L.U.E.S., B.L.U.E.S. Etcetera, the Wise Fools Pub, Kingston Mines and Buddy Guy's Legends. It's always advisable to check in advance with these popular clubs to see if booking is necessary; on weekends or when well-known performers are playing there, tickets can be tight.

But that's on the North Side and downtown. You cannot book or make advance reservations on the South Side. For a real plunge into urban blues, nothing compares with the South Side, particularly the Checkerboard, also known recently as the New Checkerboard Lounge. For years, the Checkerboard has been the unofficial headquarters of the Chicago blues for the South Side bluesmen themselves, but it's in a tough neighborhood where visitors should take care. Most white people prefer to arrive at the club in cabs, though frequent visitors drive themselves and then park in the club's own off-street parking lot, which is located nearby and even has a security guard in attendance.

The cover charge at the Checkerboard is usually only a few dollars. Once inside, the club is remarkably small for having such a big reputation. It has seats for perhaps 100 and standing room (which is more usual) for about 300, but in fact it only takes about 30 people to make the place look crowded.

Though the neighborhood outside may be threatening to some, once inside it's easy to make friends among the locals and the bluesmen themselves, who especially appreciate out-of-towners and love the idea of someone crossing an ocean to hear them play.

For the hard-core late-night prowlers, Kingston Mines, with its two alternating stages, can be a gold mine for the blues. One of Chicago's northernmost blues clubs (on North Halsted Street), it's not exactly a fancy club, but it's one of those places that looks better as the night goes on. And the night does go on at Kingston Mines, usually until 4 a.m. On Saturday nights and Sunday mornings, the music rolls until 5 a.m. Other blues performers around the city finish their regular gigs at two or three in the morning and then head for Kingston Mines, where they jam and "talk country" at each other, much to the delight of aficionados.

One of the best places to catch the blues is at Wrigley Side, on Clark Street just around the corner from baseball's Wrigley Field. A specialty here are the shows, often by top Chicago bluesmen such as Lefty Dizz, that begin as soon as the last score is registered in afternoon games at Wrigley Field. Some fans leave the game before it's over to make sure they get a good stool near the band.

In 1990, the city granted landmark status to the building at 2120 South Michigan Avenue that once housed well-known Chess Recording Co. and its legendary music studios.

A former Chess studio musician, Gerald Sims, bought the building and announced plans to turn it into a "living music museum where artists can record, where the public can hear lectures on the blues and where tourists can visit." Interested fans should check to see if it's open.

Another blues stop that isn't in most of the official tourist information is the Old Town School of Music, situated at 909 West Armitage, which not only has a blues school, but features a shop, workshops and occasional acoustic performances.

And, of course, the Chicago Blues Fest has become an avidly awaited annual tradition in early June. It's free, held in downtown's grassy Grant Park, and typically features dozens of artists from both Chicago and elsewhere.

Chicago is a sporting kind of town, from what people read in the morning newspaper and what they talk about during the day to what they do after work and where they eat and drink at night. In the city's poorer neighborhoods, many young people see a career in sports as their best hope of claiming a slice of the American dream. Public officials recognize the importance of sports in Chicago, from the millions in tax money that helped build a new baseball stadium for the White Sox to the late-night basketball leagues aimed at keeping kids off the streets between the hours of 10 p.m. and 1:30 a.m.

Chicagoans love their professional teams – baseball's Cubs and White Sox, football's Bears, ice hockey's Black Hawks and basketball's Bulls – but they love to play themselves, too. The South Side pick-up basketball games are known for their "no autopsy, no foul" style of rough play, and the lakefront is a haven for runners, cyclists, bodybuilders and volleyball players. Parks all over Chicago feature a popular local variation of softball, baseball's slower cousin, that features a balloon-sized 16-inch ball compared with the 12-inch regulation softball and the 9-inch baseball. (It's probably fitting that since the players are fatter, the ball should be, too.)

Back in time: For many visitors, and for many Chicagoans as well, the quintessential Chicago sporting experience is an afternoon baseball game at Wrigley Field, home of the Chicago Cubs. A Cubs game is a high priority for visiting Americans because it's a chance to savor the national game, to step back in time to the days before World War II when all baseball games were played in the afternoon instead of at night, under lights. Wrigley Field is one of the oldest baseball parks in the major leagues, and fans revel in its ivy-covered walls where balls sometimes become lost and entangled in the vines, and in the way its erratic breezes can turn harm-

less fly balls into important home runs.

For foreign visitors, even those who know or care little about baseball or sports in general, a visit to Wrigley is a prime opportunity for people-watching, for sizing up the style of these ruddy creatures who call themselves Chicagoans. Perhaps more than any other big US city, the people of Chicago represent the great middle class of America – in size, shape, apparel, speaking voice, economic standing, political attitudes and

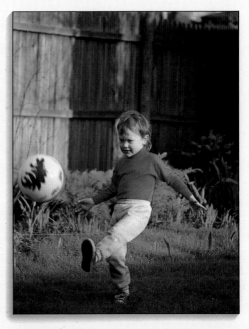

social concerns – or lack thereof. And there is perhaps no better place than an afternoon baseball game at Wrigley Field to observe folk who are so cheerfully, relentlessly, unabashedly *American*.

Wrigleyville is a middle-class, aspiringly gentrified North Side neighborhood of large, solid-brick apartment blocks and one-time family homes that have been carved into flats and unassuming duplexes. It is also not the most accessible place Chicago could have put a ballpark. But for many fans, the El (elevated railway) ride to Addison, a short walk from the park – it never seems right to

Preceding pages: Bear-faced battle. **Left**, eye on the ball. **Right**, kicking kiddie.

call this little bandbox a stadium – is as much a part of the game as hot dogs and popcorn and beer.

Safe at home: Most afternoon games are sellouts, due to the remarkable allegiance that Cubs' fans show for their long-suffering team. Yet tickets can be had, and usually for not much more than $5 to $20 above face value, depending on the location of the seats. Ticket scalping is illegal, but there are usually plenty of touts slyly making deals across the street or around the corner from the official ticket windows.

Also, people without tickets can strike up a conversation with one of the Cubs' usher-

prefer to catch a couple of innings from the lower grandstand, a couple more from the upper deck and a couple more from the underground stands where they can munch nachos, pizza, bratwurst, burgers and other fast food while watching the game on over-head closed-circuit TV. For the worst view of the game but perhaps the most fun, adventurous fans prefer the outfield bleachers, where the infamous Bleacher Bums cheer maniacally, strip off their shirts at any hint of sunshine and typically end up soaked in beer, inside and out.

The real show at Wrigley Field is not the baseball on the field, but the fans themselves.

guards outside the entrances; these guys have the uncanny ability to scan the entering crowd for people with extra tickets who will sell them at face value or sometimes simply give them away.

For visitors who just want to sample the atmosphere and look around a bit, the best bargain is probably a standing-room-only ticket, purchased even on sellout days for a few dollars from the regular ticket windows. These tickets do not guarantee a seat (though seats are often available due to no-shows) but they do afford decent views from the many aisles. Many people with SRO tickets

Huge men bearing trays of beer and junk food carefully belly their way through the crowds. Bespectacled, serious young men concentrate on the game, scribbling in their scorebooks as they chart the action play by play. Seemingly oblivious to both the game and the cheers of young men, buxom young women strut confidently up and down the aisles just ahead of the broad-beamed, child-dragging matrons they will probably eventually become.

No one should leave before the middle of the seventh inning, the famous "stretch," when Harry Caray, the venerable Cubs TV and radio announcer, sticks his head out of the overhead broadcasting booth and leads the crowd in singing a horribly off-key version of "Take Me Out to the Ballgame." Caray, a hoary septuagenarian whose words have become a little slowed and slurred since he suffered a stroke a few years ago, is not a typical American glib, blow-dried sportscaster. But his common-man looks and plain-speaking enthusiasm have helped qualify him as one of Chicago's all-time sports personalities.

Local heroes: There are other sports heroes, of course, and they say a lot about Chicago and its makeup. In the 1950s, the baseball

players such as Chet Walker and Bob Love and hard-nosed, scrappy white players such as Jerry Sloan.

The heroes of the 1980s and '90s have been the Cubs' (now-retired) white Ryne Sandberg and black Andre Dawson (now traded to another team), both quiet sluggers known for their off-field charity work; the now-retired Bears' football player Walter Payton (rightly nicknamed "Sweetness") and the Bulls' ex-star Michael Jordan, whose high scoring and soaring slam-dunks made him perhaps the most exciting basketball player of his era.

Drinking in sports: The Chicago Bulls'

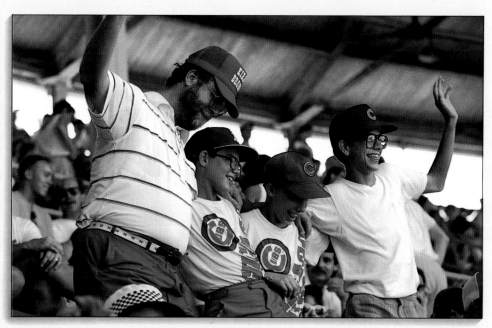

heroes were the Cubs' Ernie Banks and the White Sox's Minnie Minoso, a pair of black sluggers known as much for their sunny dispositions as their home runs. In the 1960s, the Chicago Black Hawks had two of the greatest ice hockey players ever, Bobby Hull and Stan Mikita, both team-oriented players who were also prolific scorers and tough guys who comported themselves as gentlemen in a game known for its thugs. In the 1970s, the Chicago Bulls basketball team was led by a combination of smooth black

Left, baseball buddies. **Right**, the Wrigley wave.

former coach, Dick Motta, once used a backhanded reference to opera to describe his team's hope in the face of despair: "It ain't over 'til the Fat Lady sings." Nowadays, after the Fat lady sings she is likely to be seen, along with other fans of both food and sports, at one of Chicago's many influential "sports" bars.

The sports bar, as originated in Chicago, was once merely a neighborhood tavern that had a TV installed so that afternoon customers could watch the Cubs in dark, air-conditioned comfort. Now, however, the sports bar has become an American "concept," much expanded and imitated across the country but still not done anywhere as well as in Chicago.

The modern sports bar still has TV, but there are likely to be several large screens that may show taped highlights or past games when nothing live is being broadcast. Besides the usual theme decorations of sports equipment, photos and memorabilia from hats to bats, many sports bars offer participation in the form of pay-per-play sports trivia games, miniature bowling, little basketball hoops and even indoor baseball batting cages. But what keeps people coming back to the most prominent sports bars

Fans across the nation prepared to follow the games, play by play, as relayed by telegraph to rented halls.

The White Sox were the overwhelming favorites. Pitcher Eddie Cicotte had won 29 games, but the hero of Chicago was "Shoeless" Joe Jackson, an illiterate former cotton-mill worker from South Carolina who wielded a huge, fearsome bat he called "Black Betsy" and had a league-leading .356 batting average.

The bribery plot was initiated by White Sox first baseman Arnold "Chick" Gandil, according to Eliot Asinof, who wrote a book that was the basis for one of the several

are the large quantities of good food, mainly burgers and pasta dishes or pizza, served up from the kitchens.

The Black Sox: Chicago, of course, wouldn't be Chicago without its history of scandal, and that extends to sports, too. The Chicago "Black Sox" baseball bribery scheme discredited the national pastime and is still America's biggest sporting outrage.

In October 1919, the Chicago White Sox arrived in Cincinnati to play the first World Series – the annual championship between the winners of the rival National and American leagues – since the end of World War I.

movies that have been made on the subject. Gandil met with a bookmaker in a Boston hotel three weeks before the series began. For $80,000 to be provided by a group of gamblers, he agreed to arrange for the White Sox to lose.

Gandil recruited Cicotte and five other White Sox players with the $80,000: third baseman George "Buck" Weaver; shortstop Charles "Swede" Risberg; outfielder Oscar "Happy" Felsch; pitcher Claude "Lefty" Williams, and utility infielder Fred McMullin. Jackson demanded $20,000 for his participation and the gamblers agreed, bringing the total figure up to $100,000.

Rumors that Chicago was going to throw the series were so widespread that the dozens of gamblers crowding into the team's Cincinnati hotel room waved $1,000 bills at the players before the first game. Ultimately, the White Sox lost five games to three (the World Series was then a best of nine games, instead of today's best of seven) in contests marred by bobbled catches and bad throws. The White Sox reportedly won their three games only out of anger when the gamblers were slow in making their bribe payments.

Gandil was eventually paid $35,000. Cicotte got $10,000 which he found under

conspiracy to defraud. The scandal devastated the baseball world. Team owners, under pressure to clean up the game, appointed Judge Kenesaw Mountain Landis as the first commissioner of baseball.

Say it ain't so: The scandal also triggered a wave of bitterness and cynicism. A Chicago newspaper reported that a young boy clutched at Jackson's sleeve as the fallen hero left the grand jury hearing and pleaded, "Say it ain't so, Joe. Say it ain't so."

"Yes, kid, I'm afraid it is," Jackson is said to have replied.

Like so many good Chicago newspaper stories of the era, this one turned out to be a

his pillow in the hotel the night before the first game. Risberg and Williams got $10,000 each, while Felsch and McMullin got $5,000 each. Jackson, too, only ended up with $5,000, despite his $20,000 demand. Weaver apparently decided not to help throw the games, and there is a strong argument that he in fact played to win. He was paid nothing.

The next year, under the goading of newspaper reporters, a Chicago grand jury indicted the eight ballplayers on nine counts of

fabrication by a reporter. But the bitterness was real. Chicago kids began to cry sarcastically, "Play bail!" to start sandlot games. The players were acquitted of the criminal charges, but Landis nonetheless suspended them from professional baseball for life. For a time they knocked around in semi-pro and "outlaw" leagues, sometimes playing under pseudonyms.

For betraying the sport, and casting it into disgrace for several years until New York Yankee slugger Babe Ruth caught the fans' fancy, the 1919 White Sox have become forever known as the Black Sox.

Left, rugby mud. **Right**, Loop cycling.

AN ARCHITECT'S PHOENIX

The collective psyche of Chicago has never recovered from the fire of 1871; one look at the city's architecture confirms it. One look up, that is.

Those rows of towering skyscrapers – from the sinewy steel spires of the John Hancock Center to the illuminated turrets of the romantic 900 N. Michigan Building – might never have been erected if Mrs O'Leary's infamous cow hadn't kicked over a lamp and started the fire that levelled the city a century ago. Today, the urge to build bigger, taller and faster hasn't abated. Another fire, these giant buildings seem to say, won't wipe *us* out.

Long after other major American cities have gasped in horror at the faceless glass slabs populating once-pleasant boulevards – and gotten fed up with the shrinking space left for people – Chicago continues to be a place where few if any obstacles are put in the way of really big real estate developments. Los Angeles might compel developers to build art museums, Boston may insist on low-income housing and New York may champion the greater good of historic preservation, but here, builders are still sitting pretty – and high.

Scraping the sky: The miracle is that, considering the running room granted developers, Chicago has any good buildings at all, let alone a collection of museum-quality edifices. The integrity of the cityscape was ensured by the early marriage of big building to cutting-edge architecture: Chicago didn't just rebuild after the fire, it invented the skyscraper – the architectural form that was to define American cities.

From that day forward, good – or a least interesting – architecture has gone hand in hand with big building. Ask Chicago developers why they hired famous architects like Cesar Pelli, Helmut Jahn or Ricardo Bofill, and they'll look at you uncomprehendingly.

Preceding pages: State of Illinois Center atrium. **Left**, Oldenburg's *Batcolumn*. **Right**, the Picasso.

The reason is self-evident: this is Chicago.

Perhaps no one epitomizes this phenomenon like local-boy-made-good Paul Beitler, a professional descendant of the men who rebuilt Chicago after the fire. Beitler started his career as a salesman before becoming a leasing broker and making the extremely rare leap to developer. In a city that already has the world's tallest building (Sears Tower: Wacker and Adams, 1,468 feet, 110 stories, built in 1974), the world's fourth-

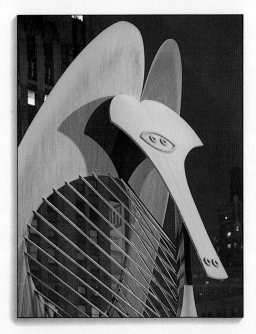

largest building (Amoco Building: 200 E. Randolph, 1,136 feet, 97 stories, 1979) and the world's fifth-largest building (John Hancock Center: Michigan and Chestnut, 1,105 feet, 97 stories, 1969), Beitler announced plans to build a new world's tallest building. Before anyone can outdo the birthplace of the skyscraper by building an inch taller than Sears Tower, Beitler hopes to head them off at the lofty pass with a reed-thin tower that locals are already calling the Sky Needle: Madison and Wells, 1,999 feet, 125 stories, sometime in the 1990s (maybe).

Beitler has already contributed some future landmarks to the city's skyline. For his Madison Plaza buildings, also at Madison and Wells, he hired Skidmore Owings and Merrill's Bruce Graham, of John Hancock Center fame, and Cesar Pelli, the architect for the planned Sky Needle.

Suburban shadows: In 1987 Beitler built the only high-rise in the Chicago suburbs, a 31-story office building in Oakbrook, for which he engaged Helmut Jahn, one of the city's and the world's most famous and controversial architects.

"Tower" is a relative term in Chicago. Examples from the dawn of the skyscraper are clustered in the city's South Loop along

been saved – and Chicago has an appalling track record on historic preservation – it's because Chicago is much better at building new landmarks than preserving old ones.

For example, all that's left of the facade of one of the city's most famous landmarks, the Stock Exchange Building designed by Louis Sullivan, is the entrance arch, saved when the building was demolished in 1972 and resettled, sculpture-like, behind the Art Institute of Chicago. There it remains, a reminder of how much the city has lost and continues to lose.

This is the double-edged sword of Chicago architecture, with its go-for-broke

Dearborn Street, a group of buildings fewer than 20 stories tall, with masonry facades. Here are the protruding bays, the spare, unornamented surfaces, the penchant for expanses of glass that would characterize Chicago building for the next century. Here are the "Chicago windows," grouped in sets of three.

These proto-skyscrapers look squat and somewhat inelegant today, sooty and down on their luck. But these buildings embody the spirit of post-fire Chicago: no-nonsense, sturdy, dependable structures with a minimum of fuss. If more of their ilk have not

mentality that spurs architects and developers to stretch the limits of the skyscraper form, but also obliterates the city's history in its path.

Building history: Of course, many early buildings still stand. The 16-story Monadnock Building at 53 W. Jackson Blvd, built in 1891 by John Root, is the world's tallest building bearing its own weight; the walls are six feet thick at the bottom. Although constructed using outmoded technology, the building has a modern sensibility. The straightforward, clean lines are what architecture critics call "honest," meaning the building doesn't pretend to be anything it isn't. Chicago architecture, if not its politics, is known for honesty.

Across the street along Dearborn are the Pontiac (14 stories, built in 1891), Old Colony (16 stories, 1894) and Fisher (18 stories, 1896) buildings, some of the earliest examples of the steel-frame skyscraper. Steel frames opened up the sky for architects, allowing them the freedom to design true high-rises.

Ironically, the Fisher Building is less modern-looking than the older Monadnock. It exhibits a nostalgia for old-fashioned forms, however, with an ornamented facade designed store exude the confidence and the skill of Chicago's architectural pioneers. Although the Reliance Building at 36 N. State is in terrible disrepair, its elegance and strength are apparent: crumbling terra-cotta, the loss of its cornice and the ugly ground-floor men's shop can't rob this Daniel Burnham building of its art.

Glass houses: The Reliance Building was built in 1895; Carson's, one of Louis Sullivan's most famous designs, in 1899. It is startling, given their age, that such a high percentage of the facades are made of glass. These are show-off buildings, bragging that so many stories can be held up by such thin

signed to disguise the swarthy steel construction beneath. The quintessential Chicago skyscraper is characterized by simplicity, a lack of "unnecessary" ornamentation; style is secondary to structure. These buildings aren't ashamed of the steel skeleton beneath the facade.

Early skyscrapers that flaunt their construction technology still stand on State Street, where the 15-story Reliance Building and 12-story Carson Pirie Scott department

Left, shimmering skyscrapers. **Right**, architectural contrasts. tendons of steel. They are only a stone's throw in spirit from the glass towers of the modernists, for which Chicago architecture is probably best known.

It is no accident that Chicago, where the value of new construction has always come before the less tangible good of saving the old and treasured, was the refuge for Bauhaus architects fleeing wartime Germany. Ludwig Mies van der Rohe was the most prominent of these architects to settle in Chicago, which proved a receptive canvas for his daring new buildings.

Perhaps nowhere is Mies' glass and steel

vocabulary better articulated than in his buildings here, from the famous 860–880 Lake Shore Drive apartments to the IBM Building at the Chicago River and Wabash Street. As these two structures prove, Mies' goal was an international style of architecture that didn't distinguish among residential, office, industrial or public uses. These are prisms, faceted jewels, beautiful in their craftsmanship and precision, but cold.

With Mies leading the way, Chicago developed an architectural style that can only be described as macho: strong and sinewy was in; warm and flowery was out. The street grid is peppered with these monumental of-

fice buildings, and the major federal and city buildings are also cut from modernist cloth.

Modernist influence: Some of the city's best modernist buildings are the least famous – Time-Life at 541 N. Fairbanks, Inland Steel at 30 W. Monroe, First National Bank at Madison and Clark streets – and the idiosyncratic: Marina City (dubbed Corncob Towers by locals) at the river and Dearborn, plus the Metropolitan Detention Center at Van Buren and Clark, a downtown jail with slits of windows splayed outward, so the prisoners get the maximum view.

Chicago's modernist buildings are ener-

gizing – dynamic and daring essays in construction. They provide a shimmering backdrop for the latest round of tower-building, in which this hard-edged city has acquired a slightly more romantic, certainly less masculine ambience. Everything the modernists believed in has been turned on its ear by the post-modernists, and while Chicago was slow to acquire some of these new designs, it has caught up with a vengeance. The result: a skyline with a little less brawn and a little more grace.

The other nice thing about these new towers is the echo of an architectural aesthetic that made Chicago famous for its building. Details like the tri-partite Chicago window, a 10-story cornice line along Michigan Avenue and a preference for rough-hewn stone at ground level are cropping up in these new designs as the architects pay homage to their building's local antecedents.

Architecture has always been one of the city's greatest exports. No more. New York architects, most notably Kohn Pedersen & Fox, have contributed some of the city's most stunning buildings in recent years; KPF's 333 W. Wacker Drive is one of the best buildings in the city. The 36-story office tower makes a virtue of its triangular site, curving along the bend of the Chicago River on its west facade and presenting a jutting, angular face to the rugged city to the east. The reflective glass, long a favorite of the modernists, is here transposed into a skin as warm as it is taut, lit up daily by the reflection of the setting sun.

There's no question that the out-of-town architects have effected a change in tone. Suddenly, for example, there's a skyline to light up. The flat tops of the Miesian buildings didn't offer much in the way of drama. But the new round of towers – 900 N. Michigan Avenue, 123 N. Wacker, the AT&T Corporate Center (100 S. Franklin), NBC Tower (200 E. Illinois) – boast distinctive tops, often fanciful turrets or spires, that lend themselves to night lights.

Night skyline: Some of the old-timers are lighting up, too. The Chicago Board of Trade (Jackson and LaSalle) and 919 N. Michigan (formerly the Palmolive and then the Playboy Building) have joined the Wrigley

Building and Tribune Tower, both located north of the river on Michigan Avenue, which have long been illuminated at night.

Chicago is lucky to have so many wonderful buildings, because it has precious few wonderful open spaces. The city has less parkland per capita than any other major city in America, and the relentless street grid precludes the grand vistas of European and East Coast cities. This is a place whose children would be startled by the sound of birds and for whom a special farm-in-the-park was built to show them where milk comes from.

While developers can produce great build-

ple, one would think the city's magnificent front yard, Grant Park, was the result of a grand scheme. In fact, it is the consequence of retailer Montgomery Ward's irritation in the late 1890s over plans to build a small city of public buildings – museums and the like – in Grant Park. The building would have obscured the lake view from his corporate headquarters on N. Michigan Avenue, so Ward dug up an old clause in the city code that decreed the lakefront should be "forever free and clear." Ward prevailed, preserving his view, and one of the city's great amenities, forever.

Although Burnham's name is invoked

ings, great spaces require planning, which necessitates putting the brakes on development. And the same zeitgeist that has nurtured the construction of tall buildings has stifled city planning in Chicago. American city planning was born here, with Daniel Burnham's 1909 plan, but it was a stillbirth. Planning may get in the way of development and, as such, has always been suspect.

Planning in Chicago has almost always, therefore, happened by accident. For example,

regularly, very little of his ambitious city plan was ever implemented. The Buckingham Fountain made it, as did the layout for the museums along the lakefront. But there's no Civic Center, few of the tree-lined boulevards and not much of the system of southern lakefront lagoons and islands that Burnham once envisioned.

Instead, it is the great planner's credo – "Make no little plans" – that is invoked, and that philosophy has shaped the city. Developers make no small plans, either, and by some magic the result is one of the world's great architectural mosaics.

Left, Marina City. **Right**, helicopter plies Sears Tower airspace.

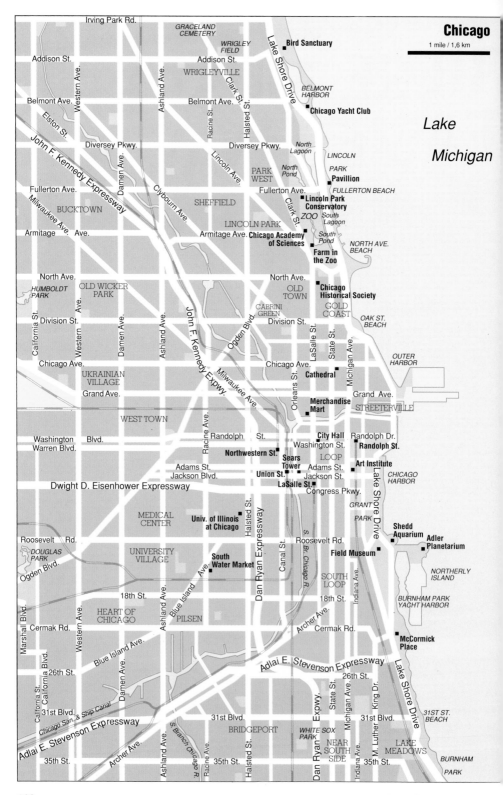

Chicago
1 mile / 1,6 km

Irving Park Rd.

GRACELAND
CEMETERY

WRIGLEY
FIELD

Bird Sanctuary

Addison St.
Addison St.

WRIGLEYVILLE

Belmont Ave.
Belmont Ave.

BELMONT
HARBOR

Chicago Yacht Club

Lake
Michigan

Elston St.

John F. Kennedy Expressway

Diversey Pkwy.
Diversey Pkwy.

North
Lagoon

LINCOLN

Lincoln Ave.

PARK
WEST

North
Pond

PARK

Pavillion

Fullerton Ave.
Fullerton Ave.

FULLERTON BEACH

Milwaukee Ave.

BUCKTOWN

Clybourn Ave.

SHEFFIELD

Clark St.

Lincoln Park
Conservatory

ZOO

South
Lagoon

Armitage Ave.
Armitage Ave.

LINCOLN PARK

Chicago Academy
of Sciences

South
Pond

Farm in
the Zoo

NORTH AVE.
BEACH

North Ave.
North Ave.

HUMBOLDT
PARK

OLD WICKER
PARK

OLD
TOWN

Chicago
Historical Society

California St.

Division St.

Western Ave.

Damen Ave.

Ashland Ave.

John F. Kennedy Expwy.

Ogden Blvd.

CABRINI
GREEN

Division St.

GOLD
COAST

OAK ST.
BEACH

LaSalle St.

State St.

Michigan Ave.

Chicago Ave.
Chicago Ave.

UKRAINIAN
VILLAGE

Milwaukee Ave.

Cathedral

Orleans St.

OUTER
HARBOR

Grand Ave.
Grand Ave.

Merchandise
Mart

STREETERVILLE

WEST TOWN

Washington
Warren Blvd.

Blvd.

Randolph

St.

Northwestern St.

City Hall
Washington St.

Sears
Tower

Randolph Dr.
Randolph St.

LOOP

Art Institute

Racine Ave.

Adams St.
Jackson Blvd.

Union St.

Adams St.
Jackson St.

CHICAGO
HARBOR

Dwight D. Eisenhower Expressway

LaSalle St.

Congress Pkwy.

Lake Shore Drive

GRANT
PARK

MEDICAL
CENTER

Univ. of Illinois
at Chicago

Halsted St.

Roosevelt Rd.

DOUGLAS
PARK

UNIVERSITY
VILLAGE

South
Water Market

Blue Island Ave.

Shedd
Aquarium

Adler
Planetarium

Roosevelt Rd.

Field Museum

SOUTH
LOOP

NORTHERLY
ISLAND

Ogden Blvd.

Canal St.

S. Br. Chicago R.

Indiana Ave.

BURNHAM PARK
YACHT HARBOR

18th St.
18th St.

Marshall Blvd.

Cermak Rd.

Western Ave.

HEART OF
CHICAGO

Ashland Ave.

Blue Island Ave.

PILSEN

Dan Ryan Expressway

Archer Ave.

Cermak Rd.

McCormick
Place

California St.

California Blvd.

26th St.

Damen Ave.

Blue Island Ave.

26th St.

State St.

Dan Ryan Expwy.

Michigan Ave.

M. Luther King Dr.

Lake Shore Drive

31st Blvd.
Chicago San. & Ship Canal

31st Blvd.

31st Blvd.

31ST ST.
BEACH

Adlai E. Stevenson Expressway

BRIDGEPORT

WHITE SOX
PARK

Archer Ave.

LAKE
MEADOWS

Ashland Ave.

S. Branch Chicago R.

Racine Ave.

Halsted St.

NEAR
SOUTH
SIDE

Indiana Ave.

BURNHAM
PARK

35th St.
35th St.
35th St.

Chicago is a city of extremes, from the weather to the politics to the architecture. Given its rambling, rambunctious history, it's not surprising that the city retains much of the spirit of individualism upon which it was built.

That individualism is reflected in the city's different districts, from the gloss of the Gold Coast and the Magnificent Mile to the dozens of neighborhoods that fan out from the city's focus, the downtown lakefront. Sociologists debate whether or not Chicago is America's "most segregated" city, but no one disagrees that it is the major city best defined as a collection of neighborhoods.

Many of the ethnic barriers of the old immigrant neighborhoods have broken down, but enough remain to make Chicago a living exhibit of the American melting pot. Fires, riots, booms and busts, strikes, atomic experiments – the landmarks of events that shaped America are literally underfoot throughout Chicago.

Another distinct aspect of Chicago is its North-South divide. The side of the river on which one is born has relatively little influence on future wealth and happiness, but everything to do with a lifelong disdain for people born on the other side.

Both North and South Siders agree, however, that the downtown lakefront is Chicago at its most extreme: a vast lake, tall buildings, great museums, popular beaches, glittering shops, renowned theaters, famous hot dog stands, classy restaurants and the Midwestern Americans who use these aspects of their city daily.

Chicago's sense of irony is reflected in the way that, after years of trying to shrug off the gangster legacy, there are now guided tours showing where who did what to whom.

Rush Street is Chicago's best-known district for nighttime revelry, but today the action has spread much wider and is more varied. Comedy and cabaret clubs are a specialty, from the Second City troupe that has produced so many TV and movie stars to the smaller spots that feature local comics and singers.

Finally, Chicago offers more festivals and celebrations of music, food and people than perhaps any other American city. Chicago is a town to be celebrated for what it is now rather than for its past, and Chicagoans are only too happy to do that kind of celebrating almost every day.

Preceding pages: flipping at the fountain; fire hydrant fun; waiting for a bus; climbing the corporate ladder.

LOOPING THE LOOP

The Loop, a reference to the circumnavigations of the elevated train system, or the El, is how Chicagoans refer to their downtown, the heart of the city.

The Chicago River, spanned by 10 bridges from Lake Shore Drive to Franklin Street, affords a good introduction to the Loop. Cruise boats, Chicago's answer to the *bâteaux mouches* that ply the Seine, dock at North Pier and Michigan and Wacker. One 90-minute Architectural Cruise chugs past Chicago's famous "corncobs," **Marina City**, the graceful trefoil curve of **Lake Point Tower**, the powerful steel-banded **John Hancock building**, and the lopsided steel-and-glass, balloon-like **State of Illinois building**.

On another worthwhile cruise, a guide provided by the Chicago Architecture Foundation covers the city's famous downtown architects from Mies van der Rohe to Helmut Jahn, and then cantilevers to energy consumption, commenting on or pointing out some 100 notable structures in the course of the journey. Less scholarly but operating more frequently, non-specialist boat tours offer 60-minute, 90-minute and two-hour cruises throughout the day and into the evening, when the light-dotted cityscape is often silhouetted against a velvety sky.

Museum buses: Another way to get a sense of the Loop is to take one of the Chicago Transit Authority (CTA) air-conditioned **Culture Buses** that stop at many of the city's most significant museums, neighborhoods and monuments. There are three non-overlapping routes, North, South, and West, and though they all begin at the Art Institute on Michigan Avenue, they ramble in and out of the Loop before returning. Culture vultures and their long-suffering companions may board the bus at one museum, get off to tour another and then catch a later bus to a third.

As an adjunct to boat and bus, or just for its own flawed charm, visitors ought to consider a loop around the Loop via the El. It won't be a quiet experience. The wheels wring banshee shrieks from the tracks as they take the curves, teenagers scream deliriously into each other's rock-deafened ears, the motorman calls out stops over a muddy public-address system and the occasional lurching drunk or wacko extemporizes for the benefit of one and all. But that's Chicago, and the El is about as non-touristy as Chicago gets.

El on Wheels: On the El, a good place to begin a Loop tour is at the **Merchandise Mart** between Wells and Orleans streets, north of the river. The Mart, closed except to the trade, wears a skin of limestone and terra cotta ornamentals, but these do little to soften its brooding magisterial aspect.

Those who board the southbound Ravenswood train one stop earlier, at Chicago, should keep an eye out for the "climbers" on the right, a startling sight

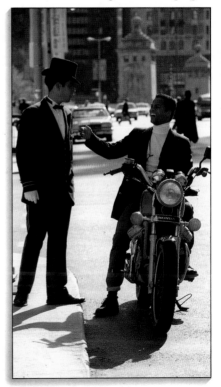

even for seasoned riders. **The climbers** (see page 106) are life-sized models, a man and woman, dressed in business suits. They appear to be pulling themselves up or, possibly, letting themselves down the somber face of a building not much more than 30 feet from the passing trains. Each clutches a realistic briefcase in one hand, and a rope that trails from an overhead fixture in the other. A cartoon balloon sagging from the man's mouth declaims, "There must be an easier way in."

It's worth a few minutes to leave the train and look around the El's **Quincy-Wells station**. Dating from 1897 but recently restored and repainted, it rises above the platforms like an art-deco bungalow. Back on the El, heading east on Van Buren, the odd but dramatic triangular building on the right is the **William J. Campbell US Courthouse Annex**, but the inmates know it better as the Metropolitan Detention Center. This innovative 27-story building, designed for prison efficiency, maximizes

the number of cells, each with its own window, in the given space. It also minimizes the hall space necessary to reach them. All in all, the center is a scientific rather than a humanistic exercise in incarceration.

Fizzy facades: Just down the street on the left is the **Fisher Building**, built in 1896 and extended in 1907. From the El, the building's facade, tiers of tall windows gathered into triplets by rounded masonry arches, appears to shimmer gently. The **Automat Building**, also on the left, acquired its jazzy facade of polychromed terra cotta in 1917 when Horn and Hardart converted it from a seedy hotel into a haven for people who didn't mind putting nickels into machines in order to get their food from behind automated windows. What they saw was what they got.

As the train swings left entering Wabash on its northward run, it passes the **CNA Center**, a deep, almost oxblood-red pair of buildings supported on steel columns – Mies van der Rohe's **Loop lines.**

1 Univ. of Chicago Campus	14 Marshall Field	24 Art Institute
2 Time Life Bldg.	15 Chic. Public Library	25 Petrillo Music Shell
3 Tribune Tower	& Cultural Center	26 Post Office
4 Wrigley Bldg.	16 Civic Opera House	27 Roosevelt University
5 Sun Times Bldg.	17 First National Bank	28 Lincoln Statue
6 Merchandise Mart	18 Carson Pirie Scott & Co.	29 Buckingham Fountain
7 Illinois Center	19 Palmer House	30 Chicago Hilton & Towe
8 Prudential Bldg.	20 Goodman Theatre	31 Northwestern Station
9 Amoco Bldg.	21 Union Station	32 La Salle Station
10 Chicago Theatre	22 Sears Tower	
11 Randolph St. Station	23 Dirksen Bldg.	
12 City Hall &		
Cook County Bldg.		
13 Daley Center		

Downtown Chicago

Subway
Elevated Train ("EL")

0.5 miles / 800 m

influence. On the left are glimpses of students poring over books at DePaul University's Loop campus, and on either side office buildings flow by as, through the windows, draftsmen move T-squares across slanted boards, dancers spin, and typists punch.

Unless you are determined to complete the loop, exit at **State Street**. "That great street," converted to a pedestrian mall, has lost some weight while gaining in breadth. Widened for its renaissance as a mall, the street gained stalls selling popcorn and fruit. But major retailers such as Wieboldt's, Lytton's, Goldblatt's, Steven's, and Montgomery Ward pulled up stakes in the 1980s, leaving a swath of schlock storefronts advertising cheap electronics and kitsch.

Amid the junk, a few oldtimers remain. Evans, selling women's clothing just south of Madison, tries to ignore the occasional anti-fur picketers. **Marshall Field's** is still an anchor, along with rival department store **Carson Pirie**

Scott & Co. Designed by Louis H. Sullivan and built by Daniel Burnham, the Carson Pirie Scott Building retains the architectural tension and grace which made it revolutionary at the turn of the century. Wide, light-embracing windows on the terra-cotta facing rise above cast-iron reliefs that lend strength to the lower floors. The grill on the southwest corner recreates, in metal, swirling floral fantasies reminiscent of Art Nouveau calligraphy.

On Michigan Avenue, just outside the southern boundaries of the Loop proper, are the Museum of Contemporary Photography and the Spertus Museum. The **Museum of Contemporary Photography**, a Columbia College project, takes light-sensitive emulsions – not to mention 19th-century coated glass plates and contemporary electronic adjuncts – seriously. Special exhibits usually complement the internationally-respected Permanent Collection and Print Study Room.

The **Spertus Museum** has a split

uckingham ountain, rant Park.

personality. Part of the collection celebrates the survival of the Jewish people as embodied in their art: the gilt Torah pointers and needlepoint Torah covers of the medieval *stetl* (village), parchment manuscripts and tableware, and modern Israeli festival lamps alongside 300-year-old Passover dishes. The rest of the Spertus collection mourns the horrors of the Holocaust, with numbing mounds of clothing, heaps of buttons and piles of human hair retrieved from the death camps. The museum is unified, however, in its drive to explain Jewish history and celebrate Jewish people.

School daze: Heading north up Michigan Avenue, the **Auditorium Building** once housed a hotel and offices as well as a major theater. The theater and its magnificent tiered ceiling remain, but **Roosevelt University**, a prime example of a city school, has taken over the rest. Theatergoers reach the steeply-banked gallery via an elevator and corridor shared with the school, and a wrong turn may lead to Sociology 101 rather than the opening curtain of *Les Sylphides*.

Further north on Michigan, the granite-and-limestone **Fine Arts Building**, originally a showcase for the Studebaker Carriage Co., now produces budding artists like Jackson Pollack and Virgil Thomson.

The nearby Santa Fe building houses the **Chicago Architecture Foundation's Shop and Tour Center**. This bookstore-cum-gallery is devoted to the history of Chicagoan architecture, The Foundation also maintains the Glessner House and the Clarke House in the Prairie Avenue Historic District, and offers more than 50 tours of architectural highlights in and around Chicago.

Two blocks on is **Orchestra Hall**, home to the Chicago Symphony Orchestra since 1904. A short walk over the green lawns of **Grant Park** east of Michigan Avenue leads to **Buckingham Fountain** which, during the summer, throws jets of water as high as 135

An engineering dedication, Daley Center

feet. At night, concealed lights turn the jets yellow, pink, blue and green, creating one of the lakeside's more spectacular kinetic effects. Outdoor concerts are a pleasant feature of the nearby **Petrillo Band Shell**.

A tree-dotted park leads to the **Art Institute of Chicago**. Inside, the Art Institute offers a wide range of exhibits, including ancient Chinese bronzes, neolithic Ban Chiang pottery from Thailand, Arthur J. Rubloff's eye-popping collection of paperweights, some of America's choicest examples of French Impressionists and Post-Impressionists, arms and armor, textiles and pre-Columbian pottery as well as hugely popular temporary exhibits.

Founded in 1879, the Art Institute moved to its present French Renaissance-style quarters in 1892, just in time for the 1893 Columbian Exposition. The famous **stone lions** that flank the building's main entrance have, according to legend, occasionally been "sold" to unwary newcomers by hustling lo-

cals. In January 1986, when the Chicago Bears went to American football's Super Bowl, the lions found themselves in oversized football helmets fashioned from barbecue kettles.

Glorious protests: Extensive renovations and additions to the Institute over the past 15 years have added a new 1,000-seat auditorium, plus the entire **Trading Room** from the now dismantled Adler and Sullivan's Chicago Stock Exchange, which dates back to 1893. In recent years, the School of the Art Institute has been the center of considerable controversy. One student gained national attention when his painting of the late Mayor Harold Washington, decked out in bra and panties, was unceremoniously yanked from the wall by a group of irate aldermen.

In 1989, another student placed an American flag on the floor, leading some unconcerned museumgoers to walk on it. Protesters crowded the front steps, and motorists, invited to "honk if you love Old Glory," created a ca-

Mao by Warhol, Art Institute of Chicago.

cophony of patriotism on Michigan Avenue. Some legislators threatened to revoke public funding, but the furor eventually flagged and died down.

The Art Institute regularly offers special exhibits and lecture series. It is also associated with the adjacent **Goodman Theater**, which most nights presents classical and contemporary drama, along with new works and training for would-be playwrights and actors.

A few blocks from the river, the **Chicago Cultural Center** flaunts Tiffany mosaics and domes resplendent with stained glass. Vast public spaces connected by vaulted arches and sweeping staircases create a satisfying interior for a public building. The Center offers programs and exhibits in the performing, visual and literary arts; architectural tours are available.

On **LaSalle Street**, roughly between Madison and Jackson but spilling over onto Wacker Drive three blocks farther from the lake, is a financial district that could well be called Wall Street West.

One landmark is the Board of Trade Building, its lobby an Art Deco tone poem in variegated marble, nickel steel and glass. The Lyric Opera's home on Wacker Drive, the **Civic Opera House**, is nicknamed Insull's Throne, so-called for both backer Samuel Insull and its fancied resemblance to a chair of monumental proportions.

Also on Wacker Drive is the 333 West Wacker Drive Gallery, part of the **Chicago Athenaeum**, a museum that aims to show how design can positively impact the human environment in architecture, industrial and product design, graphics and urban planning. Its resource center is at the Daniel H. Burnham Center, 1165 N. Clark Street and Gallery I is at 515 N. State Street.

Plaza art: The **Dirksen Building** and the **Kluczynski Building and Post Office**, both on Dearborn Street and named after prominent native sons, are frequently cited as two examples of Mies van der Rohe's most successful designs. Alexander Calder's *Flamingo*,

Alexander Calder's *Flamingo*.

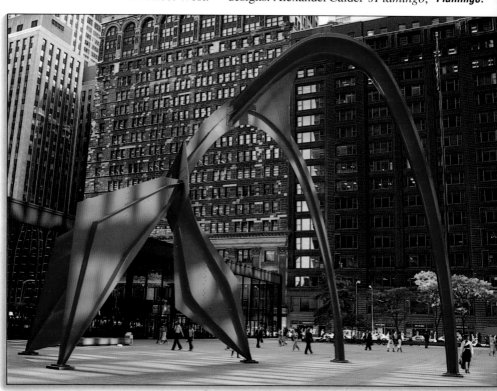

a series of deep-red arcs whose lightness and grace belie the work's 50 tons, occupies a large, open square between the two buildings.

Meanwhile, at the **Daley Center Plaza**, 162 tons of rusted steel rise 50 feet high. Known only as *The Picasso Sculpture*, it has been the butt of jokes and the subject of criticism since it was first erected in 1967. What is it? The consensus says a woman, though some say a bird, a dog or a range of obscene suggestions. On the south side of Washington Street, directly across from the Picasso, stands **Joan Miró's *Chicago***, a highly-stylized female figure formed from steel-reinforced concrete. Her skirt is a lively mosaic, and she shows no signs today of the vivid red spray paint with which vandals greeted her controversial arrival in 1981.

Scraping skies: The tallest bank building in the world, the **First National Bank**, soars in a gentle, pale-gray arc above a plaza that opens a few steps down from street level in the fibrillating heart of Chicago's commercial center on Dearborn and Madison. Around noon, on sunny days, the plaza around the **Hamal Fountain** rapidly fills up with office workers, lunching al fresco.

On the Dearborn Street side, **Marc Chagall's** *Four Seasons* mosaic mural, 70 feet of multi-colored marble, glass and stone, squats uncomfortably. It's best seen at night, illuminated, when it doesn't have to compete with the graceful curves of the building or the plaza's spacious sweep.

The 16-story **Monadnock Building**, on Dearborn between Van Buren and Jackson, built in 1891, is the highest ever erected using wall-bearing masonry construction instead of the modern metal-frame method of construction. Named after a picturesque mountain in northeast Vermont, the Monadnock Building remains a personal triumph for architect John Root, and one of the last great examples of a now obsolete technology.

Sears soars: In describing the world's

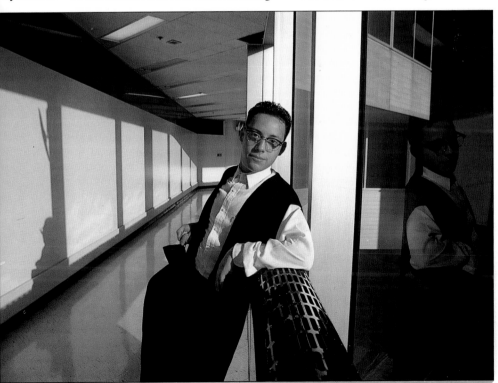
Arty student.

tallest office building, one is tempted to borrow from Alexander Pope, who wrote that he "lisped in numbers for the numbers came." Completed in 1974, the **Sears Tower**'s 110 stories soar 1,454 feet, enclose more than 4 million square feet of floor space and accommodate some 16,500 people daily. From the 103rd-floor **Skydeck**, 1,353 feet above the ground, you can see four US states on a clear day (a rarity in Chicago). Roughly 16,000 bronze-tinted glass windows and 28 acres of black anodized aluminum cover a framework of 76,000 tons of steel – and enough concrete for a five-mile long, eight-lane highway.

Admission to the Skydeck includes a multi-image slide show, *The Chicago Experience*, and a brief lecture on the building's main features with the help of a nine-foot model, built to 190th scale, that illustrates and elucidates its nuts-and-bolts workings. Go for the view and the lecture; the slide show is disappointingly uninformative, though

mercifully short. Stop in on the Calder level to see **Alexander Calder's** *Universe*, a sculpture 55 feet wide, 33 feet high, consisting of a series of geometric shapes in red, yellow, orange and black, that swing and turn independently.

If hunger pangs strike in the Sears Tower, and a hot dog or doughnut will not do, pop into Mrs Levy's delicatessen for some gefilte fish, or a bagel with cream cheese and lox. Should a south-of-the-border flavor be more appealing, amble over to Dos Hermanos for tacos and enchiladas. Those who cannot leave without a tote bag, ashtray, T-shirt or souvenir mug will find 30 accommodating shops in the tower.

On the hot track: Walking east to Clark and then north brings you to the **State of Illinois Center**, which finally opened on May 6, 1985 amid negative publicity, escalating costs and many design and maintenance problems. Some called it designer Helmut Jahn's homage to megalomania. Others merely noted that 17 stories of glass encircling a huge rotunda topped by a shortened glass cylinder could be expected to play havoc with internal temperatures. And it does. Office workers on upper floors, forced to wear sunscreen and dark glasses on bright days, suffer from temperatures in the high 90s F during the steaming summer months, despite an air-conditioning system working to capacity. And when the air-conditioning breaks down, the building has to be virtually evacuated.

More than 50 state agencies are housed in the center, as well as three levels of restaurants and shops. An art gallery exhibits primarily Illinois artists and artisans, and is well worth a visit. So is the building itself, despite its drawbacks as a place to work. A glass-enclosed elevator provides a thrilling, stomach-lurching ride to the top floor, not recommended for acrophobes. A tour of the building may be had by asking at the information booth. Outside, at the main entrance, **Jean Dubuffet's** *Monument With Standing* Field Museum of Natural History.

Beast, 10 tons of white fiberglass outlined in black, stands guard.

The museum district: South of the formal boundaries of the Loop, the Field Museum of Natural History, Shedd Aquarium and Adler Planetarium draw crowds of travelers and scholars. The **Field Museum**, whose classical lines separate the north and southbound lanes of Lake Shore Drive with majestic calm, contains more than 19 million artifacts. Named after Marshall Field I, a principal benefactor, the museum was built in 1921 from a Daniel Burnham design, and is regarded as one of the best museums in the world for anthropology, botany, zoology and geology.

A pair of enormous dinosaurs welcome visitors to the high-ceilinged entrance hall, along with an African elephant that, for many Chicagoans, is a symbol of the museum. One of the most spectacular exhibits, the life-sized **tomb of Unisankh**, scion of the Fifth Dynasty Pharaoh, has been carefully reconstructed, down to two original tomb chambers excavated in 1908. The labyrinth's display cases, including faïence amulets, tools and mummies, merge into a human-scale model of an ancient Egyptian village.

Elsewhere, there's a full-scale reproduction of a South Pacific island. Gem lovers gravitate through the extensive array of precious stones to gawk at the **Chalmers Topaz**, resplendent in all its 5,890 carats. The jade room has a superb collection of Orientalia, tempered by a small sampling of ancient jade. This stone comes not only in green but also in rich oxblood red, mustard-seed yellow and white flecked with carmine.

In the swim: Nearer the lake, in the **Shedd Aquarium**, 90,000 gallons of sea water provide a home for sharks, eels, sea turtles and other denizens of the Caribbean deep in the world's biggest public fishbowl. Divers swim among the creatures twice a day, doling out food as spectators crowd around, cameras ready to snap a hammerhead shark or moray eel literally eating out of

Detail from the ancient Egyptian Book of the Dead, Field Museum.

a diver's hand. In all, more than 6,600 specimens inhabit 200-plus separate environments. The Shedd Aquarium's **Oceanarium** duplicates a Pacific Northwest environment for whales, dolphins, sea otters and seals.

The **Adler Planetarium** peers up at the heavens from the northern point of **Northerly Island**, a five-minute walk from Lake Shore Drive via Achsah Bond Drive. The planetarium can project pictures of the night sky as it appeared when Tyrannosaurus Rex and his ilk roamed the Cretaceous swamps and forests of the American Midwest. The show suggests events that scientists believe may have occurred in the first few seconds of Time, and it also casts a speculative eye forward, up to 20 billion years in the future.

Friday nights, weather permitting, which, unfortunately, it seldom does, the show culminates with a closed-circuit TV panorama of the sky through a direct feed from the 20-inch **Doane Observatory telescope**. There's also a three-story museum that includes a **moon rock** collected by the *Apollo 15* astronauts, and the telescope through which Sir William Herschel first sighted the planet Uranus.

Those in need of sustenance might like to return to Michigan Avenue for elegant *cucina Italiana* amid the restaurant La Strada's lushly overstated ambience. Or they could mosey on over to **Printer's Row**, a place and a restaurant, the latter showcasing the skill and talent of Michael Foley, whose combination of traditional French and American nouvelle styles yields some of the most satisfying serious dining in the Loop. A spiffy, up-and-coming area it would be churlish to brand yuppified, Printer's Row does offer the young and affluent a neighborhood to call their own. Outdoor sculpture is all around, and the **Printing Museum** on South Plymouth makes an enjoyable low-key interlude from the likes of the highbrow Art Institute with its display of ponderous bronzes.

Left, **Chicago photographed by NASA.** *Right*, **Dan Aykroyd, left, and John Belushi in** *The Blues Brothers.*

CHICAGO IN THE MOVIES

The human drama, comedy and crime of Chicago, along with a cityscape ranging from lovely lakefront and soaring skyscrapers to grim ghettos and sordid stockyards, has been a fertile playground for American filmmakers.

The play *The Front Page* by Ben Hecht and Charles MacArthur described the comic rough and tumble of Chicago newspaper life in a style that has spawned several movie versions, including a largely unfunny Burt Reynolds-Kathleen Turner vehicle, the 1988 *Switching Channels*, that had the stars working in cable television news.

The original 1931 film *The Front Page* was one of the best of the early talkies, starring Pat O'Brien as an ace reporter and Adolphe Menjou as his editor, doing battle against civic corruption and one another. But a 1940 remake, *His Girl Friday*, directed by Howard Hawks, became one of America's favorite movies of the era by making the ace reporter a young, attractive woman (played by Rosalind Russell) with whom the editor (Cary Grant) falls in love while trying to stop her retiring from the paper.

The Front Page spawned a tradition of transforming Chicago's vibrant experimental theater onto the big screen. One of the more successful examples in recent years was local playwright David Mamet's modern romance-comedy of manners, *Sexual Perversity in Chicago*, which was the basis for the 1986 movie *About Last Night*. That film provided springboard roles for several rising young actors, including Demi Moore, Rob Lowe, Jim Belushi and Elizabeth Perkins, and brought to the screen a vivid picture of yuppie life in Chicago, from the sports bars to the softball along the lakefront. Later, when Mamet began writing and then directing his own screenplays, he set much of the 1988 mob comedy *Things Change* in Chicago.

Another 1986 flick that used Chicago locations well was *Ferris Bueller's Day Off*. The John Hughes comedy – one of several he has directed locally about Chicago's suburban teenagers –

starred Matthew Broderick as the truant living out everyone's dreams of the way high school should have been but rarely was. Other John Hughes teen-screen hits filmed in Chicago include *Sixteen Candles* in 1984, *The Breakfast Club* and *Weird Science* in 1985 and *She's Having A Baby* in 1988.

Perhaps the quintessential Chicago movie in recent years, however, has been *The Blues Brothers*, the 1980 comedy starring John Belushi and Dan Aykroyd as Jake and Elwood Blues. The story – the outlaw boogie brothers must save their old orphanage – is corny and there are too many car crashes, but the two stars are at their best and some classic music scenes are provided by Aretha Franklin, James Brown and Ray Charles.

In 1987, *The Untouchables* was a blockbuster depiction of the Chicago story that the rest of the world knows best: crime fighter Eliot Ness's battle against the Capone mob.

One of the interesting things about the cinema in Chicago is the way big talents who came up in the town – the Belushis, Aykroyd, John Candy, David Mamet and others – return to their roots when they acquire a kind of creative control needed to dictate where their movies are shot.

Well-known movies in recent years that were filmed in or around Chicago include *Silver Streak* in 1976, *Looking for Mister Goodbar* in 1977, Robert Altman's *A Wedding* in 1978, and *Somewhere in Time* and *My Bodyguard* in 1980. *Ordinary People*, the film directed by Robert Redford that won an Oscar for best picture in 1980, was filmed in its entirety in Chicago and its North Shore suburbs.

Other locally made films include: *Four Friends* in 1981; *Endless Love* and *Continental Divide* in 1981; *Doctor Detroit*, *Bad Boys* and *Risky Business*, another teen movie that made a star of Tom Cruise in 1983, and *Streets of Fire* in 1984. Also filmed in Chicago were *The Color of Money*, the Paul Newman-Tom Cruise sequel to *The Hustler*, and Cruise-vehicle *Top Gun* in 1986; a rare John Hughes non-teen comedy, *Planes, Trains and Automobiles*, in 1987; *Major League*, *Uncle Buck* and *Music Box* starring Jessica Lange in 1989, and another Jessica Lange film, *Men Don't Leave*, released in 1990.

THE FINANCIAL DISTRICT

Chicago's financial district is best known for its colorful, raucous futures markets. Amid the seemingly manic action of the trading pits, world prices are set for corn, wheat, soybeans, pork bellies and live cattle, to name just a few of the commodities involved. These century-old markets have become increasingly sophisticated and now include financial instruments such as US Treasury bonds, foreign currencies from Japanese yen to German marks, Eurodollars, stock options and stock indexes.

LaSalle Street is Chicago's answer to Wall Street, lined by somber bank buildings and glistening skyscrapers that are filled with brokerages and law offices. The financial district runs from roughly **Madison Street** on the north to **Jackson Street** on the south, where LaSalle stops at the foot of the towering **Chicago Board of Trade** to form an architectural canyon. The district has been expanding westward to **Wacker Drive**, where the **Chicago Mercantile Exchange** occupies a newer 40-story twin tower.

It makes sense that commodity trading was invented in Chicago, which grew up as a transportation crossroads nestled in the Midwestern breadbasket. In the 1800s, wagons, oxcarts, barges, canalboats and railroads hauled crops here from fields across the prairie. At harvest time the streets and waterways were choked with loads of grain as local farmers scrambled to find buyers. Often there were surpluses in which case spoiled grain was often dumped into Lake Michigan. The exchanges evolved to provide an orderly marketplace for agricultural commerce.

Pit bulls: With the growth of financial futures, futures trading has spread to New York, Tokyo, London, Hong Kong and other international cities. But Chicago remains the industry's center.

Traders are easy to spot, their bright-colored trading jackets unmistakable in the financial district's bars and coffee shops, such as **Lou Mitchell's Restaurant** on W. Jackson Boulevard, where they gather to brag about their trading acumen or debate whether grain prices are heading up or down.

Inside the exchanges, traders and brokers gather in octagonal, stair-stepped rings called "pits," which allow buyers and sellers to see one another. Each pit is for a specific commodity and the biggest are crammed with hundreds of traders who at first glance seem to be simply jumping up and down, frantically waving their arms and shrieking at each other. The activity looks chaotic, but there's method to the madness. Fortunes are at stake here and millions of dollars have been made and lost in a split second.

This fast-moving game lures high-rollers: a seat on the Board of Trade, for example, costs about $400,000. But the prospect of a big score has attracted players from practically every background: ex-cops, former football players, lawyers, teachers, doctors, even professional gamblers have tried their luck in these trading pits. The Jaguars and Porsches parked in surrounding lots attest to the success of many. The unlucky lose their seats and sometimes, literally, their shirts.

On the exchange floors, there are legendary tales of brash traders who won or lost huge sums trying to corner the markets. Traders still tell stories about the time the action in the soybean pit got so crazy that a trader's leg was broken – and no one noticed him writhing on the floor in pain until after the closing bell had sounded, ending trade for the day. Or the one about the time a fire broke out on the Chicago Mercantile Exchange floor and the traders refused to stop buying and selling.

Crying out loud: The physical commodities – wheat, corn and so forth – don't actually change hands. Instead, trading takes place in the form of futures contracts, which are agreements to deliver or take delivery of a certain commodity during a specific month at a price agreed upon in the pit.

It all happens under the open-outcry method, a free-form auction in which each trader shouts out a bid or offer, often red-faced and screaming to be heard over the din. They bellow in pit lingo unintelligible to outsiders: "Ten July at a quarter!" To attract other traders' attention as they try to make themselves understood, they gesture with hand signals symbolizing their prices and the number of contracts they want to buy or sell. Traders stand in specific areas of each pit according to the contract delivery month for which they're trading.

Surrounding the pits are banks of telephones operated by brokerage houses. Most trade orders originate from customers outside the exchange and are phoned in. They are recorded by order-takers, time-stamped and then rushed by floor runners to brokers in the pits.

Continental Illinois Bank Building.

128

Though it seems little more than a game of dice, the daily hysteria performs a necessary economic function. Traders are buying and selling futures contracts on farm products that may not yet have been planted or harvested. The business is largely speculative and highly risky. But futures trading makes it possible for farmers, processors and wholesalers to lock in a price for their products; they can sleep soundly at night knowing they are protected against damaging price swings regardless of drought or flood.

Future money: Since the 1970s, the biggest growth has come in the area of financial futures, now accounting for more than half the futures exchanges' business. Stock-index futures, used by traders to speculate on general stock market trends rather than specific share prices, came under the spotlight of controversy during the Wall Street market crash of 1987; some argued that the futures' pessimism made the crash worse than it might have been. Today, the relationship between futures trading and stock market volatility is still a subject of debate among experts.

To accommodate their enormous growth, the Chicago exchanges have built shiny new trading floors with video and electronic signboards enabling traders to monitor developments in stock, bond and futures markets around the world. Despite the high-tech surroundings, floor trading practices actually have changed little since the 1800s. But historic changes are in the making. The exchanges are developing automated systems so that trading can take place via computer screens as well as in the pits, a contemporary development which may have unforeseen effects on transactions.

At the heart of the district, at 141 W. Jackson Boulevard, lies the venerable **Chicago Board of Trade**, the world's oldest and biggest futures exchange, founded in 1848 by a group of local businessmen. Even for those bored by financial matters, this landmark Art-

Deco skyscraper is worth a look. Designed by Holabird & Root and built in 1930, its lobby elevator doors are graced by golden bundles of wheat. A 32-foot statue of Ceres, the Roman goddess of agriculture, sits at the building's very top.

Just off the lobby is the **Ceres Café** (formerly the Sign of the Trader), a bar and restaurant where traders gather to drown their sorrows, celebrate their profits, or simply take a break, their eyes glued to the commodity prices flashing by on electronic boards punctuating the walls.

Night trading: The Board of Trade is one of the few exchanges open at night. Evening trading sessions are held Sunday through Thursday, catering to businessmen in the Far East dealing in US Treasury bond contracts.

The **Chicago Mercantile Exchange**, established in 1919, began as a tiny butter and egg market and grew into the world's largest trading center for livestock and foreign currencies. In 1972,

Hailing a cab that never comes. Following pages: braced for the financial future.

the Merc pioneered financial futures, used by banks and investors to manage risk. Its stock-index market, based on the Standard & Poor's 500, is the industry's biggest.

Several years ago the Merc moved to a new, glitzier home on South Wacker. In a corner of the exchange, butter and egg prices are still recorded, though only out of nostalgia. The brass spittoons once used by cattle traders are now gone. But the jargon of the pits lives on: a popular gathering spot at the Merc is the **Limit Up** bar, its name taken from the traders' term for a big swing in price that causes a market to temporarily shut down.

Just south of the Board of Trade on LaSalle and linked by bridge is a red, polished-granite complex known as **Exchange Center**. This houses the city's two securities exchanges, the Chicago Board Options Exchange and the Midwest Stock Exchange.

The **Chicago Board Options Exchange** is a mere youngster compared to the city's other exchanges. Founded in 1972 as an offshoot of the Board of Trade, it is the birthplace of stock options trading. Some traders maintain that trading options to buy and sell shares requires more tactical finesse and knowledge of mathematical theory than the futures game. Traders in the pits can be seen clutching notes outlining complicated strategies devised by computer.

Compared to the rollicking commodities markets, the 104-year-old **Midwest Stock Exchange** is almost church-like. Its more staid atmosphere, however, belies a thriving activity level. It is the nation's largest stock exchange after New York's.

Other points of interest in the area include the **Continental Illinois Bank and Trust Building** on South LaSalle, a massive block-square building with a "classic" design said to be copied from early Roman baths. It's Chicago's oldest bank. Across the street is the **Federal Reserve Bank of Chicago**.

COOLER BY THE LAKE

Nothing defines Chicago more than its lakefront. **Lake Michigan** is the city's front yard: an urban vacationland, outdoor sports playground and important cultural center.

Chicago is situated at the southern tip of Lake Michigan, one of the five freshwater Great Lakes formed by melting glaciers at the end of the last Ice Age. With the coming of the European explorers in the 17th century, the site quickly became a trading center because of the transportation crossroads formed between the lakes and nearby inland rivers.

More than 900 feet deep in places, 300 miles long and 118 miles across, Lake Michigan is the second largest of the Great Lakes. It has a profound effect on the city's weather, acting as a sort of insulating blanket that keeps lakefront neighborhoods cooler in summer and a bit warmer in winter. It unleashes fierce winds that come sweeping down over the water, picking up moisture and sometimes dumping "lake effect" snow on the city.

Coasting: In the minds of Chicagoans, the city's 29-mile **lakefront** is the country's third coast. Visitors are surprised by its breadth and beauty. Other cities may boast waterfronts that are in fact more magnificent, but die-hard Chicagoans will argue, with good reason, that none surpasses their own in terms of sheer fun.

Chicagoans make the most of mild (and sometimes hot) summer temperatures by flocking to the lake for a day of play. Even in the coldest weather, when steam rises eerily from the icy water, some hardy souls regularly bundle up in their heaviest winter gear for a peaceful lakefront stroll. In the chill of spring, smelt fishermen along the shore huddle to keep warm.

Weather permitting, Chicagoans can lie on a beach, sail, visit a zoo, picnic, windsurf, hear a concert, see a play, watch a ballet, hit a bucket of golf balls, play chess, eat brunch, jog, roller skate, ride a bike or see an airshow, all within a few square miles.

Architect Daniel H. Burnham in the early 1900s was the first to visualize the lakefront's possibilities as a recreational center. He rejected the typical waterfront development pattern which was dominated by shipping and other industrial users.

The immense scale of the lake inspired Burnham to draw an ambitious plan for a chain of parks, beaches, cultural facilities and pleasure boat harbors along the shore.

A trip along **Lake Shore Drive**, a thoroughfare skirting the shoreline on one side and skyscrapers and parks on the other, is a glorious way to take in the lakefront, city skyline and nearby sights. The drive stretches 124 blocks from Hollywood Avenue on the north to Jackson Park on the south.

But better yet, those with the time should take a walk or a bike ride. The lakefront is laced with jogging paths and bicycle trails scenic enough to entice even the most dedicated couch potato into at least a little exercise. There are many museums, harbors and historic points along the way.

Bikes can be rented in Lincoln Park at **Fullerton Avenue** just west of Lake Shore Drive. The bike path pretty much parallels the course of Lake Shore Drive on its east side. But beware: bike paths and beach areas often become dangerously crowded in the summer. It will take a little practice to avoid all the roller skaters, runners and sun worshippers. The best time to escape the mob scene is early in the morning or late in the afternoon.

Another picturesque way to enjoy the lakefront is to view it from the water itself. There are a half-dozen or so good **boat tours** of the city, including several offering lunch or dinner cruises. They leave from Navy Pier at Grand Avenue and the lake, and from the Chicago

River, next to the Wrigley Building (410 N. Michigan Avenue).

On the edge of the Loop, **Grant Park** is home to several of the city's most famous museums (see the preceding chapter of this book, on the Loop, for more on the Art Institute, Field Museum and Shedd Aquarium). The center of the violent 1968 antiwar riots during the Democratic National Convention, Grant Park's biggest crowds these days come to the **Petrillo Band Shell** (Columbus Drive and Jackson Boulevard) for its lively array of free concerts. The Grant Park Symphony performs here on weekends during the summer. Its weekend-long music festivals – the **Blues Fest** in early June and **Jazz Fest** in late August – draw fans from around the world.

Thousands of picnickers bring blankets and candles to enjoy the music, dance and savor one of the finest views of the city's skyline. In the week leading up to the Fourth of July, scores of local eateries sell their Chicago-style and ethnic cuisine at the **Taste of Chicago** festival. On Independence Day itself, fireworks light the sky and the symphony plays a rousing version of Tchaikovsky's 1812 Overture.

Another nearby draw is the opulent **Buckingham Fountain**, with a colorful light show each evening at 9pm. Modeled after a fountain at Versailles, it was given to the city by heiress Kate Buckingham in memory of her brother, Clarence, a director of the Art Institute.

Varied past: To the north, at Grand Avenue, **Navy Pier** stretches almost two-thirds of a mile into the lake. Its tip provides what some people claim is the best lakefront vantage point in the city. A multi-million dollar facelift begun in 1990 changed dilapidated to dazzling. The city spruced up the pier's image with picnic tables and flowers. Art classes, puppet shows and free concerts under the canopy are just a few of the pier's expanded summertime programs. Bicyclists, skateboarders, roller

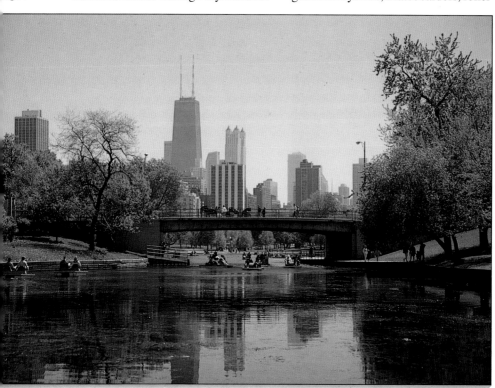

skaters and fishermen are welcome. The public can also tour US Navy and Coast Guard vessels which are docked at the pier.

Olive Park, surrounding the city water filtration plant at Ohio Street, has a small but good beach and tree-shaded area for lounging on the grass. It was named for a soldier, Pfc. Milton Olive Lee, who died in Vietnam in 1966 by throwing himself on a hand grenade to save the lives of four friends.

Farther north, the 1,000-acre **Lincoln Park**, Chicago's largest park, borders the lake between North and Hollywood avenues. The park has been called Chicago's Central Park, and in fact the two were designed by the same landscape architect, Frederick Law Olmstead. It's a fine grassy park suited for strolling and picnicking, complete with rambling walks, lagoons and ponds, footbridges, gardens, bronze statues, two museums and a zoo. Three cafés are tucked among the trees and ponds: Café Brauer at the south end of the zoo, Park

Place Café at Deming Place and Brett's at Waveland Avenue by the golf course.

At the park's southern tip, at North Avenue and Clark Street, sits the red-brick **Chicago Historical Society**. Its exhibits highlight the city's colorful history and characters, including pioneer life, the Fort Dearborn Massacre, the Chicago Fire and the gangster era. Especially good are its collection of materials on Abraham Lincoln and the Civil War, and copies of the inaugural gowns of US presidents' wives.

Nearby, half hidden by shrubbery, is the **Couch family mausoleum**, a reminder of the days when the park was a municipal cemetery. At the time of the Chicago Fire, the city was moving coffins to private cemeteries. When the fire roared north, families took refuge here, climbing into open graves to escape the blistering inferno.

A little farther north on Clark Street is the **Chicago Academy of Sciences**. Its exhibits focus on the natural history and wildlife of the Great Lakes region, depicting Chicago as the dense coal forest that it was 350 million years ago.

The free zoo: The park's best-known attraction is **Lincoln Park Zoo**, which is open daily. Remarkably, admission is free. The zoo is home to more than 2,000 mammals, reptiles and birds, from koala bears to elephants to giraffes. It's famous for its great ape house, with the world's largest collection of gorillas.

The **Farm-in-the-Zoo** consists of several big red barns that offer visitors a sample of rural life, including cows being milked and chicks hatching. The **Zoo Rookery** provides a peaceful respite for a variety of land and water birds that come to feed and nest. Located south of the regular zoo is a children's petting zoo, open most days during the summer months.

The park is also home to some of the city's nicest gardens: the **Lincoln Park Conservatory**, lush with ferns, palms, flowers and other plants; and the **Grandmother's Garden**, between

Chrysanthemum display, Lincoln Park Conservatory

Stockton Drive and Lincoln Park West which is full of old-fashioned flowers.

Not far away is an unexpected find: an interesting, if somewhat age-worn, **Viking ship**. Dating from the Columbian Exposition of 1893, it is a copy of a 10th-century ship built by Norway for the exposition and sailed across the Atlantic by a crew of 12.

At Fullerton Parkway, right on the lakefront, is the **Theatre on the Lake**, which stages Broadway plays in the summer months. Strictly community theater, it's nonetheless delightful on a warm evening under the stars.

Sports: The park has something to offer sports enthusiasts of all kinds, whether their interest is in tennis or 16-inch softball, Chicagoans' favorite.

At Diversey, west of Lake Shore Drive, is a **driving range** for golfers. The **golf course** itself is just north of Addison Street.

The Chicago Park District maintains **30 sandy beaches** along the lakefront, bordering some of the city's richest and poorest neighborhoods. They are officially open (that is, manned by lifeguards) from June 15 to September 15. But swimmers can plunge in at their own risk any time the weather allows. The beaches are free, easy to find and very accessible – they are generally named for the nearest cross-street. On peak summer sunning days, finding nearby parking may be impossible, so walking, taking a cab or using public transportation is a good idea.

The city's most famous stretch of sand is **Oak Street Beach**. Located across Lake Shore Drive from the posh high-rises of the city's Gold Coast neighborhood and only steps from Oak Street's exclusive boutiques, this is where the beautiful people go. There is also some serious beach volleyball played here. To get to the beach, use the pedestrian underpass at Michigan Avenue and Oak Street.

Other popular beaches at North Avenue and Fullerton Avenue are frequented by the youthful, arty and so-

Bald eagle, the US national symbol, in Lincoln Park Zoo.

phisticated residents of the nearby Lincoln Park neighborhood. A bit south of the North Avenue beach house (hard to miss because it resembles a steamship) is an open-air **chess pavilion** where aficionados come to test their gamesmanship. Farther north, Foster Avenue Beach, popular among urban youths, is known for its **pick-up basketball**.

The most crowded weekend of the season is in mid-July, when Chicago holds its yearly **air-and-water show**. Hordes of spectators jam the beaches to view the aerial parade featuring daredevil stunts and aircraft of all kinds.

Just south of Grant Park are two of the city's most-visited facilities: **Soldier Field**, home of the Chicago Bears football team, and the enormous **McCormick Place**, convention capital of the world.

Shipping: Visible out in the lake just north of Grant Park is the system of locks which enabled engineers to reverse the flow of the Chicago River. In the late 19th century, sewage from the river flowing into the lake had so polluted the water that there were frequent typhoid outbreaks. A massive digging project lowered the river level below that of the lake, diverting its flow into the Illinois River and downstream to the Mississippi River.

Today, most shipping is done by rail or air. But Lake Michigan remains a vital part of the city's life and commerce. Most important, Chicago pumps its drinking water from the lake through intake cribs located two miles offshore. Grain, ore, chemicals and other bulk commodities still move through Chicago's busy docks to other ports around the world.

The **Port of Chicago** is located near the steel mills of the industrial southeast side at the Calumet River. The St Lawrence Seaway connects the Great Lakes to the Atlantic, making the city a mid-continent port for ocean-going vessels. Inland, barge traffic on the Illinois and Mississippi rivers links Chicago to the Gulf of Mexico.

Beach bubbles.

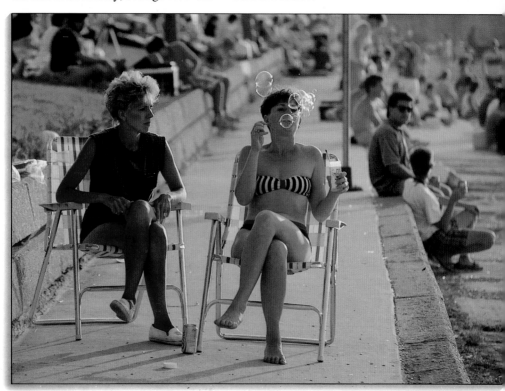

STUDS TERKEL

Studs Terkel is best known for his five books of oral history including Working *and* The Good War. *But Chicago also knows Studs for his daily radio interviews on* WFMT. *Here, speaking into someone else's tape recorder for a change, is Studs Terkel talking in his inimitable style about the lake and the neighborhoods of his adopted city.*

"Chicago is the double-headed city. Our god is Janus, the two-headed god. Nelson Algren, of course, spoke of that often, most eloquently in *Chicago: City on The Make*. He spoke of the city of the night and the city of the day. He wrote of the winners and the losers, of the Jane Addameses and the Al Capones.

"I'm just reading a book now about the Chicago Fire, and what came out of the fire. The myth, the legend, of course, is that after the fire they – all the people of Chicago – worked together. Nonsense. The fact is there was a split, a big split. Why, the Haymarket Riot came just 15 years later.

"Chicago has always been split. The first fur traders – prototypes for our great robber barons – were gypping the Pottawattomies. It was a new land, a new country. Then John Kinzie and his Anglo-Saxon Protestant crowd came here from back East, and the immigrants shortly after that, and everybody was stepping on the next guy.

"The Germans had a tough battle against the WASPs, fighting for Sunday beer. And the Irish had it tough – 'No Irish Need Apply.'

"Who came to Chicago? Hands. I call Chicago a city of hands. 'Hands' is an old-time word for working person. 'Fifty hands wanted.' You read that in rural communities. Farm hand. Hired hand... also factory hands, industrial hands. Chicago is a city of hands, not paper. Some other city, let's say Washington, is a city of paper.

"And yet a crazy thing happened here with the rich men and their wives at the turn of the century. Mrs Potter Palmer and the other wives longed for culture. Whether or not they knew what it was, they wanted it. And so Chicago became a center for culture because of the wives of guys who were meatpackers.

"A guy named Alson J. Smith, a writer, he used the word 'seedbed.' He said Chicago has been a seedbed of various art forms. Take jazz and blues. Back in those early days, before the two big black migrations to Chicago, jazz and blues only had one audience – black people. But when the audience moved north the artists moved north, so Louis Armstrong and King Oliver came to Chicago. And young white kids, like Bud Freeman and Jim McPartland and the whole Austin High gang, heard these guys play. They learned and went East, where all the dough was. Chicago was a seedbed of jazz.

"So what's to see in Chicago? Well, let me tell you. You've got to see the lake, the goddam lake, so magnificent.

"And just stand on the corner of Oak and Michigan, where you've got this crazy juxtaposition. You've got this magnificent lake, and right next to it are these crazy buildings where Xerox copies of things are being made. There is no other city that has a lake, this natural wonder, right in the heart of it. And there's the beach, a common beach, a democratic beach. The poor, the middle class, blacks and whites – they're all on the beaches.

"And you should take an automobile ride through the bungalow neighborhoods and maybe, as Mike Royko would say, go *fast* down South State Street. Drive down there and see the biggest housing complex in the world. It could be an asylum, an orphanage, a prison; it's all these thrown into one.

"And the Art Institute. Go there. Isn't it remarkable? And look at the goddam buildings, the architecture. Isn't it remarkable?

"You know, I was born in New York City and I had asthma as a kid. But I was cured of asthma when I got to Chicago. It was a summer day. I remember. We had a rooming house at Ashland and Flournoy. And I could smell the south wind from the stockyards.

"I just needed something, I think, and Chicago had the energy I wanted, and the feeling. Just something.

"And then it got exciting."

THE MAGNIFICENT MILE

Chicago's **Magnificent Mile**, the city's premier shopping and strolling street, stretches along N. Michigan Avenue between the Chicago River and Oak Street.

The mile earned its nickname largely because of the array of shops that are the match of any upscale retail area: Tiffany, Cartier, Elizabeth Arden, Burberry, Brooks Brothers and on and on. Within five blocks are five of the world's best-known department stores: Saks Fifth Avenue, Neiman-Marcus, Marshall Field's, Lord & Taylor and I. Magnin.

In any season, the only way to sample the Mag Mile is to promenade with thousands of others; even in the dead of winter, the tiny white lights on the branches of the leafless trees give the avenue a warm holiday feeling.

A little history: Start at the **Michigan Avenue Bridge** over the Chicago River, and with some history. Near the northeast pylon of the bridge is a plaque commemorating the passage through the Chicago River in 1673 of the first white men – Jesuit missionary Father Jacques Marquette and Canadian-born explorer Louis Jolliet. On their way north from their explorations on the Mississippi River, they entered the Des Plaines River. There, Indians guided them through the Chicago Portage, a stretch of mud that the explorers realized connected the Great Lakes with the Mississippi River and the Gulf of Mexico.

Across the street a plaque near the bridge's southwest pylon notes the passage in 1681 through the Chicago River of Cavalier Robert René de La Salle and Henry Tonty on their way to the Mississippi River and the Gulf of Mexico. During that trip they claimed the Mississippi Valley for France, naming it Louisiana after their king, Louis XIV. La Salle built a fort near the present site of Chicago, and in a letter referred to its location for the first time on record as "Checagou."

On the north bank of the river and the east side of Michigan Avenue, now the site of a wide pedestrian plaza, the city's first non-native settler built his cabin in 1781. He was Jean Baptiste Point DuSable, a French-speaking black man. He established the city's first commercial enterprise, a river trading post.

Set in the sidewalks on the bridge's south end, across Wacker Drive, are markers outlining the site of Fort Dearborn, the first US Army garrison in Chicago, which was built in 1803. In 1812 the fort was destroyed, and about two-thirds of its settlers and soldiers were killed by Indians incited by the British army during the War of 1812. A bas-relief on the southwest bridge pylon commemorates the event. The three other pylons have bas-reliefs commemorating Jolliet and Marquette, fur trader John Kinzie and the rebirth of the city after the Great Fire of 1871.

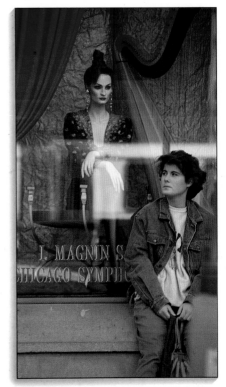

The Magnificent Mile was originally a dirt path called Pine Street, used primarily by lumber wagons that loaded at the Chicago River. Once lined by warehouses, by the 1880s the area farther north of the river had become a popular building site for merchants' large homes; the streets were lined with wooden paving blocks.

Bridgeworks: The building of the Michigan Avenue Bridge, accomplished with great civic fanfare in 1920, ignited the spectacular growth of the street, by then attached to Michigan Avenue and thus renamed. The bridge itself is a fine example of the double-leaf trunnion bascule bridge, so common over the Chicago River that it is known internationally as a "Chicago style" bridge. "Bascule" is from the French for "see-saw," which is what a bascule bridge does. Its two halves rotate up and down on a pair of horizontal shafts called trunnions. The movement of the two sides, or leaves, can be accomplished with a relatively small motor because the weight of the leaves is precisely balanced by iron or concrete counterweights sunk into a pit below street level. The double-decker Michigan Avenue Bridge's leaves weigh 6.7 million pounds each. The counterweights are balanced so finely that they must be rebalanced every time the bridge is repainted.

Engineering aside, the bridge is a stellar attraction when it is raised and lowered, a frequent occurrence around midday during the spring and summer, enabling tall-masted sailboats to pass to or from their winter storage yards up the river. The sight of the roadbed hovering at nearly a 90-degree angle is astounding to visitors, although office workers impatiently waiting to cross to the other side find it infuriating.

Standing sentry at the south end of the Magnificent Mile are two landmark buildings constructed at the same time as the Michigan Avenue Bridge. On the west side, just north of the river, is the **Wrigley Building**, built in 1921 with an **North Michigan Avenue from the bridge.**

annex added in 1924. Its lacily decorated white terra-cotta facade, modeled after the Giralda Tower of Seville Cathedral, is floodlit at night, making it resemble an ornate wedding cake.

Pressing business: Across Michigan Avenue to the east is the **Tribune Tower**, a Gothic revival skyscraper complete with a topping of flying buttresses. Built in 1925, its design was chosen by a nationwide competition held in 1922. It houses the offices of the *Chicago Tribune*, but the newspaper's printing plant is along the north branch of the Chicago River, at Chicago Avenue and Halsted Street. To see the giant presses rolling, cross Michigan Avenue, pass between the two Wrigley Building halves and enter the home of Chicago's other major daily newspaper, the **Chicago Sun-Times Building**, where a glass-walled corridor overlooks the press room.

The Tribune Tower, on the other hand, offers a marble lobby inscribed with quotations from famous personages ranging from Euripides to the powerful former *Tribune* publisher Robert R. McCormick. And the sides of the building are studded with hunks of famous buildings and historical sites around the world, including the Parthenon, the Taj Mahal, Westminster Abbey and the Mosque of Suleiman the Magnificent in Istanbul. The stone fragments were gathered by *Tribune* foreign correspondents at the request of McCormick, who reportedly asked them to pursue only "honorable means" in acquiring these invaluable and irreplaceable stone fragments.

Just east of Tribune Tower is **NBC Tower**. Its similarities to Rockefeller Center in New York are no coincidence. The architect Adrian Smith, of Skidmore, Owings and Merrill, studied the Art Moderne-style Rockefeller Center complex, along with nearby Chicago buildings including the Tribune Tower, before designing the NBC Tower. The result, wrote architecture critic Paul Gapp, is "the best-looking masonry-clad skyscraper constructed in Chicago since the 1930s."

A pier-less detour: Descend the stairs just north of the NBC Tower, and walk three blocks on Illinois Street to **North Pier Chicago**. It is not really a pier, but was originally a nondescript brick warehouse built between 1905 and 1920 for lake boats to tie up in the adjacent slip and unload their cargo. Today's cargo consists of tourists, for the warehouse has been transformed into a complex of restaurants, exclusive shops, art galleries and leisure attractions, including an indoor golf course. Enjoy a snack on a porch overlooking the water, or munch fresh fudge while walking along the landscaped waterfront promenade.

Parents traveling with fidgety children will find the nearby **Chicago Children's Museum** a godsend, with exhibits aimed at children from pre-schoolers to age 14. Toddlers can play on a big wood fantasy vehicle, crawl through squares lined with various touchable treasures or play in a miniature kitchen or Three Bears' House. For older children, there are child-sized versions of a post office and the Art Institute of Chicago, and a hands-on bubble-making exhibit. Diaper-changing areas are provided in both the men's and women's rest rooms.

North Pier Chicago also offers the **Chicago Maritime Museum**, with exhibits on Midwestern maritime history, including shipping on the Great Lakes and the St Lawrence Seaway, and navigation on Midwest rivers and canals. North Pier also offers 90-minute boat tours focusing on Chicago architecture. Just east of North Pier, past Lake Shore Drive, is **Lake Point Tower**, a curving, three-lobed condominium building whose architects took their inspiration from a 1921 Mies van der Rohe proposal for a Berlin skyscraper.

Elder citizens: The Magnificent Mile has seen such a dizzying pace of development in recent years that it is difficult to picture what it looked like in more

Leafy lunch on the Mag Mile median

genteel, bygone times. But a few elegant buildings remain on the west side of N. Michigan Avenue, featuring mansard roofs and neoclassical detailing. And history can be seen in more ways than one at the **Hotel Inter-Continental**. Built in 1929 as the Medinah Athletic Club, it features a gilded onion-shaped dome and a floor-by-floor history of the world in interior design, from the Assyrian lions carved into marble balconies on the second floor to the 13th-century Florentine mosaics in the stairwell to the Renaissance paintings above the elevators on the fifth floor.

A touch of modern elegance can be found at the **Terra Museum of American Art**. This narrow building, with a marble facade interrupted by several simple expanses of windows, houses a compact museum of American paintings from the collection of industrialist Daniel J. Terra, who opened the museum in 1987. The museum specializes in 19th-century paintings.

Lovers of modern art will want to visit the **Museum of Contemporary Art**, a block and a half east of Michigan Avenue on E. Ohio Street. In addition to provocative, changing exhibits, the museum offers an excellent gift shop featuring fun jewelry and T-shirts making witty proclamations.

Squatting: The surrounding blocks, between Grand and Chicago avenues, and St Clair Street and the lake, are known as **Streeterville**. The area is named after George Wellington Streeter, who claimed squatter's rights here for more than 30 years. Streeter and his wife were excursion boat operators whose boat ran aground in 1886 in the lake south of Chicago Avenue. Instead of freeing the boat, they decided to fill up the lake around it. Nearby residents brought dirt, garbage and trash, and soon built a 180-acre shantytown. Streeter "sold" some of the real estate to other squatters, and it was not until 1918 that he was forced out by court order.

At Chicago Avenue, on the west side of N. Michigan, is the **Water Tower**,

aying for ssersby.

one of Chicago's most famous landmarks – and possibly one of the least attractive. It is an elaborate, pseudo-Gothic tower surrounded by crenellated medieval turrets. Oscar Wilde, on visiting Chicago in 1882, called it a "castellated monstrosity with pepper boxes stuck all over it." The tower was built to conceal a standpipe that equalized the pressure of the water pumped from the **Pumping Station** to the east, a less elaborate structure made of the same yellow Joliet limestone. Both structures were built two years before the devastating Chicago Fire of 1871, and are among the few buildings in the area that survived the fire. The tower is locked and empty, but the pumping station is still in use. It also serves as a tourist information center.

The area near the Water Tower seems to attract Chicago street artists. One notable example in recent years is Lee Godie, a gray-haired, toothless bag lady earning a nice living from selling her childlike drawings to passersby. She even made a deal with a nearby high-fashion boutique to cash checks from her customers, including a number of major art galleries and prominent private collectors.

Good views: North of the Water Tower, between Pearson and Chestnut streets, is **Water Tower Place**, renowned as an upscale downtown shopping mall. Just north of Water Tower Place is the **John Hancock Center**. The third-tallest building in Chicago (and fifth-tallest in the world), it is a tapered black tower marked with external X-shaped braces that support the building against wind. At 1,105 feet, the John Hancock offers a lower observation deck than that of the 1,468-foot Sears Tower. But some aficionados say the view is better, for it includes vast panoramas of lake, with tiny white dots which are sailboats. On a clear day, visitors can see the states of Wisconsin to the north, Indiana to the south, and Michigan straight across the lake.

At the junction of Michigan Avenue,

Sleeveless; strolling.

and Chestnut Street is **Fourth Presbyterian Church**, an elegant Gothic church built in 1912 and featuring a cloistered walk and a quiet courtyard with a stone fountain. Farther north are some of the more spectacular examples of recent North Michigan Avenue development. The **900 N. Michigan Building** houses Bloomingdale's and an atrium which includes elegant shops such as Christofle, purveyors of fine silver, and Cacharel, French designer clothing. **One Magnificent Mile**, at the corner of Michigan Avenue and Oak Street, has several shops and fine, somewhat expensive restaurants.

Once a guiding light: For a blast from the past, there's the former Playboy Building, now known as the **919 N. Michigan Building**. This 37-story Art Deco-style skyscraper was built in 1930, and features a revolving beacon on top that was used to guide airplanes to safety until taller buildings rendered it obsolete.

At the northernmost foot of the Magnificent Mile, at Michigan Avenue and Walton Street, is the **Drake Hotel**. Built in 1920, it faces Lake Michigan and Oak Street Beach on the north, and offers the weary walker a lobby in the manner of the grand hotels of Europe. For a relatively inexpensive taste of perhaps the best view in all of Chicago, have breakfast or lunch in the hotel's Oak Terrace dining room.

On its north side, the hotel anchors **E. Lake Shore Drive** – a one-block street said to be the single wealthiest block in Chicago, and one of the wealthiest in the world. Some of the amenities in the elegant buildings, constructed between 1912 and 1929, include bedroom vaults for furs at 209 E. Lake Shore Drive; a turntable on the garage floor of the Drake Tower, just east of the Drake Hotel, to turn incoming cars around swiftly so they can drive right out again; and refrigeration for garbage at the Mayfair Regent Hotel, lest it develop an unfortunate smell. Advice columnist Ann Landers lives here. Television per-

Mag Mile
oy shop.

SHOPPING CENTERS

Once you've got them by the malls, their hearts and minds are sure to follow. Indeed, nowhere has the "malling" of America been more apparent – or accepted more enthusiastically – than in the shopping centers of Chicago.

To those who study such trends, the American mall – a collection of stores under one roof – is variously seen as a shrine to the national urge to acquire, or perhaps as the new "town square," where elderly people walk, teenagers loiter and people with causes set up their petition tables and hand out their leaflets.

There is no doubt, however, that most Americans see their local mall – and, indeed, any mall they encounter – as a place to explore: "Let's go check out the mall." Studies show that more and more families now regard shopping as a leisure activity and view a trip to the mall as a "day out" for the entire family, especially as malls add skating rinks, cinemas, bowling alleys and amusement centers.

Within Chicago, the crown jewel is Water Tower Place. Buttressed by Marshall Field's to the north and Lord & Taylor to the south, this vertical shopping emporium features seven levels with 125 boutiques, salons, eateries, and cinemas in a dazzling array of steel, glass and marble.

The best way to tackle Water Tower Place is to take one of the glass elevators to the top floor, and then work down by escalator, floor by floor: jewelry by Christian Bernard; shoes by Pappagallo, Connie and Florsheim; luggage by Louis Vuitton, and cookies by Mrs Fields.

Other shops offer whatnots for the bath, the dining room, the office or the person for whatever kind of statement one wishes to make. And for the child who has everything but a handmade, 6-foot tall stuffed toy giraffe, FAO Schwartz will happily supply one for a mere $5,000 or so.

Go for the glitter, the crowds, the variety of vendibles, the upper-crustiness of it all. For the exhausted, the Ritz-Carlton Hotel rises 859 feet above the east wing of the complex.

Across Michigan Avenue, Bloomingdale's bestows its aura on more than 50 shops. Despite a colorful 60-foot mural in its atrium and the Four Seasons Hotel looming 58 stories tall in the same structure, despite even Gucci and Henri Bendel, this mall has neither the panache nor the stylish elegance of its Water Tower counterpart.

Nearby, at 700 N. Michigan Avenue, is a newer but equally glitzy mall called Chicago Place. The 80 shops, spread over eight levels and 320,000 square feet, include stalwarts such as Saks Fifth Avenue and high-ticket emporia such as CD Peacock and Luis Vuitton. An eighth-floor food court wraps around an indoor garden. The barrel-vault dome and Prairie School-inspired trappings provide visual relief for shoppers jaded by the relentless retail landscape.

Northwest of the city, the suburb of Skokie offers the Old Orchard Center, an outdoor, low-slung, neatly arranged set of boutiques and department stores. A pool, stone islands, delicate Japanese bridges, flower beds and welcoming benches add a cool touch during hot summer months.

Arcades protect shoppers from the elements and afford a rambling path past the stores, and the whole complex is kept scrupulously clean by workers who seem to scoop up gum wrappers before they hit the ground. Old Orchard's 60-plus shops include Saks Fifth Avenue and Marshall Field's.

Farther north, Northbrook Court is a grande dame of malls – enclosed, bi-leveled, unmistakably tennis-set suburban. The 144 stores arrayed around broad intersecting aisles and plazas with modernist sculpture include Neiman-Marcus, Circle Gallery, I. Magnin and Mark Shale.

Toward the center of the Northbrook mall, an interesting design concept is realized by an interlocking set of steel polygons, painted canary yellow, that form an angular spheroid looking up toward clouds drifting over the skylit roof.

Finally, for the truly dedicated who do not mind the long trek to Schaumburg, there's Woodfield Mall, a granddaddy of US malls containing 235 shops. During the summer, up to 200 buses a day bring in customers from a four-state area to shop at Schaumburg's stores.

sonality Oprah Winfrey lives here. Nancy Reagan lived here as a girl. Abra Wilkin, a granddaughter of John D. Rockefeller, lives in the Drake Tower penthouse, and once hired helicopters to bring up building materials for a redecorating job.

Walk east, then turn back south on Lake Shore Drive to see **860 and 880 N. Lake Shore Drive**, two apartment buildings designed in 1952 by Mies van der Rohe. To reach **Oak Street Beach**, double back to the southeast corner of Michigan Avenue and E. Lake Shore Drive, and duck down the pedestrian underpass beneath Lake Shore Drive. Return to the underpass, this time veering right to the west side of Lake Shore Drive. Emerge at the corner of the drive and **Oak Street**, a block-long stretch of small high-fashion shops, most notably Ultimo Ltd and the Giorgio Armani boutique.

Rushing out: At the end of the block, turn right and head north on **Rush Street**. Once known as Chicago's

nightclub district, it is now popular with suburban teenagers who pack taverns near Rush and Division streets. Some of the bars play great rock 'n' roll, and often have hundreds of patrons singing raucously along. If that sounds good, try some of the bars on Division Street such as She-Nannigans, Butch McGuire's Tavern or Mother's.

Just north of Division Street, on State Parkway, is a charming Art-Moderne apartment building constructed in 1938 with glass blocks wrapped around its curved corners. This area along Lake Shore Drive is known as the **Gold Coast**, a preserve of wealth and elegant architecture. On the lakefront itself are a mixture of modern high-rises and beautiful old apartment buildings where some of Chicago's oldest families have lived. One block west is Astor Street, and the **Astor Street District**, the heart of the Gold Coast. The six-block walk is filled with elegant townhouses.

At the northwest corner of Burton and

unchtime
ooking.

Astor streets stands the district's largest building, **Patterson House**, a Renaissance revival home designed by New York architect Stanford White. It was commissioned in 1892 by *Chicago Tribune* publisher Joseph Medill as a wedding gift for his daughter and son-in-law.

Also notable are the **James Charnley House**, at 1365 N. Astor Street, designed by Frank Lloyd Wright; the **James Houghteling houses** at 1308-12 N. Astor, designed in neo-Elizabethan style by John Wellborn Root in 1887, and the French Renaissance revival **Joseph T. Ryerson House** at 1406 N. Astor, built in 1922.

There is also the Art-Deco **Edward P. Russell House** at 1444 N. Astor Street, designed by Holabird and Root in 1929, and two Art-Deco apartment buildings at 1301 and 1260 N. Astor Street. At the northern end of Astor at **North Boulevard**, is the earliest house on the block, a large Queen Anne mansion designed by Alfred F. Pashley in 1880 as the residence for the Roman Catholic Archbishop of Chicago.

Around the corner, at 1524 N. Lake Shore Drive, is one of the city's more unusual museums. The **International Museum of Surgical Science** tells the history of surgery using graphic paintings of tumors and amputations and a gruesome variety of surgical instruments, not to mention a death mask of Napoleon.

Heading back west, do not miss the lovely, lacey apartment building at **1550 N. State Parkway**. It was designed in 1912 by Benjamin Marshall and Charles E. Fox, who also designed the Drake Hotel, among other prominent local buildings. The building features enormous, high-ceilinged apartments with *petits salons, grands salons* and *orangeries*, and once housed such well-known families as the Fields and the Shedds.

Old Town: Walk west on North Boulevard, which becomes North Avenue. One block past La Salle Street is Wells Street and the heart of **Old Town**, a neighborhood that has veered from wealth to seediness and back up to wealth again. The side streets north and west of the intersection are lined with pretty townhouses that have been lovingly restored.

Just north of North Avenue, on Wells Street, is the longtime home of **Second City**, the innovative comedy improvisation club that served as a training ground for such stars as Elaine May, Alan Arkin, Joan Rivers, John Belushi and John Candy.

South of North Avenue, is **Wells Street**, which was once Chicago's hippie haven, a place to buy cigarette papers, water pipes, psychedelic magazines and tie-dyed T-shirts. Now Wells Street is a strip of fancy shops and restaurants. For a slight whiff of the past, visit Uno's Bizarre Bazaar, which has been in the area since 1966. The shop still sells tie-dyed T-shirts and peace-sign jewelry.

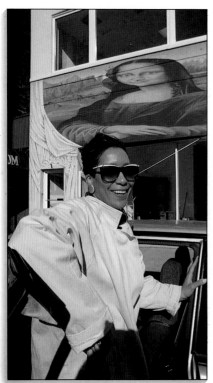

Left, modern Lisa. **Right**, getting directions outside one of the newer Mag Mile malls.

CHICAGO PLACE

◆ SAKS FIFTH AVENUE ◆

Above—The Capone-Guzik-Fusco wildcat brewery at 1642 South 48th avenue, Cicero, that was raided yesterday by prohibition agents under Elliott Ness, aid of W. E. Bennett, chief of the special prohibition corps. C...

Ness Raiders 'Knock Out' Capone Breweries in Quick Succession

The Gang's All Here

Crime historian William J. Helmer said that those people concerned about Chicago's image never had a chance when they tried to purge the city of its association with gangs and gangsters, with firebombs and tommy guns.

"I think that Americans have always had a rebellious streak that permits them to identify with certain kinds of lawbreakers," Helmer suggested. "Gangsters, like Capone, and outlaws, like Dillinger, seem enviably self-confident, unafraid of authority and unafraid of death, and to have an admirable ability to handle stress. If they also have style and élan, they discover that crime may not pay, but it can be a shortcut to immortality."

In the 1950s and '60s, Mayor Richard J. Daley and other city fathers tried to make the world forget about "Scarface" Capone and the Thompson submachine guns that made the Twenties roar.

But times have changed and today the city is no longer demolishing any site associated with gangland lore, and the Chicago Historical Society no longer answers Capone queries with a blank, "Al who?"

Biograph ambush: In the last few years, Chicago has begun learning to live with, if not love, its gangland reputation through tours, exhibits and restaurants. Ironically, the city's only structure with **National Historic Landmark** status and a link to gangster lore has nothing to do with the infamous Capone.

The **Biograph Theatre** at 2433 N. Lincoln Avenue became famous on July 22, 1934 when bank robber John Dillinger was gunned down by federal agents. Dillinger was not part of any crime syndicate; he was a freelancer who resembled Humphrey Bogart and came across as a regular guy. His dramatic flair in relieving banks of their money, the gallantry he sometimes displayed and his success at playing cat-

and-mouse with law enforcers contributed to his popularity. Dillinger's brooding good looks and reputation as a dashing playboy only enhanced his standing among women admirers all over America.

When he was betrayed by the "Lady in Red" and ambushed by G-men, Dillinger died in an alley, just south of the Biograph. Women reportedly rushed to the scene to dip their handkerchiefs in the pool of his blood.

Tourists interested in the pivotal events and colorful personalities of Chicago's most exciting and dangerous era can visit **Capone's Chicago**, a museum of the Roaring Twenties, at 605 North Clark Street.

Gang society: Hardcore gangster enthusiasts can even join the John Dillinger Died for You Society, a tongue-in-cheek fan club started in 1966 for followers of gangster lore. "Some called him Public Enemy Number One," noted Horace Naismith, the society president. "Actually, John

Dillinger was a prominent economic reformer with unorthodox banking methods."

Applicants to the society receive a membership card, a history of the group, a catalog of gangster accoutrements and notices of meetings where an empty chair is always left for the club's namesake.

Chicago's oldest crime structure stands at Dearborn and Hubbard streets. It is the old **Criminal Courts Building**, an imposing, gray stone fortress that has been renovated for private offices. Behind it, where a firehouse now stands, was the old jail where executions were carried out.

It was here, on November 12, 1887, that the four celebrated Haymarket anarchists went to the gallows. (Eight activists were originally charged with incitement to murder after a political riot which ended in several deaths. But sympathy for the accused led to the pardoning of the four survivors.)

In all, 92 prisoners were hanged in the old jail between 1882 and 1929. It would have been 93, but in 1921 "Terrible" Tommy O'Connor, condemned to hang for murdering a police detective, escaped four days before his date with the hangman's knot.

The perpetrators of gangland murders were rarely arrested by the police, however, let alone sentenced to death. Their courtrooms were the smoke-filled headquarters of gangster bosses, and their executions were carried out in public or private by gunmen whose own days were numbered.

Flavored death: During the 1920s, most of the death sentences delivered by gangsters were the result of territorial wars that began over bootlegging and quickly expanded to extortion, gambling, prostitution, labor racketeering and corruption of public officials. The methods of punishment were swift and often ingenious, like rubbing the bullet tips with garlic so that if they missed a vital organ the victim could still die of gangrene.

The aftermath of the St Valentine's Day Massacre, 1929...

At first, the gangs were content to keep to their own sides of town, but greed got the best of them and entrepreneurs sparked open warfare.

In July of 1921, independent businessman Steve Wisniewski hijacked a beer truck belonging to Dion O'Banion. Deanie, as close friends knew him, had been an altar boy and a singing waiter. But by 1921, O'Banion was the undisputed crime boss of the city's North Side. His top lieutenant, Earl "Hymie" Weiss, forced Wisniewski into a car at gunpoint at the corner of **Halsted** and **14th streets**, now the edge of the Maxwell Street flea market district. Wisniewski got his brains blown out and made history by being the first victim to be "taken for a ride."

O'Banion ran his operation from a flower shop at 738 N. State Street, now a parking lot. He himself had become a thorn for South Side crime boss Johnny Torrio. On November 10, 1924, Capone – who at the time was Torrio's top lieutenant – sent a trio of killers into O'Banion's flower shop to silence the Irish tenor forever.

Weiss took over O'Banion's gang, but not for long. On October 11, 1926, Weiss and his driver, Sam Peller, died in a storm of machine gun bullets on the steps of **Holy Name Cathedral** at 735 N. State Street. Both Weiss and O'Banion were taken to a mortuary at 703 N. Wells Street, now an art gallery. Back then, it was the site of some of Chicago's most lavish gangster funerals. O'Banion's funeral procession included 122 cars and 26 trucks loaded with flowers.

Scarface surfaces: By now, Al Capone had taken over from Torrio, who survived an assassination attempt and decided to retire amid the city's longest running gang war. Its violence was so blatant that Tony Lombardo, Capone's *consigliere*, was gunned down on a Friday afternoon, September 7, 1928, walking east on the south side of Madison, between State and Dearborn. At the time, **State and Madison** was known as

...and a police recreation shortly after the massacre.

"the world's busiest corner."

But the most notorious of all gangland attacks, the one that would forever burn Capone into Chicago's history, came on St Valentine's Day in 1929. At 2122 N. Clark Street, now a grassy lot in front of a senior citizens' home, stood the SMC Cartage Co. It was at this garage that Capone's boys, masquerading as cops, lined seven members and associates of the rival Bugs Moran gang against a brick wall and riddled them with machine gun bullets. Moran, who had inherited the O'Banion-Weiss organization, was not present at the massacre, and so lived to learn what others already knew: Chicago had become Capone's city.

Capone, whose estimated income surpassed an astonishing $105 million in 1927 – still a Guinness world record six decades later – was finally convicted in 1931 of income tax evasion and served eight years in prison.

His final headquarters were at the corner of Michigan Avenue and 22nd Street, now a vacant, 10-story eyesore building with a sign over the boarded entrance that reads the **New Michigan Hotel**. It used to be the Lexington Hotel, where Capone's office was on the fourth floor, behind the rounded turret windows at the front corner. Several would-be developers over the years have managed to keep the wrecker's ball out, but haven't brought in enough capital to restore the hotel.

Capone died in 1947 in Florida, his body ravaged by syphilis because he was deathly afraid of needles, even those backed by penicillin. He is buried in the family plot at **Mount Carmel Cemetery** in the western suburb of Hillside, about 40 minutes from downtown Chicago.

As for "Machine Gun Jack" McGurn, who masterminded the St Valentine's Day Massacre, his life came to a close on the seventh anniversary of the event. The building at 805 N. Milwaukee Avenue now houses an office furniture store. In 1936, it was a bowling alley, where two remnants of the Moran gang mowed McGurn down with tommy-guns. Into his lifeless left hand, they pressed a blood-red valentine.

Guided tours: Untouchable Tours, a theater on wheels, offers a nostalgic two and a half hour trip to many gang-era landmarks.

The tour's dinner package winds up at **Tommy Gun's Garage**, 1237 S. State Street. Tommy Gun's, a block from Chicago Police Headquarters, offers dinner and an entertaining floor show set in the 1920s. There's a machine gun-toting bouncer and plenty of flappers. The place is usually packed with both locals and visitors from around the globe who buy up the "I Got Massacred" T-shirts.

"Any place in the world, people will associate Chicago with Al Capone. That's what Chicago's known for, like it or not," says Sandy Mangen, proprietor of Tommy Gun's Garage. "Right now, it's a negative image. Let's make it a fun one."

Left, John Dillinger, the people's favorite outlaw, 1934 **Right**, Evelyn Whitney, flapper, 1929.

THE NORTH SIDE

In the 1860s, the fattest madam on Chicago's North Side was Gentle Annie Stafford, who weighed 300 pounds and liked to put on airs. So successfully did she drill her prostitutes in proper manners and refined conversation that, at the opening-night party of a new brothel, one backslapping girl bellowed at every man she met: "Who's your favorite poet? Mine's Byron."

More than 130 years have passed since Gentle Annie's day, but the North Side remains Chicago's classy side of town, flush with restaurants, nightclubs, galleries, theaters, concert halls and people who like to put on airs. Naturally, this tends to grate on South Siders, who talk about North Siders the way some Canadians talk about Americans – all the time, with great emphasis on the "us" and "them," defining themselves by the contrasts. North Siders, on the other hand, talk about South Siders the way Americans talk about Canadians – almost never. They forget the South Side exists.

Diverse lifestyles: But, if truth be told, Chicago's North Side is by no means a uniform world of wine snobs and effete theatergoers. To think so is to think like a South Sider. The North Side is a collection of diverse neighborhoods, ethnic groups and lifestyles, from the third-generation bungalow dwellers of the far Northwest Side to the Vietnamese of Argyle Street to the Koreans of Lawrence Avenue to the Poles of Milwaukee Avenue.

One good way to tour Chicago, especially north of Lincoln Park, is to follow old Indian trails. Most of the major diagonal streets, such as Clark and Milwaukee, run along the former trails. Because they are among Chicago's earliest roads, they bisect many of the city's oldest and most interesting neighborhoods.

The first neighborhood as you ven-

Chicago and Suburbs

10 miles / 16 km

Round Lake Beach
Great America
Gurnee
Gages Lake
Waukegan
North Chicago
Des Plaines
Loch Lomond
Butler L.
Rondout
Wauconda
Mundelein
Lake Forest
Countryside L.
Diamond L.
Fort Sheridan
Tri-State Tollway (94)
North Branch Chicago
Indian Creek
Highland Park
Lake Zurich
Deerfield
Ravinia Park
Barrington
Buffalo Grove
Chicago Botanic Garden
DEER GROVE
Skokie
Northbrook
Palatine
Northwest (14)
Skokie Lagoons
Winnetka
Des Plaines
Glenview N.A.S.
Arlington Heights
Northwest Tollway (90)
Glenview
Mount Prospect
Morton Grove
Hoffman Estates
NED BROWN PRESERVE
Des Plaines
Niles
Skokie
Evanston
Schaumburg
Elk Grove Village
Park Ridge
N. Br. Chicago
North South Channel
Lincolnwood
Chicago O'Hare International Airport
John F. Kennedy Expy. (90/94)
Bloomingdale
Schiller Park
Lake Shore Dr.
Montrose Harbor
Salt Cr.
River Grove
Belmont Harbor
Addison
Addison Cr.
Maywood Park Race Track
LINCOLN PARK
Elmhurst
Lombard
Maywood
Oak Park
Eisenhower Expw. (290)
GRANT PARK
Wheaton
Berwyn
Cicero
Chicago Stadium
Meigs Field Airport
Brookfield Zoo
Hawthorne Race Course
Chicago
East-West Tollway (88)
Brookfield
LaGrange
Riverside
Stevenson Expw. (55)
University of Chicago
JACKSON PARK
Downers Grove
Chicago Midway Airport
East Branch
Woodridge
Tri-State Tollway (294)
Burbank
Chicago State University
ILLINOIS
INDIANA
Calumet Harbor
Chicago Skyway (90)
Longjohn Slough
Oak Lawn
Evergreen Park
Bolingbrook
Palos Hills
Calumet Expwy. (90/94)
L. Calumet
Indiana Harbor
Saganashkee Slough
Calumet Sag. Channel
Des Plaines
Hastings
Alsip
Wolf L.
L. George
Joliet (55)
Long Run
Orland L.
Little Calumet
Blue Island
East Chicago
Orland Park
Dolton
Calumet City
Indiana Toll Road (90)
Oak Forest
(571)
Harvey
Hammond

Lake

Michigan

ture north of Lincoln Park on Clark Street is **Wrigleyville**, perhaps Chicago's most torridly trendy residential district. Everything about Wrigleyville – roughly bounded by Diversey Parkway, Irving Park Road, Ravenswood Avenue and the lake – has changed in recent years. Even its name.

Fifteen years ago the neighborhood was rough and gritty and called Lake View. But then young white-collar professionals, priced out of comfortable Lincoln Park, began moving in. Older blue-collar Germans, Swedes, Hungarians and Puerto Ricans began moving out. Fashionable espresso bars and restaurants staked claims, like squatters in a gold rush, on seemingly every corner.

Gentrification marches on, but Wrigleyville remains – if only for the moment – one of Chicago's most varied neighborhoods, a place where people of different tongues, colors and incomes live side by side. The cultural heart of Wrigleyville is **Wrigley Field**, a baseball park as quaint as any corner café.

Wrigley Field, more than any other ballpark in the nation, is an integral part of its community, crowded on all sides by houses, apartment buildings and bars. Rooftop Cub fans along Waveland Avenue enjoy a free and unobstructed view of every game, and home runs sometimes break front windows.

For more than a decade, a majority of Wrigleyville residents fought all efforts by the Chicago Tribune Co. – owners of the Cubs – to bring lights and night baseball to the old ball park. They worried that drunken fans might rock the night with noise, urinate on lawns and tie up traffic.

They feared, at bottom, the Great Wrigleyville Revival might falter. As it happened, the Tribune prevailed, and night baseball came to Wrigley Field in the summer of 1989. It did, indeed, create a good deal of noise, rowdiness and gridlock. But the Great Revival never missed a beat. Property values continue to soar in the 1990s.

For a pleasantly refined dining experience after a game, try Thai Classic for seafood, at 3332 N. Clark.

One of the best bars in Wrigleyville is Sheffield's Wine and Beer Garden at 3258 N. Sheffield. This bar somehow manages to strike a pleasant and improbable balance between the yuppie need for fancy bottled beers and jazz music and the old neighborhood's traditional informality.

The 3700 block of N. Clark Street is one of Chicago's most avant garde. Check out Cabaret Metro for cutting-edge rock music; or Pravda Records next door for the sort of independently-recorded music you might not get back home; or the Ginger Man for its big pool tables and exotic imported beers, or the Smart Bar for the hipsters with hair dyed jet-black, chalk-white complexions and dark clothing.

Victoriana: A block north of Wrigley Field is a one-block stretch of Victorian England, incongruously out of place and out of time. **Alta Vista Terrace**, listed on the National Register of Historic Places, is a narrow side street of 40 striking houses, built in 1900 and modeled after a street in London. The ornate facades of the houses are paired, one on each side of the street. A few blocks farther up the old Indian trail, at Clark Street and Irving Park Road, lies **Graceland**, Chicago's most stately and historically significant cemetery. You can pick up a map at the front office and walk through Chicago's past. (Foreign visitors should not confuse this Graceland with the Memphis mansion of the same name which is the final resting place of its former owner, Elvis Presley.)

The tombs at Chicago's Graceland include those of John Kinzie (1763–1828), the city's most prominent early settler, farm-machinery inventor Cyrus H. McCormick, meatpacking mogul Phillip D. Armour, heavyweight boxing champions Jack Johnson and Bob Fitzsimmons, retailing giant Marshall Field, architect Louis Sullivan and the founder of baseball's National League,

William A. Hulburt. Near **Lake Willowmere** in Graceland stands perhaps the most impressive monument in the cemetery, the intricately detailed **Carrie Eliza Getty Mausoleum**, designed by Sullivan and built in 1890. The limestone monument is considered by many to be a landmark of modern architecture.

Home of the stars: Graceland's elegance stands in dramatic contrast to the shabbiness of the community immediately to the north: **Uptown**. Until about 1950, Uptown was one of Chicago's most exclusive communities. Wealthy businessmen lived in spacious Victorian, Prairie, Queen Anne and Georgian-style homes in Uptown's most exclusive lakefront neighborhoods. Movie stars of the silent era, including Charlie Chaplin, Gloria Swanson, Douglas Fairbanks and Mary Pickford, worked at the Essanay Film Studio on West Argyle Street. Big Band-era stars such as Tommy Dorsey, Glenn Miller and Frank Sinatra per-

Graceland Cemetery.

formed regularly in the famous **Aragon Ballroom**, 1106 W. Lawrence.

But Uptown's glamorous image was shattered by a post-World War II housing shortage. Many of its finest homes and apartment buildings were converted into low-rent rooming houses. The community was flooded with penniless newcomers, including Appalachian coal miners and Native American Indians. Uptown today remains synonymous with winos, the immigrant and migrant poor, flophouses for the homeless and half-way houses for the mentally ill.

Like Wrigleyville, however, Uptown has been rediscovered of late by the forces of gentrification – real estate speculators, housing rehabilitators and young professionals. The Aragon, serving up professional wrestling for many years, is once again a hot concert and dance hall. The lakefront neighborhoods, particularly, are luring back a moneyed crowd. Former Illinois Governor James Thompson, for one, makes his home here. Thanks to gentrification and the recent arrival of thousands of remarkably ambitious immigrants from the Far East, Uptown is making a comeback. Two Uptown neighborhoods in particular stand out: Andersonville and New Chinatown.

Swedish models: Centered at Foster and Clark streets, **Andersonville** is Chicago's last Swedish community and a fast-disappearing one at that. Swedish bakeries, delis and restaurants still dot Clark Street, but have been joined by Japanese, Thai, Korean and Assyrian establishments. When Andersonville celebrates *Midsommarfest* nowadays, blocking off Clark Street for an all-day Old Country summer fair, it assumes something of an international flavor. Walking down Clark, you can nibble on Swedish meatballs, Assyrian *falafel* or Turkish *baklava*, washed down with Thai iced coffee.

At one time Chicago had more Swedes than Stockholm. They settled in five neighborhoods, founded more than

cyclist
out to
terrupt a
shion
oot.

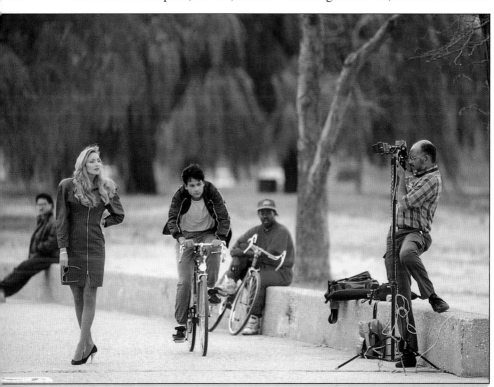

50 churches and printed several daily newspapers. But their grandchildren moved to the suburbs. Now, by some estimates, as many as 50,000 Chicago-area residents – including former Governor Thompson – can claim predominantly Swedish ancestry. But relatively few still live in Andersonville.

When touring the neighborhood – as the king and queen of Sweden did in 1988 – stop by Svea Restaurant, at 3258 W. Foster, an Andersonville landmark known for its authentic Swedish pancakes with lingonberries, herring salad, *limpa* bread and boysenberry cobbler. The 5300 and 5400 blocks of Clark Street have many Swedish landmarks, such as Wikstrom's Scandinavian American Gourmet Foods, at 5247 N. Clark, which features a spicy potato sausage called *potatis korv*, and Nelson's Scandinavian Bakery, known for its *limpa* bread and buns.

Also on Clark Street, a good Turkish restaurant is Konak, where Turkish carpets and tapestries decorate the walls.

Try the eggplant salad and a kebab. Then there's Beirut Restaurant, known, like Konak's, for its great kebabs.

A hip place to relax and browse for travel books, maps and wearables – many from Third World countries – is Kopi, A Traveler's Café, at 5317 N. Clark in Andersonville. It has a full espresso bar and offers snacks, hearty soups and fresh-baked desserts which you can enjoy while sitting at a hand-painted table.

The best stop-off for souvenirs in Andersonville might be the gift shop of the **Swedish American Museum**, at 5211 N. Clark. The museum features a permanent exhibit illustrating, through pictures and artifacts, the Swedish contribution to the building of Chicago. In the next block, the Swedish Style Gift Shop and the Swedish Style Knit Shop are two other good stops.

For those last-minute gifts, head to The Landmark of Andersonville at 5301 N. Clark, a cooperative with three floors of shops selling country kitsch,

Dual focus; Baha'i Temple.

clothing, ethnic crafts and collectibles.

Chinatown: Four blocks east of Andersonville lies an immigrant settlement that is as new to Chicago as Andersonville is old: **New Chinatown**. This two-block stretch of Argyle Street, bounded by Broadway on the west and Sheridan Road on the east, pulsates with the verve and entrepreneurial spirit of Vietnamese and Cambodian refugees, a majority of whom are ethnic Chinese. Vietnamese and Chinese restaurants, grocery stores and clothing stores line the street. Thousands of Asian customers, ignoring seedy Uptown drifters, pour into the area on weekends for the good prices on 150-pound bags of rice among other things, and the authentic smells and sights of home.

Argyle Street is a microcosm of the American immigrant experience. After the Vietnam War, Vietnamese and ethnic Chinese living in Vietnam fled to America and Chicago, choosing to settle on Argyle because rents were cheap. They pooled their meager resources and

opened small stores and restaurants. Thousands now live in Uptown's tenements. A few have moved on to better city neighborhoods and the suburbs.

Trung Viet Grocery offers a wide selection of traditional Vietnamese foodstuffs. The store was started by a family that came to Chicago from Saigon in 1979. Kinh Do's Gift Shop, a few doors away on West Argyle, is crammed from floor to ceiling with imported Chinese wares, including exquisite Chinese silks. Two critically acclaimed Vietnamese restaurants in New Chinatown are Pasteur, a café-style establishment, and Lao Vien, a long and narrow storefront restaurant. The food is good, and you can stare out the windows as all of Uptown straggles by. Chinese carry-out dinners and desserts are available all along Argyle Street.

The other Chinatown, first settled by Chinese immigrants around 1912, is centered around Cermak Road and Wentworth Avenue and continues to serve as a Midwestern receiving area

hinatown
vins.

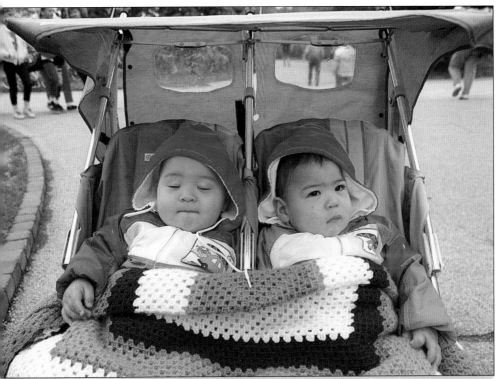

for immigrants from mainland China.

Around the corner from Argyle Street is one more Uptown treat – the **Green Mill Jazz Club**. The Green Mill, at 4802 N. Broadway, is a legendary Chicago late-night jazz and jam-session bar once owned by "Machinegun Jack" McGurn and frequented by Al Capone. In the 1940s, when Big Band musicians and torch singers finished a job at the Aragon or the Edgewater Beach Hotel, they would shed their tuxes and jam til dawn at the Green Mill. Among those who sat in were Frank Sinatra, Billie Holiday, the drummer Gene Krupa, trumpeter Roy Eldridge and drummer Claude "Hey Hey" Humphrey, who later died homeless, frozen in a grocery store parking lot in Uptown.

The Green Mill went sour in the 1960s and '70s, when Uptown was at its seediest, but has come back strong. It offers excellent jazz on almost every night except Monday, when the Poetry Slam is featured. The Slam is a Green Mill original, where local poets with strong constitutions take the stage and serve up their best verse for the mixed crowd of locals and tourists. When they're good, the crowd cheers. When they're not, the crowd jeers.

Devon divide: Argyle Street is one of Chicago's most homogeneous immigrant strips – virtually everybody here is Vietnamese or Cambodian. In contrast, **Devon Avenue**, two miles to the north, is perhaps Chicago's most culturally diverse – not to say confusing – strip. To walk down Devon between Oakley Boulevard and Kedzie Avenue is to wander through another land. But which land?

On the east side of the strip are the shops of the New Guard – Indians, Pakistanis, Greeks, Turks, Palestinians, Syrians, Lebanese and Filipinos. On the west are the shops of the Old Guard – Eastern Europeans and Russian Jews. In between, everything is up for grabs.

The best time to visit Devon Avenue is on a Sunday morning, when the sidewalks are jammed with crates of

A Milwaukee Avenue restaurant.

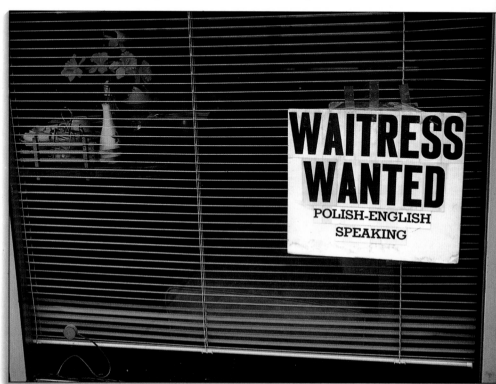

produce and men in *yarmulkes* and women in saris. In summer, the air is spiced with the intermingled odors of the Arab fruit markets, Jewish bakeries, tandoori chicken, hummus and espresso. For urban romantics, there is no better place to be.

Jews were among the first and last immigrants to settle on Devon. The first wave came from Eastern Europe in the early decades of the century. The most recent poured in from Russia in the 1980s, when the Soviet Union relaxed restrictions on immigration. Asians began settling along Devon in the early 1970s. Devon is known informally as Sari Row because it is lined with stores carrying Indian saris, fabrics, chiffon scarves and jewelry. Taj Sari Palace, at 2553 W. Devon, is one of the largest. Devon also boasts quite a few Jewish and Arab butcher shops.

On the west end of the strip, Miller's Meats and Poultry sells meat that has been slaughtered and prepared in accordance with Jewish kosher law. On the other end of the strip, Sawzi Suleiman and his brothers, the proprietors of Farm City Meats, supply fellow Arabs with meat butchered according to Islamic dietary law.

In the 2900 block of W. Devon, the Shaevitz Meat Market claims a cult following for its kosher hot dogs and salami. The Midwest Fish Market still smokes its own white fish and grinds fillets for gefilte fish.

By general consensus among the local critics, Devon's best Indian restaurant is Standard India, an unpretentious and relatively inexpensive purveyor of subcontinental specialties.

While in the neighborhood, especially if you have children, consider venturing a few blocks further north to **Indian Boundary Park**, at 2500 W. Lunt. The 13-acre park, two blocks west of Western Avenue, has a terrific playground and its own small zoo which features alpacas, yaks, reindeer, swans, and goats, among other animals.

Poles apart: A second old Indian trail

Polish neighborhood bakery.

in Chicago – Milwaukee Avenue – embodies the history of the single largest ethnic group in the Chicago area, Polish Americans. An estimated one million Poles and people of Polish descent live in the six-county Chicago area, the greatest concentration of Poles outside of Warsaw. Within the city, they have tended to settle in five geographically dispersed areas, the largest number historically have made their homes on or around Milwaukee Avenue.

The heart of America's Polish diaspora, **Polonia**, is on Milwaukee Avenue from Belmont Avenue to Central Park Avenue. Here, in an area called Jackowo, live Chicago's newest Polish immigrants, the best-educated and most sophisticated in the city's history. They love jazz and never learned to polka. Typically, these people may be certified accountants who are often forced to work as janitors.

The intersection of Milwaukee Avenue and Division Street, immediately northwest of the Loop, was called Chicago's **Polish Downtown** after the first Poles moved into the area in the 1860s. Unskilled laborers, they worked in the tanneries and factories along Milwaukee and the banks of the Chicago River. As Scandinavians and Germans worked their way northwest up Milwaukee Avenue, moving on to better lives in better neighborhoods, the Poles followed them through the neighborhoods.

Today, the old Polish downtown is gone. Its last landmark is a gourmet Polish restaurant, the Busy Bee, at 1550 N. Damen, frequented by people who live somewhere else. Second and third-generation Polish-Americans still live along Milwaukee, but in suburban-style neighborhoods on the far edge of town and beyond.

The biggest Polish restaurant on Milwaukee – and in all the Midwest – is in suburban Niles. Przybylo's White Eagle Banquet Hall, at 6845 N. Milwaukee, claims that it can handle around seven wedding receptions at one

A fruit and vegetable shop.

time, and is frequently put to the test.

The new Polish Downtown is the **Jackowo** business district. Polish bakeries, taverns and restaurants crowd the streets. Jackowo (pronounced *yahts-koh-voh*), is Polish for "hyacinth neighborhood." It takes its name from **St Hyacinth**, the local Roman Catholic Church. The Orbit, at 2940 N. Milwaukee, is a popular and boisterous restaurant in Jackowo, known particularly for its *pirogi*.

The **Polish Museum of America** hangs on in the old Polish Downtown, at 1000 N. Milwaukee. It features paintings of famous Polish patriots, as well as exhibits of traditional Polish crafts and Polish weaponry. And for a sense of Chicago Polonia then and now, visit **St Stanislaus Kostka Catholic Church**, at Evergreen and Noble in the old neighborhood. This majestic Renaissance-style church, built in 1881, served more than 8,000 Polish families in 1890. Today, it tends to fewer than 850 families, a testament to changing neighborhood boundaries rather than changing values.

EVANSTON: The first town north of Chicago's city limits is **Evanston**, the city's most cosmopolitan suburb. It has a racially diverse population, a famous university, superior restaurants, unique shops, a tradition of progressive politics, big-city sophistication and small-town warmth. It's an all-round good town, especially now that you can buy a beer there.

Evanston is the national headquarters of the Women's Christian Temperance Union, the folks who gave America Prohibition, the national alcohol ban that perhaps inadvertently allowed the gangsters to flourish. Until only a few years ago, it was illegal to sell packaged alcohol in Evanston and, even now, the town has no taverns.

Local legend has it that, thanks to Evanston's teetotalers, the ice-cream sundae was invented here. Seltzer water was banned on Sundays in the 1880s, so when the local druggists removed it

fter services
t St
ladimir's.

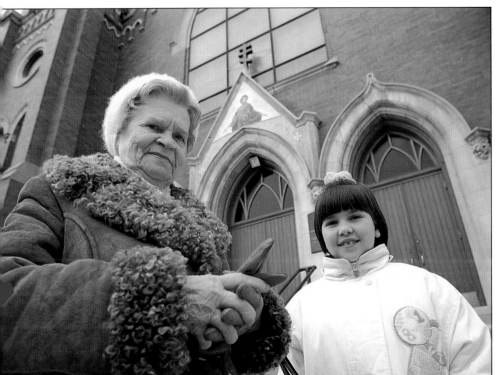

from their ice-cream sodas, they called what was left – ice-cream with syrup – a "sundae."

Evanston is also special because of **Northwestern University**, its cultural and economic anchor. Founded by Chicago Methodists in 1855, the university has grown from 10 students in one three-story building to almost 11,000 students and more than 160 buildings. Its football team, the Wildcats, is perennially unlucky, but its academics are superior. In the area, only the University of Chicago has a better reputation and Northwestern surpasses the school downtown in several areas.

On campus, **Pick-Staiger Hall** offers regular classical, folk and pop concerts. Its acoustics are excellent. A lesser known treat on campus is the lush **Shakespeare Garden**, just south of the Technological Institute. It is as peaceful as it is beautiful.

Evanston is a walker's town, with miles of stately mansions along its lakefront. One of the finest is open for public viewing, the 28-room **Charles Gates Dawes House**, at 225 Greenwood Avenue. Dawes was America's vice president from 1925 to 1929 under President Calvin Coolidge. The **Evanston Historical Society**, which has offices in the mansion, offers a list of other landmark homes that are also worth viewing.

For good French provincial dining in Evanston, try the stylish Café Express, at 615 Dempster, a slightly bohemian favorite of both students and townies. For a store with a difference, check out Dave's Down To Earth Rock Shop, at 704 Main Street, which sells rocks, precious and otherwise. If you're looking for a semi-precious stone or just a nice paperweight, it's worth a visit.

The **Baha'i Temple**, at Linden and Sheridan in Wilmette, is just over the Evanston town line. This 1953 architectural masterpiece by Louis Bourgeois, with its lacy walls and delicate bell-like shape, is on the National Register of Historic Places.

On the Northwestern University campus.

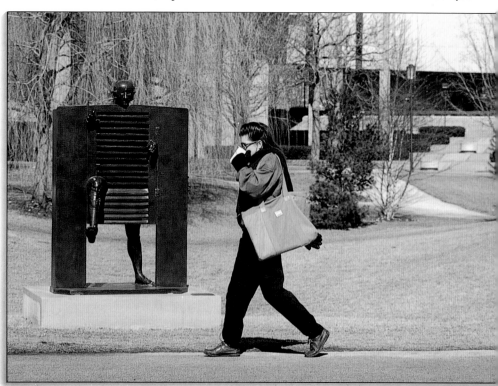

URBAN WOODLANDS

Loosely ringing Chicago along much of its north, south and west borders is a green belt of natural lands, known as the forest preserves, set aside for conservation and recreation.

While other large cities have dedicated land to similar purposes, the Cook County Forest Preserves, comprising 66,746 acres of woodlands, recreation facilities and open space, is probably the oldest and largest forest preserve system in any US metropolitan area.

In addition to forests and fields, the preserves boast 13 golf courses and driving ranges, 33 fishing lakes and ponds, plus swimming pools, boat ramps, bicycle trails and picnic areas.

Unlike the preserve systems in other cities, where forest land was set aside only after urban populations began moving away from the central downtown areas in the 1950s, the concept of a forest preserve system for Chicago began before the turn of the century on the initiative of some of the city's most prominent citizens.

Their mission was to establish nearby areas where city dwellers could find the pastoral recreation and peace afforded by open space filled with natural flora and fauna. Rather than simply acquiring open tracts, they were interested in preserving naturally beautiful areas "for their own sake and... scientific value, which, if ever lost, cannot be restored for generations."

Only three forest preserves – the Edgebrook/Caldwell woods and the Indian Boundary preserves, both on the northwest side of the city, and the Dan Ryan Woods on the South Side – are actually located within the city limits.

Run as a separate government agency, independent of both the city and the county, the Cook County Forest Preserve District is funded by taxes levied on all county property owners, and by small fees charged to those who use its facilities.

However, the Forest Preserve District board is made up of the same people who are elected to the County Board of Trustees. As a result, the district, like the City of Chicago and the County of Cook, has long been a haven of patronage for the local Democratic party. In Chicago, even when you escape to nature, it's hard to leave behind the political machine.

Until the mid-1970s, the forest preserves were used mostly on Sundays for family outings, company picnics and the like. With so much of the metropolitan population moving into the suburbs, however, the demand for picnic groves, bike and bridle paths is now creating crowds for much of the week, and district managers are trying to cope with overcrowding.

In fact, one problem the district faces is that many suburbs with nearby forest preserves have foregone setting aside extra open space within their own municipalities, relying instead on adjacent forest preserves to provide recreational space for their residents.

Overcrowding isn't the only problem caused by encroaching urbanization. Once-rural roads that in past decades had little impact on natural life within the preserves have been expanded into major highways to serve the ever-growing outlying population and dormitory communities. At the same time, housing and commercial developments have been built around forest preserve district holdings.

Fortunately, about 5 percent of the Cook County Forest Preserve District is set aside as part of the Illinois Nature Preserve system, which is even more conservation-oriented than the forest preserves. The nature preserves, spread throughout the forest areas, are protected regions of unique natural, geological or environmental habitat, crucial to such processes as spring seepage or home to endangered species.

But the preserves aren't used for daytime family fun alone. In the evening they are a favorite place for teenagers to find romantic privacy, and are occasionally dumping grounds for murder victims. Some preserves have also become known for the sale of drugs.

The district has its own police force and, even in the thickest woods, civilization is never far away. Still, for safety's sake, it's best not to visit the forest preserves alone, especially when hiking or biking wooded paths.

YEAR-ROUND PERFORMANCES

There is no slow season on the Chicago entertainment scene. Whether large theaters or small cabarets, whether lavish ballet and opera productions or one-man shows, Chicagoans are accustomed to a wide choice for a night out. They are also accustomed to seeing live people on stage; in much of the Loop and its neighboring downtown areas, it's much easier to find a play or a music act on stage than it is to find a movie house. Cinema-goers typically head for outlying residential areas and the multi-screens at the shopping malls.

Despite the January-to-October nature of Chicago entertainment, a few attractions are necessarily seasonal. Some of Chicago's 120 theater companies, for example, concentrate on **summer stock** or **Shakespeare in the parks** during June, July and August. Similarly, the summer brings many concerts, day and night and often free, at the band shell in **Grant Park**.

The **Blues Fest** in early June and **Jazz Fest** in August are enormously popular weekend events, attracting internationally known stars like Dizzy Gillespie and John Lee Hooker. Another summer highlight are the outdoor concerts, from big bands and touring symphonies to jazz and pop stars, at **Ravinia** in the north shore suburb of Highland Park. The autumn cultural offerings include the **Lyric Opera of Chicago** and the **Chicago Symphony Orchestra**.

For many Chicagoans and visitors alike, however, the ultimate night out in the Windy City includes the theater and one of the handful of swanky nightclubs or cabarets that serve up sophisticated songs along with the nightcaps.

Stepping out: A few years ago a *New York Times* reviewer wrote: "What is the current state of the American theater? Illinois!" Because there is so much theater in Chicago at any one time, at any time of year, it's best to plan

ahead. Both major dailies, the *Chicago Tribune* and the *Chicago Sun-Times*, have extensive Friday entertainment listings for the weekend. In addition, there's a lengthy theater guide in the *Reader*, a 150-page free Chicago weekly found in downtown and lakefront bookstores and coffee shops.

Theater bargains for those who don't plan ahead are available from **Hot Tix booths**. The booths are run by the League of Chicago Theatres, a trade association for 123 theaters and theater companies in the Chicago area. The booths are at 24 S. State Street in the Loop; 1616 Sherman Avenue in Evanston, and 1020 Lake Street in Oak Park. Theater and dance tickets are available the day of the performance at half price, on a cash-only basis. The booths also sell full-price advance tickets for theater, concerts, sports and other events.

The Hot Tix booths offer free copies of the *Theatre Chicago Guide*, with its current listings of productions, ad-

Preceding pages: Edward Hopper's *Nighthawks*. Left, waiting in wings. Right, a vaudeville landmark.

dresses and telephone numbers for member theaters and detailed maps of playhouse locations.

Long history: Many of the best known Chicago companies of the 1990s started in the 1960s and '70s, but the city's stage history goes back more than 150 years. The first plays were presented in 1837, when Chicago was incorporated as a city. By the time Abraham Lincoln won the Republican nomination in Chicago in 1860, the city had several permanent theaters. The waves of immigrants who came to a brawny Chicago brought with them spirited productions in their native tongues and the city was soon a port of call for an international roster of performers – a tradition that continues today with touring troupes from Broadway and London shows.

However, there's much more to Chicago theater than touring shows in Loop playhouses. In the early 1960s, controversial, avant garde director Bob Sickinger came to Chicago to create a community-based theater for Hull House, seeking a company in the city's heart, nurtured by neighborhoods. From among those artistic roots came actor Mike Nussbaum and playwrights David Mamet and Alan Bates.

The **Body Politic Theatre** was created in the mid-1960s, offering theater games for actors to learn body language. Its executive director, Jim Shiflett, had been taught by the legendary improvisationist Viola Spolin. One of its first program directors was Paul Sills, Spolin's son and a master of improvisation in his own right.

Sills had been a director of The Compass Players in 1955, a group that borrowed from *commedia dell'arte*, a Renaissance style in which actors improvised on scenarios. The Compass Players were characterized by an explosion of creative energy, rehearsing scenarios during the day, performing at night, then taking audience suggestions for more improvisations. From this group, which spawned the Second City improv group, came Mike Nichols,

A T-shirt display; *The Nutcracker* at the Aire Crown.

Elaine May, Shelley Berman and Barbara Harris.

Variety of venues: By the mid-1970s, there was rich competition for the Body Politic. **Victory Gardens Theater** focused on Chicago playwrights and made a commitment to black and Hispanic theater. **Wisdom Bridge Theatre** vibrated with youth, originality and inventiveness. The Evanston Theatre Company, now the **Northlight Theatre**, performed contemporary works, fresh interpretations of classics and forgotten plays with ambitious, thought-provoking productions. And there was David Mamet's **St Nicholas Theater Company**, producing early, highly praised works by the playwright. There was also the irreverent **Organic Theater**, which created a living cartoon on stage with *Warp*, a campy, science-fiction serial.

The number of Off-Loop theaters increased rapidly and by the time they exceeded 100, critics were saying Chicago theater was becoming a major force. Emerging in the late 1970s was a distinctively gritty, visceral mode of performance and in-your-face directional style that came from the **Steppenwolf Theatre Company**. Productions left audiences spent and critics raving. From this theater of realism have come the later writings of Mamet and the acting of John Malkovich and Glenne Headley.

While the Steppenwolf style of lean linguistic vernacular and intense acting has often been used interchangeably with the phrase "Chicago theater," this is not the case. And while the dramatic community still argues over a definition of "Chicago theater," its basic components consist of an energizing strength and a collective heart.

"Chicago theater artists were unable to succeed, and they were unable to fail. And both those things were blessings," wrote Robert Falls, artistic director of the Goodman and former artistic director of Wisdom Bridge. "You couldn't really fail, because it didn't really mat-

avement *iper;* *ernando* *ones' tribute* *o Junior* *Vells.*

ter, whereas in New York or Los Angeles if you failed, that was it. In Chicago, people approach it more as their work, as their art. They're continually writing, acting, designing and directing plays. They're interested in a body of work."

Second to none: One of the things that makes the term "Chicago theater" so immensely difficult to nail down is that it must also include Second City, without doubt its most famous company. The city's theaters of realism and improvisation have links in language and situations. They both make profound use of colloquialisms and of placing the common man in uncommon situations. But whereas one plays for intensity, the other does so for sophisticated laughs.

There's a full history of the homegrown genre available in the **Chicago Theater Collection** for reading and viewing at the Chicago Public Library. It's open to the public and includes original scripts and videotapes of famous performances. In the meantime, there's plenty of live theater to enjoy.

Steppenwolf productions should not be missed. Victory Gardens, Wisdom Bridge, Northlight and the Organic also have reliable productions. There are also several noteworthy companies. The **Court Theatre** in Hyde Park has a repertory which includes innovative productions of classics, rarely-seen masterpieces and significant works by contemporary authors. The season of the **Pegasus Players** in Uptown might include modern and classical productions, a musical and a new script.

For more traditional performances, there's the **Shubert Theatre**, just off State Street in the Loop. Most of the Broadway touring companies play here for longer runs. For shorter runs, of perhaps a week, they play the **Aire Crown** at McCormick Place. But unless you're absolutely dying to see the show, skip the Crown. Its enormous layout loses the intimacy of theater past the first several dozen rows, and theatergoers have always complained of the hall's acoustics.

John Lee Hooker at the Chicago Blues Festival.

There are several theaters in the round and dinner theaters within driving distance of the city. Among the best is the **Candlelight Dinner Playhouse** in southwest suburban Summit. It's about a 15-minute expressway drive from downtown and worth the journey for those fond of musicals.

Tough tickets: Two on the city's "must see" list are usually among the toughest tickets in town to come by: the Goodman and Second City. Virtually any production at the **Goodman Theater**, located behind the Art Institute of Chicago on Michigan Avenue, will be difficult for non-season ticket holders. Recent seasons were nearly sold out, but tickets are sometimes available through agencies and touts.

Opened in 1925, the Goodman is Chicago's oldest and largest resident theater. Its stage has hosted the American premieres of Mamet's Pulitzer Prize-winning *Glengarry Glen Ross* and Nobel Laureate Wole Soyink's *Death and the King's Horseman*. The Midwestern premiere of August Wilson's Pulitzer Prize-winning *Fences* was also performed at the Goodman. An annual sellout and Chicago tradition is *A Christmas Carol*, adapted from Charles Dickens. As a last resort, try going directly to the Goodman for occasional returns from season holders. Another option for those with the time or with budget constraints, especially if in town for at least a few weeks, is to call the Goodman and offer to be a volunteer usher.

Also tough to get are seats for **Second City**, where improvisation became a household word. The setting is a simple one. Six or seven actors work the stage with a few chairs and very limited props. They create topical sketches in a slice-of-life environment and throw in some original songs. The very first show in 1959 took on President Eisenhower, grand opera, the medical profession and the cultural pretensions of FM radio. The troupe never stopped breaking ground and television's *Saturday*

Dizzy Gillespie at the Chicago Jazz Festival.

Night Live might never have become so successful without the influence of Second City and a cast that included so many former Second City regulars.

The acting is called improv because current revues were put together with improvisations that came from audience suggestions after the regular show. Those who stay after the revue for the late improv show can add their suggestions for the actors to tackle. The Second City atmosphere is a pleasant one, with cabaret-style seating and drinks.

Located in **Old Town**, some of the country's best comedic talent developed here. Alumni include Alan Arkin, Dan Aykroyd, John and Jim Belushi, Peter Boyle, Barbara Harris, Bill Murray, Joan Rivers, David Steinberg and many more whose faces on television and in movies are more familiar than their names. The secret to good seats here is to go to performances during the week. Plan on staying for the late improv show, and moving up for better seats when the revue crowd departs.

Theater's future in Chicago looks bright. Several large new theaters are under construction, and the Goodman plans to move into a new North Loop theater complex by the end of 1998.

Cabaret: Sure-bet cabarets are more difficult to recommend in Chicago, not because they are few, but because they open and close like matchbook covers. The tiny cabaret where the willowy singer interpreted Gershwin may have closed because it was never discovered. The elegant room where long-familiar names were booked may have closed because its coziness meant they couldn't charge a big enough cover to pay the performers and still make a healthy profit. Again, check the newspaper listings and call the clubs for more information. Here is a couple of nightspots that are worth mentioning, depending on the entertainment.

The **Park West**, 322 W. Armitage Avenue, will sometimes book cabaret as well as rock groups; and **The Improv**, 504 N. Wells Street, the larg-

Night lights.

est club in Chicago, features nationally recognized stand-up comics and a variety show for children on Saturday afternoons. Here, however, is a solid trio of the city's best cabarets that have been around for years and look set to last years more.

The granddaddy of them all is **Milt Trenier's Lounge** in the basement of 610 N. Fairbanks Court, the building that once housed the legendary Chez Paree nightclub. Milt, who always wears a tuxedo and ranks among the best lounge hosts in the country, has been in the business more than 40 years. He started singing with his brothers as a teenager in the vanguard of rock 'n' roll in the early 1950s, preceding the Temptations and the Four Tops. His brothers settled in Las Vegas, where they have won awards performing show tunes, swing and blues. The Treniers, a band which now includes sons and nephews, usually play Milt's club in June and shouldn't be missed. Milt made Chicago his home, and with his wife, Bea,

offers a warm and welcoming gathering place for entertainers and lounge fans.

Because of the late-hour license – the joint is often open till near dawn – this is the place where musicians come to unwind after their gigs. There's a wall of photographs near the entrance, a sort of Who's Who of national nightlife, that testifies to past guests. Della Reese, Dizzy Gillespie and Bill Eckstine have "sat in." Bill Cosby once did a two-hour act and Sammy Davis Jr took away Milt's mike and did a whole show. Regular performers include singer and impressionist Bill Acosta and songstylist Paula Ramsey. But whoever's playing, don't leave until Milt himself sings. Backed by the Classic Swing Trio, "mellow and laid-back" were terms coined for Milt and his place.

The **Gold Star Sardine Bar**, in a chic building at 680 N. Lake Shore Drive, was named for its elegance and tiny size. But co-owner and impresario Bill Allen wouldn't have it any bigger. He wanted a cozy café that paid homage to

efore
ey're
acked in at
e Gold Star
ardine Bar.

LIVE!
ON STAGE
AT THE
GOLD STAR
SARDINE BAR

TONY BENNETT
•
LIZA MINNELLI

the sleek spots of New York, *circa* 1940. He's also particular about who performs and what is sung.

Frequent acts include Tony Bennett, Chicago comedian Tom Dreesen and jazz-artist-in-residence Patricia Barber. But Allen's uncanny knack for success has to do with taking entertainment risks that regularly show big payoffs. Shelley MacArthur, a high-demand runway model and a prominent Chicago socialite, was first booked at the Gold Star and developed by Allen, recalling the notable socialites featured in Manhattan's café society of the 1930s and 1940s. Her *Embraceable You* and *Unforgettable* are fine, but Bill won't let her sing *Fly Me to the Moon* because it doesn't fit the room's style. One night he might feature a young jazz pianist from the Soviet Union, and the next a university women's *a cappella* group. The Gold Star always makes for an entertaining evening.

And finally, because it's often one of the best ways to wind up an evening of theater or an elegant dinner, there's **Pops for Champagne**, 2934 N. Sheffield Avenue, a short cab ride from Michigan Avenue. This elegant room has a rose and green motif with a low bar that forms a crescent around the raised stage. Upholstered chairs surround the bar, so patrons can relax without having their legs dangle from stools. The rest of the room is given to comfortable table seating. And when the weather's warm, there's a romantic outdoor garden.

Pops has a light menu and delicious desserts such as fresh berries and mousse to fill the little holes in a late-night sweet tooth. Local performers take to the tiny stage nightly, weaving through the crowded tables to thank music lovers for coming. Sometimes it's a veteran jazz pianist. At other times, it may be a trio or a stylish blues vocalist. The giant bottles of champagne near the entrance make it clear that the club is serious about bubbly – serious to the tune of 120 varieties on the menu, many available by the glass.

Dancing at the Loop.

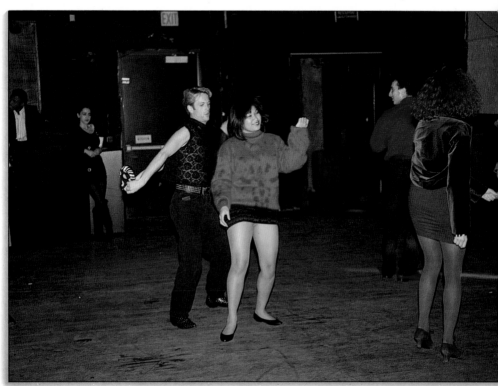

GETTING INTO "OPRAH"

"Do you know how to get on national TV?" George the audience coordinator asks the crowd of about 200 people, mostly women, who want to do exactly that.

"Act like you're very excited to be here, and hang on to the edge of your seat," says George. "See that cameraman behind me? He's looking for interesting reactions. So ask a question. Look interested."

George works for Oprah. In most circles, no more identification is needed. Talk-show host Oprah Winfrey is known worldwide, an industry unto herself.

While George loosens up the crowd, the TV lights go on to brighten the studio where *The Oprah Winfrey Show* is taped twice a day, three times a week, and aired a week later for around 15 million viewers.

The subject of this morning's taping is bachelor parties. Oprah, barely 5 feet tall, slips into the studio unnoticed, encircled by producers and assistants. She is busy scanning blue note cards when the audience sees her and immediately begins clapping.

Oprah looks slightly embarrassed, smiles, makes a small wave and says, "How y'all doing?"

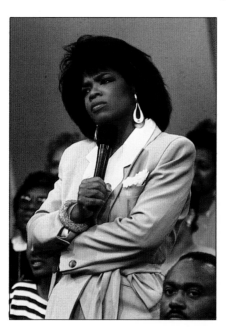

She is, after all, a Chicago celebrity, adored for her wit, her empathy, her charm, and most of all, her curiosity and eagerness to ask the most personal questions. Oprah is allowed to say what everyone else is thinking but wouldn't dare say.

To her obvious dismay, a makeup man dabs at her face with a sponge. "May I have some water, please?" she asks no one in particular. The bottle arrives promptly and she sips through a straw while the audience watches intensely. "I hate water. I really do." They laugh, having suffered with her as she shed 65 pounds in a nationally-monitored diet and then regained most of it.

Now Oprah is ready. She clears her throat, the theme music plays and she starts reading from the teleprompter.

"We'll talk to one woman who found out there were prostitutes at her husband's bachelor party," says Oprah. She turns to the woman in the audience who sent her fiancé off to his prenuptial bash with long underwear taped to his body.

Things are off to a good start, the audience provides plenty of zest and then there's a commercial break. More sips of water, more dabs at the face and the show resumes, with Oprah questioning a couple on stage. The wife says she was seriously traumatized upon hearing that strippers were at her husband's bachelor party. "It was a violation. I couldn't be intimate with him for a while," she says.

Now Oprah runs up the aisle with her microphone to where three strippers have been planted in the audience. "I'm a performer and I'm not there to do anything else," one declares. "It's clean, dirty fun," another says firmly, to the obvious dismay of some of the wives nearby.

Oprah encourages this kind of provocative banter because she knows it works. It's good theater. Since September 1986 when the program went into national syndication, she has logged more than 1,000 shows.

An hour passes quickly and the producer tells Oprah there is just one minute left. "Do you want the last word?" he asks. She doesn't. She opts instead to let members of her audience argue among themselves – and they do – as the credits roll.

The producer thanks the audience and then invites everyone to shake Oprah's hand on the way out. Most take up the offer, if only to get a closer look at their idol. One Oprah addict is teary-eyed after the experience.

Oprah moved to Chicago in 1984 at the age of 30 to host a faltering local talk show called *AM Chicago*. By 1985, it was the top show in its time slot and had been renamed, appropriately, *The Oprah Winfrey Show*.

In 1988 her HARPO (Oprah spelled backwards) Productions Inc. took over ownership and all production responsibilities, making her the first woman to own and produce her own talk show.

HARPO Studios, where the TV show is filmed, is located at 110 N. Carpenter Street. There is usually a week-long wait for audience reservations, but admission to the show is free.

THE WEST SIDE

Lacking a true center, Chicago's West Side offers students of urban development different focuses. Taylor Street at times resembles Lower Manhattan, complete with street eats and a carnival atmosphere each June when Taste of Italy erupts for a three-day gastronomic orgy of pizza, pasta, zuppa and vino. Wicker Park's perennial dilemma is whether to yuppify its aging frame house and gray stone ambience and set itself up as Newtown South, or to become a nest for the artistically and culturally dispossessed.

Maxwell Street, Greektown and Ukrainian Village are remnants of an ethnic Chicago that, urban renewal notwithstanding, retain some of their original color and character. Haymarket Square played a pivotal role in the early struggles of the American labor movement. The University of Illinois at Chicago nibbles away at the surrounding community. Cabrini-Green is a failed experiment in public housing where an unchaperoned elevator ride is risky during the day and downright dangerous at night.

The **University of Illinois at Chicago** began in 1946 at Navy Pier as a collection of temporary classrooms catering primarily to returning veterans. The move into the nucleus of today's campus at Harrison and Halsted, something akin to Godard's Alphaville or one of the more extreme Wagnerian stage sets, took place in 1965 amid hopes of establishing "a Harvard of the Midwest." The reigning pundits recruited a crop of promising young scholars to make it happen. Alas, it was not to be.

When money got tight in the early 1970s, threatened senior faculty members dismissed – though not without a fight – their brighter, more productive juniors who were approaching tenure. The English Department, a bastion of aging fellows, male and female, jettisoned 19 junior staff in one year against the recommendation of the university's own faculty Senate, which prompted a flurry of student protests.

Dominated by an inverted ziggurat that houses administrators and some faculty, the campus is a hodgepodge of structures. The **Behavioral Science Building** spirals like a labyrinthine concrete bunker, leading one professor to remark that he always expected a pellet of food to appear when he found his way to his office. Suspended walkways connecting the ziggurat, **University Hall**, with modular classrooms were supposed to provide cover during wet weather. As in so many Chicago projects, politics intervened. Substandard materials gave the walkways a sieve-like quality, and they leaked water from the beginning.

Settled in: Amid the stylistic mishmash, **Hull House** seems an oasis of dignity. A square brick 19th-century home now in the shade of the university,

receding
pages: a
Hispanic
neighborhood.
Left, back
yard boogie.
Right, leg
men.

its gabled two stories rising over white colonnades, Hull House started life at 800 S. Halsted. Jane Addams and Ellen Gates Starr converted the stately edifice into a settlement house in 1889. Now a museum, Hull House unfolds the history of the West Side's ethnic population, from Jews at the turn of the century, through the enclaves of German, Bohemian and Irish immigrants who contributed to the area's colorful melting pot.

West of the university, the thoroughfare of Taylor Street is known as **Little Italy**. Italian ice can be purchased on the sidewalks in summer and fine Italian food can be had year-round at some of the 30 restaurants spread through this community of about 8,000 Italians. Two of these are Rico's Restaurant at 626 S. Racine Avenue and the Rosebud Café at 1500 W. Taylor Street. There's another superb Italian dining area nearby, around 24th and Oakley.

Street shopping: Say the two words "Maxwell Street" in Chicago and an image of ethnic urbanites haggling over prices comes to mind. **Maxwell Street** is less a location than it is a culture, which began as a push-cart produce market that miraculously survived the Chicago Fire of 1871, said to have been started by Mrs O'Leary's cow kicking over a lantern.

While Maxwell Street has been home and shopping district to many nationalities and ethnic groups, immigrant Russian Jews who came in the late 1880s provided the most pronounced ethnic flavor to the area. Licensed vendors from most Chicago neighborhoods sell everything from hubcaps and bicycles to second-hand clothing and old record albums here.

The **Maxwell Street Market** is worth a walk-through, particularly on a Sunday morning, if only to watch a grassroots laissez-faire economy transcend racial and cultural barriers. From behind stalls and out of doorways, blacks and whites, Jews and Greeks, Latinos and Latvians conduct business.

A Ukrainian Village wedding.

Though bargains may exist, *caveat emptor* rules. The gold chain may be 24-carat, as claimed, but the gold isn't likely to be more than a few microns deep, and the "Rolex" or "Patek Phillipe" watches lining a hairy forearm are almost certainly from a Korean or Taiwanese factory.

Locals and nostalgic suburbanites shop for kitchenware, garden tools and the other prosaic stuff of daily life. Lounging Chicago policemen add their bit to the scene at Jim's Hot Dog Stand, 1320 S. Halsted, a stopping-off point for cheap franks or a Polish sausage traditionally washed down with orange soda or root beer.

Bows to Kiev: Another holdover from the past, **Ukrainian Village**, occupies a chunk of territory in the vicinity of Chicago Avenue and Oakley Boulevard south of Wicker Park. Pride of place in the community goes to **St Nicholas Ukrainian Catholic Cathedral** on Rice and Oakley, an exotic, Byzantine construction among the humdrum wood-frame and brick family houses that predominate in the area. Surmounted by a fanfare of ornate cupolas modeled on a Kiev original, the cathedral, built in 1913, embodies the community's continued commitment to traditional values and virtues.

The Milwaukee corridor, a onetime Indian trail that waves of immigrants gradually turned into a bustling mercantile microcosm of the developing city, leads northwest to **Wicker Park**, an island of substantial gray stone buildings saddled with the description "mansion" by their original owners. A magnificent example of "gingerbread," the **Hermann Weinhardt House**, has been impressing passersby at 2137 W. Pierce since 1893.

The Wicker Park Association has touted its turf for a decade or so as an integrated, socially advanced center for alternative lifestyles, but not much along the lines of Oak Park's ethnic sangfroid has emerged. Yuppies buy and renovate buildings along Logan

noisy
evolutionary
ar re-
acted.

Boulevard to live in or to rent out, while blue-collar workers and the young unemployed gather in bars on Leavitt, Wabansia and Concord Place.

Polish pride: A mile from Wicker Park, **St Stanislaus Kostka Church** is called "the mother church of all Polish Roman Catholic congregations in Chicago." Considering that Chicago's Polish population reputedly has been – and still may be – second only to Warsaw's, that's no small matter. Like St Nicholas, St Stanislaus reflects an Old World prototype, in this case a church in Krakow. Noble Street is also home to **Holy Trinity Church**, the focal point of fights, physical in more than one case, among parishioners of St Stanislaus and Holy Trinity over parish rights, as well as the German Catholic **St Boniface Church**.

Although burritos and pizza are now more common street food than kielbasa, two prominent repositories of Slavic culture fit comfortably into the area. To the west, on Chicago Avenue, the **Ukrainian National Museum** displays the intricately colored Easter eggs and bright folk costumes that Ukrainians remembered and reproduced in their new homes.

Documentary photographs of the life they left and the life they found in the New World promote a sense of unified cultural history that gives life to Ukrainian customs and provides a context for the folk art.

Reversing on Milwaukee and stopping at Augusta, the **Polish Roman Catholic Union of America** shares a building with the **Polish Museum of America**. Here, special exhibitions and film festivals explore and help maintain the sense of ethnic identity shared by Chicagoans of Polish ancestry. A library of archive material draws historians of diverse interests to this scholarly cubbyhole just off the expressway.

Riot history: A few blocks south and east of the museum, **Haymarket Square** straddles Jefferson Street. The square was the site of an 1886 bomb

Annual Greek-American Parade.

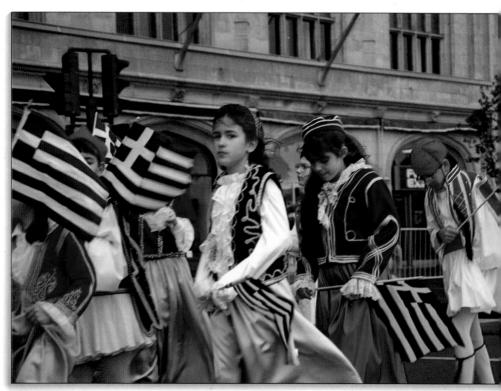

blast that killed 10 people, including seven policemen, and provoked Chicago's most sensational and agonizing display of civic unrest before the 1968 Democratic National Convention and the Days of Rage. The Haymarket Statue, however, having twice (in 1969 and 1970) been knocked from its pedestal by student radicals, no longer adorns the historic patch of ground. The old statue, a likeness of policeman Thomas Birmingham, left hand raised in an age-old gesture of admonition, with helmet and belted coat reminiscent of London's bobbies, now holds court at the **Police Training Academy** on Jackson Boulevard.

Another statue of more historic than artistic interest is the "Pillar of Fire" at the **Chicago Fire Academy**, at Jackson and DeKoven. History is still unclear on whether Mrs O'Leary's cow did or did not kick over an oil lamp that started the great Chicago Fire in 1871. It is indisputable, however, that the O'Leary barn, originally on the site of the Fire Academy, did go up in flames, along with the buildings covering 1,600 acres of the city. Curiously, Mrs O'Leary's adjacent home was spared.

Urban failure: Though hardly a source of civic pride, the **Cabrini-Green housing project** must be included in any survey of the West Side. The present 15-building high-rise cluster replaced a two-story project raised in the early 1940s and leased mainly to returning servicemen and war workers. Black and Italian families, fairly representative of the neighborhood, also rented apartments in Cabrini Houses, as they were then named.

The Cabrini Extension high-rises and William Green housing project were linked in the early 1960s, creating an island of low-income, chronically unemployed and underemployed tenants. The surrounding area, defined roughly by Division, Halsted, Chicago and Wells, deteriorated into a segregated slum that is regarded as one of the worst neighborhoods in the United States.

Pilsen
eighborhood
ar.

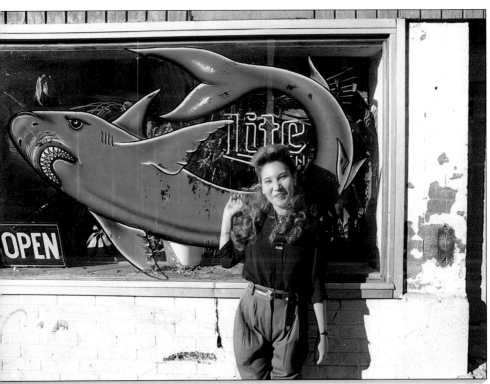

The quality of life in the ghetto has continued to worsen as a result of several factors: the West Side riots in 1968, following the assassinations of Malcolm X and Dr Martin Luther King Jr; the development of gang fiefdoms; the isolation of the homes from nearby residential communities by a series of small stores and the commercial-industrial properties to the west on Halsted. Former Mayor Jane Byrne's two-week stay in the Cabrini-Green projects during the early 1980s had no effect on the problems, though it amused some tenants and garnered national publicity for the mayor.

But things have deteriorated since then. Nowadays, police do not rush into Cabrini-Green when shooting is reported. Instead, they close off the area until the gunfire stops and then go in to tally up the dead and the wounded. This policy surprises no one. Not tenants, not the media and certainly not other cops. Unfortunately, it's one of the facts of life in Chicago.

Rail, post: Nearer the lake, in a corridor bounded east and west by Wacker and Clinton, are three major Chicago centers for transportation and communication: Union Station on Adams, the Northwestern Station used by Metra at Washington, and the main **Post Office** facing north on Van Buren.

Union Station was intended to form the foundation of a high-rise, but the project never got that far off the ground. The station is worth seeing, however, for its exterior arcade supported by massive stone columns beneath a facade of rectangular windows, and for its somewhat seedy waiting room where the steel truss-and-plaster vault soars overhead to combine grace with grandeur in mid-air.

The **Northwestern Station** on West Madison is a relatively new replacement for the old Chicago and North Western Railway Terminal, an architectural landmark where the classical portico and tesselated barrel vaulting in the main waiting room gave dignity to **Freight train.**

the whole idea of rail travel. In contrast, the present structure acts merely as a place for trains and passengers to meet.

Hard underbelly: The belly of Chicago, **South Water Market**, extends from 14th to 15th streets between Miller and Racine. Bays for refrigerated trucks, called "reefers," face each other across a boulevard-wide space where produce distributors take delivery of Georgia peaches, Maine cranberries, Texas and Florida oranges, Chilean grapes, lettuce and almonds from California, and broccoli, green beans and asparagus from all over the country. While primarily wholesalers, some distributors are not averse to a quick cash transaction, and early morning visitors often trudge back to their cars clutching a tray of dew-glistening raspberries or a hundred-pound sack of new potatoes.

Not so much a complement to the South Water Market as an addendum, the **South Loop Marketplace**, at 509 W. Roosevelt, has become the scene of an interesting social and economic ex-

periment. The National Black Farmers Harvest and Business Corporation, the "Black Farmers' Market" in common parlance, rents space at SLM on weekends from which it sells produce trucked in by black farmers from a 10-state region. Prices are low, fruits and vegetables are fresh and the goal is a laudable effort to reduce and eventually reverse the decline in land farmed by blacks. In addition to produce, bargain hunters pick through shelves and tables of oddments at the adjacent flea market, discovering battered Coca-Cola trays and faded tintypes, mechanical banks and Barbie dolls, yesterday's junk that has experienced a sea change and emerged as today's antiques and collectibles.

Greek eateries: Nearby **Greektown**, also known as the Delta due to its triangular shape, lies east of the University of Illinois. For immigrants working in the markets on Randolph Street, Greektown offered a comfortable enclave of coffee houses, compatriots,

atching aseball rough the ence.

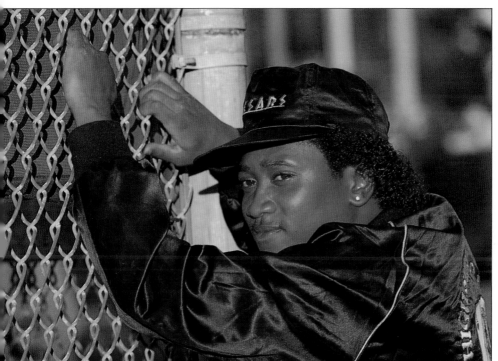

shops dealing in Greek Orthodox vestments, candles, sacred images, Greek books and newspapers, but most of all a lively group of restaurants that remind them of their former homes.

Visitors today often seek out those restaurants, a dense patch along Halsted where the Dan Ryan and Eisenhower expressways wind about each other like fishing line before continuing their headlong flight into the suburbs. In restaurants with names like the Parthenon, Greek Islands, Dianna's Island Opaa and Rodity's, food and "neoclassical" theater mix well and customers join with waiters in celebrating the joys of eating, and smashing crockery, in good company.

Saganaki, Greek cheese doused with brandy and set aflame, is extinguished by lemon juice squeezed at the table, eliciting a loud shout of "Opaa!" in unison from staff and clientele. Most restaurants offer a family meal for four at very reasonable prices.

Staples include *taramasalata*, a

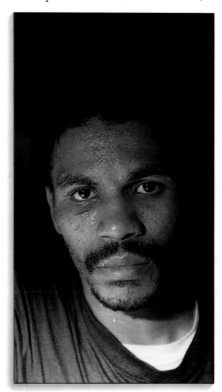

tangy pink fish roe spread; Greek olives and marinated eggplant; lamb braised with string beans or cauliflower, or baked; *pastitsio* and moussaka, noodle and potato-eggplant casseroles, respectively; and, finally, walnut-studded, honey-soaked *baklava* or rosewater-scented *galactoboureko* washed down with minuscule cups of sweetened Greek coffee.

Along the way, of course, there'll be ouzo, the anise-based aperitif that prepares the palate for the feast – or, some say, deadens it to the assault. Retsina wine, young and bracing, and spiked with resin, is a common dinner drink, along with the frankly sweet Mavrodaphne for the faint of heart. There'll also be lots of talk and smoke, perhaps some singing and once in a while even some spontaneous dancing and plate-smashing.

Bohemia: Neither **Pilsen**, near the southern edge of the West Side, nor Heart of Chicago, a few blocks farther south and west, present such ebullience. Pilsen's mostly bohemian population contributed significantly to Chicago's history during the freewheeling period of labor unrest in the 1870s. Today, the **Pilsen East Artists Colony** at 18th and Halsted provides a quieter avenue of expression for graphic artists, sculptors, actors and writers, who hold individual exhibitions throughout the year and take to the streets in October for their annual art fair.

Walkers will also find Mexican culture in contemporary Pilsen, notably at **Casa Aztlan**, 1831 S. Racine. Over a three-year period, Ray Pattan painted an exuberant panoply of Mexican themes halfway up the building's face. But it is **St Paul Church** that makes the strongest impression in this essentially residential area. Buttressed, vaulted, and topped by five needle-fine spires, Henry J. Schlacks' Gothic fantasy at 22nd Place and Joyne Street embodies a passionate vision more usually associated with Gaudí or Horta than a 19th-century Midwestern church architect.

Left, after pumping iron. **Right**, fire escapes.

SUBS

SOFT FROZEN YOGURT ON TAP

scrumptious
ice cream cones

PLAYS

TASTES OF CHICAGO

Befitting a citizenry that considers eating out a serious business – right up there with sports and politics – Chicago is home to hundreds of unusual, interesting and otherwise just plain good restaurants ranging from elegant eateries to simple hot dog stands.

That's why **Taste of Chicago** has proven so successful since getting started in 1982. This annual downtown lakeside party, attended by hundreds of thousands of people, features live entertainment and dozens of restaurant booths, allowing feasters to wander the grassy grounds sampling barbecued ribs, pizza and egg rolls. Taste, which runs from the end of June through July 4, is considered the largest food festival of its kind in the world.

Generations ago, when Chicago's stockyards were in their prime, the city was known as a steak town. Though new immigrant groups have left their culinary marks on the city and diners are more diet conscious, one restaurant that still prides itself on the perfect cut of beef is **Morton's of Chicago**. On Rush Street, the steak house takes its name from Arnie Morton, a colorful city restaurateur who founded Taste of Chicago. Morton is the third of four generations in the Chicago wining and dining business. His namesake reflects those decades of experience.

Morton's offers a clubby atmosphere with dark wood, celebrity photos, white table cloths and an intoxicating aroma of grilled meats. Fork-tender porterhouse steak is the house specialty. But the double fillet, charcoal dark outside and moist red inside, is another favorite cut among beef lovers. "Giving people a good deal seems to have paid off," says Morton, the grandson of a West Side saloon keeper.

Hullo, I'm Your Waiter: Humorist and gourmand Calvin Trillin once noted that Italian restaurants in America can be divided into those whose waiters have names like Vinnie and those that hire fellows named Travis or Dwayne. **Bravissimo**, one of Chicago's finest Italian restaurants, lives up to its name and those who doubt the heritage can discuss it with owner Nick Corey over *grappa*, the potent, colorless Italian brandy.

While some Italian restaurants in Chicago favor the heavy cream of northern Italy and others feature the tomato sauces to the south, Bravissimo pays homage to both with creative flair. The fresh roast duck ravioli comes with a red pepper cream sauce and the traditional spaghetti Napoletana is served with fresh spinach, tomatoes and a homemade pork-and-beef sausage. The list goes on, but two items are the best in the city – the flavorful Wyoming rack of lamb and the calamari, squid lightly fried in peanut oil.

Corey selects his own meats and produce, often from the Randolph Street market. Together with his partner

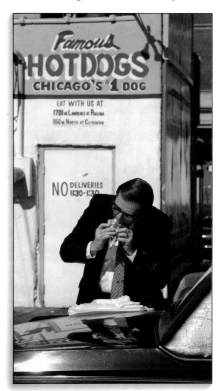

Robert Fink, the pair provide diners with inspired cuisine and a warm atmosphere in a two-level dining room, graced at the entrance by white columns. Be sure to save room for the *tiramisu*, a happy marriage of sweet mascarpone cheese, Kahlua and shaved chocolate. Fink swears he eats one daily and manages to stay slim.

Fiesta: For Mexican food, the hot spot in town is the **Frontera Grill**, in the trendy River North area. They won't take lunch reservations for fewer than six, and dinners need to be booked several days in advance. Owners Rick Bayless and his wife Deann opened their tribute to South of the Border fare in 1987, simultaneously publishing a book, *Authentic Mexican: Regional Cooking from the Heart of Mexico.*

Don't lose confidence due to the couple's non-Hispanic names. They spent eight years researching food in Mexico, and a taste of their cooking in the earthtone restaurant wins over any skeptics. Rather than limit the menu to Northern

Mexican dishes such as tacos and enchiladas, they offer a full range of Mexico's grand cuisine. From Oaxaca, they serve a *sabaroso*, seared turkey breast in rich red *mole*, a sweetened chili sauce. From Central Mexico comes charcoal grilled swordfish with a light cream sauce. The menu changes weekly, but diners always find something delightful to go with the homemade tortillas.

Eastern Europe: Hungarian restaurateur Ivan Kenessey, of **Kenessey's**, is another liberator of cuisine. He notes that culinary recipes created for wealthy families disappeared in Eastern Europe after World War II because of constant food shortages and political repression. "We're going back before war time and bringing back recipes from the good old days of Hungary," says Kenessey, who with his wife, Katalin, look the part of an aristocratic couple.

Their rediscovered recipes are tasty. The fillet mignon Eszterhazy, named for a famous Hungarian family, graces the beef with a white wine cream sauce. The Palacsinta family is honored by walnut-filled crepes, covered with a rich chocolate sauce and served in rum *flambé*. There is also the traditional lamb shank with *letcho* – green peppers, tomatoes and onion with smoked Hungarian sausage in a light paprika sauce.

Kenessey has the most impressive wine list in Chicago: 1,500 different varieties, all stored on wall-to-floor shelves around the grotto-style dining room. Walk around and pick vintage merlot, mersault or Hungarian Siklosi chardonnay. Then pay retail, plus a small uncorking fee. It's the best wine bargain in town. Located across from Lincoln Park, Kenessey's will also put together a variety of picnic lunches, from bread, cheese and wine, to pâté, caviar and Dom Perignon.

Dining in style: Old timer: For four-star gourmet fantasy, Chicagoland has its share, including the legendary **Le Francais** in suburban Wheeling. But perhaps the most outstanding is The

Chicago's classic German restaurant-brewery.

208

Everest Room, which takes both diners and food to elegant heights.

Located in the city's financial district, **The Everest Room** commands a spectacular, 40th floor view of Chicago's West Side. It is gorgeous at sunset and powerful at night, when cars on the Eisenhower Expressway create an expansive, twinkling vista.

Inside, the nationally acclaimed restaurant surrounds its guests in an ivory-toned ambience of understated elegance and attentive service that remains unobstrusive. The cuisine is inspired. Award-winning chef and owner Jean Joho has drawn on his Alsatian roots to present the magical and magnificent from his kitchen.

There may be light, Maryland crab salad in a thinly sliced cucumber box; succulent Maine lobster with Alsace Gewurztraminer and ginger; exquisite wild pheasant, wrapped in cabbage with basil; and flavorful venison medallions, served with a tart huckleberry sauce.

Don't leave without sampling a dessert. Some recent favorites include lovingly sautéed raspberries in Alsatian raspberry liqueur and the chocolate fantasy, an assortment that includes chocolate-honey sorbet in a molded, maple syrup basket.

Old timer: With restaurants opening and closing in Chicago like menu covers, an exception is the **Berghoff Restaurant**, scheduled to celebrate its 100th anniversary in 1998. Across the street from the elegant Palmer House in the heart of the Loop, the Berghoff offers the best German meals in the city.

The huge dining rooms, with oak paneling and tables, are always crowded, no easy feat for a restaurant that seats 800 diners. Service? The term "hustle and bustle" could have been coined for the Berghoff waiters who always seem to be carrying several plates of tart *sauerbraten*, smoked *thuringer* with sauerkraut, tender *weiner schnitzel* and savory German pot roast, or delivering foaming steins of Berghoff beer.

usage
aking.

The Berghoff serves some 2,500 meals plus 3,000 steins of their Dortmunder-style beer daily. Actually, it sold the beer first. Herman Joseph Berghoff, a German immigrant, opened an Indiana brewery in 1887 and brought his beer to the 1893 World's Columbian Exposition. It was such a success that he opened the Berghoff and was issued Chicago Liquor License No. 1, now on display in the main dining room. The Berghoff also makes its own root beer.

Picking winners: In terms of new restaurants, it's impossible to predict what will be trendy, or even open next month. Some chic spots have been packed one day and literally closed down the next. But if you had to pick, any venue owned by restaurant genius Richard Melman would be an odds-on favorite.

Two of his restaurants, **Shaw's Crab House** and **Shaw's Blue Crab Lounge & Oyster Bar**, next to each other just off State Street, serve some of the best seafood in Chicago. The House offers white tablecloths and 1930s decor, with

daily specials such as grilled *mahi mahi* and soft-shelled crabs. The Lounge puts diners on wooden stools for gumbo, chowder or stew. Fresh oysters and clams vary daily and the Maryland crabcakes are always moist.

Bub City Crabshack & Bar-B-Q, another Melman creation, is a lively and spacious eatery fixed up to look like a roadside honky-tonk in Texas. There's even Lone Star and other Texas beers. The cookin' includes stuffed *jalapeno* peppers, oyster and hot sausage po' boys, pick 'n' lick shrimp, blackened fish, dungeness crab, steamed with or without garlic, and plenty of barbecue. Ordinarily in the Midwest, barbecue means ribs. But at Bub's, as in the American South, barbecue means a delicious smoked beef brisket.

Rib tickling: If you're looking for Chicago barbecue – meaty pork ribs slathered in a very messy and zesty sauce – **Twin-Anchors Restaurant and Tavern** has none other than "the chairman of the board" singing its praise. When Frank Sinatra comes to his kind of town, he asks Twin-Anchors, which doesn't ordinarily deliver, to bring him plenty of ribs. Naturally, it's an offer they can't refuse.

Opened in 1932 in a former Old Town speakeasy, Twin-Anchors seems to get better with age. Many consider the ribs the best in Chicago because they are picked with care, served as a slab that overhangs the plate and can be easily pulled from the bone. The friendly, bustling tavern also serves a great burger.

For something completely different, **Mama Desta's Red Sea Restaurant** serves some excellent authentic Ethiopian fare not far from Wrigley Field. The savory food is that of the Amhara and Tigrean peoples, the ruling classes, whose cuisine is among the most sophisticated in East Africa. The spices are reminiscent of East Indian curries, but savory, not sweet.

The more guests at a Mama Desta's table, the better to try more dishes. On **Fish** each table, the waitress places a pan **formation.**

covered with spongy bread called *injera*, which resembles unbaked pizza crust but tastes something like sourdough. Orders are then spooned onto the bread in a decorative arrangement. Diners tear some bread from a side serving and pinch the food with it, rather like making a taco, and then eat with their hands. It's part of the fun.

Couples would do best to order the *Alitcha* combo and the hot combo. The *Alitcha* dish offers chicken, lamb and beef, cooked separately in a thick, mild green sauce. The hot combo has the same meats, but they are cooked in a spicy, red pepper sauce. Cold beer goes very well with the meal, as does a glass of honey wine.

Chinese choice: For Chinese food, also more enjoyable with larger parties, go to Chinatown. Cermak and Wentworth streets are the starting point. Walk through the ornate arch on Wentworth and take in the groceries, kitchen supply houses and souvenir shops. The aroma of garlic and ginger is heady.

A local favorite that is all but unknown among tourists is the **Three Happiness Restaurant** on Cermak. It's a tiny storefront with a few formica tables and cheap prices for, among other things, the best Singapore fried-rice noodles in Chicago. The noodles, which look like spaghetti, are fried in a pan with Szechuan peppers and aromatic spices. Barbecued pork, shrimp and green peppers are added to this to make up a huge single serving. For those preferring Cantonese, Three Happiness offers plump *egg foo yong*, tasty chicken with pea pods and several good beef dishes.

Get along, little doggies: The best hot dogs can be found at **Demon Dogs**, under the Fullerton Avenue El stop. Owner Peter Schivarelli uses top-line Vienna beef hot dogs. The difference is that the better dogs come in a casing that keeps them from shrinking while they're being steamed. Besides the clearer flavor, there should be a slight crunch when that first bite breaks the

Butcher shop.

casing. Chicago has many Vienna stands, but not all have the firmer, non-shrink casing.

A true Chicago dog must be loaded with "the works" – mustard, relish and onions. The tiny peppers are optional and very hot. Demon Dogs, named for the Blue Demon mascot of nearby DePaul University, sells 5,000 hot dogs a week. The french fries, cooked in vegetable oil instead of animal fat, are also excellent. Demon Dogs, opened in 1982, is regarded by many as the best hot dog stand in Chicago because it hasn't diluted its identity by adding salads or grilled chicken sandwiches to the menu. It also has free parking in a congested part of town. The decor is appealing: Schivarelli grew up with members of the rock group Chicago and has decorated his place with many of their gold and platinum records.

Deep dish original: Chicago is famous for deep-dish pizza, a hefty concoction of chunky tomato sauce over a thick baked crust with plenty of mozzarella cheese. Add favorite ingredients, such as pepperoni, sausage, green peppers or mushrooms, and call it a meal.

A pizza war has been running in Chicago for decades among restaurants, critics and customers all claiming different winners. Visitors might want to begin their own research by returning to where it all started back in 1943. **Pizzeria Uno**, a couple of blocks from Michigan Avenue, is the birthplace of Chicago-style deep dish pizza. **Pizzeria Due**, established in 1955, is the sister restaurant and just as good. Creator Ike Sewell, the man most responsible for teaching Americans that pizza could be a meal rather than just a snack, makes pizza with a coarse, crunchy crust, a thick layer of mozzarella and a natural, perfectly seasoned sauce – a good foundation to build on.

No chips: A great burger and a correspondingly great character – or maybe it should be characters – are the attraction at **Billy Goat Tavern & Grill**, a neighborhood bar on lower Michigan

Big hot dog, with relish; a doorman-chef-babysitter welcomes customers of all ages.

Avenue that is the city's hangout for newspapermen and women. They simply call it "the Goat" and their legions include Pulitzer Prize winner Mike Royko, the *Chicago Tribune* columnist whom many regard as Chicago's conscience. Visitors often order cheeseburgers in groups, so they can hear the Greek grillman shout, "cheezborger, cheezborger, cheezborger," as he slaps patties on the sizzling grill, just like in the famous *Saturday Night Live* TV skits featuring the late John Belushi.

The burgers are juicy and excellent value. Try the double cheeseburger, served on a Kaiser roll. Take it over to the counter, load it up with pickles, onions, ketchup and mustard, and then survey the tavern's history on its walls. Way before *Saturday Night Live* the place was famous for William "Billygoat" Sianis, who opened the tavern in 1934 and welcomed sportswriters to drink there. One day a goat wandered in and was adopted as a mascot. Sianis, his goatee and goat made good pictures for the several daily newspapers of the day and many of those snaps are displayed along the walls of the tavern. The original Billygoat's nephew, Sam Sianis, runs the place now and keeps the publicity going.

The juice is loose: The best Italian beef sandwich can be found at **Mr Beef** on Orleans. What's an Italian beef? Thinly sliced roast beef is slowly cooked in its own juices with a hint of garlic and packed into a fresh slice of Italian bread. On this, Mr Beef piles sautéed green peppers, hot peppers or both, and offers the choice of "wet," with extra juices, or "dry," without. Owners Dominic and Joseph Zucchero, who opened the beef stand years before the River North area got trendy, use fresh sirloin tip roasts. Their fans, who always pack this daytime-only place, include local and national celebrities alike, such as comedian Jay Leno, who once showed up on a nationwide talk show eating Mr Beef sandwiches. The Italian beef sandwich is a Chicago classic.

A burger with all the trimmings.

OAK PARK

Oak Park is a curious place – or perhaps two places. The inhabitants of this suburb 10 miles due west of Chicago's Loop divide into two groups. One group includes all the normal citizens who get up, get dressed, go to work, clean the house, yell at the kids and run red lights when the street seems clear of police. The second, smaller group is a priestly class, the dead-serious Frank Lloyd Wright fans for whom Prairie School architecture ranks no lower than second or third in the history of great ideas.

Norman Mark, a Chicago broadcaster and a member of the latter group, reverently proclaimed, "To walk through Oak Park is to touch genius." He continues: "Oak Park reverberates with the ghost of Frank Lloyd Wright, an architectural genius who lived there, [and who] revolutionized residential building design…"

Which is true as far as it goes. Mark and other Wright advocates often fail to mention how dark and constricting his interior spaces may be as living quarters, how the flat roofs he gave to some Midwest houses implode under the weight of repeated snowfalls, or how ergonomically unsatisfactory some of his built-in chairs and tables appear on close acquaintance.

Wright turns: Most visitors reach Oak Park via the suburban Metra commuter line from downtown. Near the station in Oak Park, the **Oak Park Visitor's Bureau** rents taped talks for self-guided tours, an ingenious idea for those who prefer a leisurely stroll to the frenetic pace often adopted by zealous tour leaders. A quick count of shelves at the Visitor's Bureau reveals 26 books devoted exclusively to FLW, his designs and his philosophy, including a *Frank Lloyd Wright Home and Studio* coloring book for children. On sale are numerous postcards and posters, as well as mugs, T-shirts and shopping bags, clear indi-

cation that FLW has blossomed from mortal architect to immortal souvenir industry.

The reason for the adulation, of course, is the conspicuous near-absence of almost anything other than the Wright and the Queen Anne and Stick houses that make a walk through "historic" Oak Park a must for architecture buffs and an agreeable diversion for the rest of us.

But there are a few other things in Oak Park, which has long been studied by sociologists who view the neighborhood as a classic American suburb, not least for the way its more liberal-minded white residents encouraged middle-class blacks to become their neighbors in the 1950s and '60s.

The Children's Curiosity Corner of the **Oak Park Conservatory and Earth Shelter Classroom** (at 617 Garfield Street) keeps smaller youngsters happy while dad and mom and the older siblings immerse themselves in exhibits that explore desert and tropical

Preceding pages: a Wright house in Oak Park. Left, mugging in Oak Park. Right, Frank Lloyd Wright with a model apartment building, 1930.

flora and the specialized biology of ferns. Collections of exotic plants, a waterfall and gardens of herbs combine with native Illinois prairie plants in this richly diverse and undeservedly neglected part of Oak Park.

Cool diversions: Opposite the Visitor's Center, **Austin Garden** is equipped with benches and lots of shade trees which can be a godsend in the heat of July and August. A trio of casual ice-cream parlors cluster nearby on Lake Street: A Taste of Culture Frozen Yoghurt, Phoebe's Frozen Yoghurt and Baskin-Robbins. The first two feature homebaked cakes and muffins as well, to be washed down with non-alcoholic potables, while A Taste of Culture also offers soup.

Oak Park and contiguous River Forest share the **Village Players**, an air-conditioned and comfortable theater small enough to foster a sense of intimacy and engagement. As the view is good from anywhere in the house, tickets only a few dollars and productions usually light and contemporary (*A Funny Thing Happened on the Way to the Forum, Stepping Out*, an angst-free *Chorus Line* with tapdancing instead of high kicking), a walking tour can segue pleasantly into a light supper and show.

Oak Park has its share of special events in the summer, many devoted to the arts, or arts and crafts, or to historic buildings, or to literati such as Ernest Hemingway, who was born here, and Edgar Rice Burroughs, author of *Tarzan of the Apes*, who lived and worked in the suburb.

Art fairs punctuate the summer calendar, along with occasional special tours that take visitors into landmark homes, including some of Wright's, that are normally closed to the public. There's also a summer country fair and the **Kettlestrings Festival**, a jamboree named after the settler who established Oak Park as a discrete urban entity back in 1839.

The pedestrian mall sandwiched between the Oak Park Metra station and

Wright's house for Mrs Thomas H. Gale.

Lake Street has gone down sadly since its halcyon days, though there are still a few specialty and fashion shops.

Housing history: Still, Oak Park's main attraction for outsiders, apart from air refreshingly free of pollutants and a social fabric notably unrent by civic dissension, are the walking tours. An entire district, the area lying between Chicago Avenue and Randolph Street on the north and south and Linden and Marion streets east and west, has been given a listing in the *National Register of Historic Places*. Almost all of the houses are private homes, so the interiors have to be imagined from descriptions or viewed via photographs and line drawings that embellish books and pamphlets.

One can, however, tour the **Frank Lloyd Wright Home and Studio**, 947 Chicago Avenue, and Unity Temple, 875 Lake Street. The former's initial structure, dating from 1889, did double duty as workshop and home until 1898, when Wright built a brick-and-shingle house next door to accommodate his expanding needs. All aspects of his architecture business, from conception to artistic design to drafted plans, were carried out here until 1909, the period to which the building – made over into a residence by Wright in 1911 – has been restored.

The 1889 home, the product of Wright's tradition-bound vision, is dominated by a bold pitched-roof second floor, an equilateral triangle pierced by diamond-pane casement windows set in a rectangular array. The studio features a squat octagonal library to go with a two-story drafting room and an inconspicuous side entrance, the latter consistent with Wright's belief, later developed and elaborated upon, that movement from an outer environment to an interior space should be an experienced transition, not an abrupt change. Furnishings designed by Wright fill the house, for which a one-hour tour is available.

The **Gingko Tree Bookstore** down-

stairs sells tour tickets, also available at the Visitor's Bureau, and any number of books on architecture in general and Wright in particular. Mostly technical works or essays in secular hagiography, at least one volume deserves singling out for its amusing sidelights on Wright's prickly personality, *Letters to Clients* – which also includes letters *from* them. To a 1934 query about thresholds and keeping flies from getting into the house under the door, Wright replies, "Dear Nancy Willey: The screen doors can be cut on the slope and filled with leather flap. A half-inch clearance at the center and about half way back is all that will be needed. The rest will be in the clearance anyway. Let us have no thresholds. Amen. Frank Lloyd Wright."

The Wright church: The construction of Wright's 1905 magnum opus, **Unity Temple**, began in 1906 and wound to a close three years later. A scarcity of money in the church coffers enabled Wright to get the commission and dic-

"bootleg" ouse.

tated, in part, his use of poured concrete, which was cheap but relatively untested. The construction has stood the test well, though visitors are cautioned not to stand under the overhanging eaves, which 80 years of weathering have rendered crumbly.

From the street, Unity Temple presents a set of cubic masses whose jutting horizontal slabs and fret-ornamented vertical blocks only in part overcome an essential stolidity and heaviness. A skylight and windows send natural light flooding over the soft earth tones of the church. The sanctuary's muted yellow, green, gray and white interior, plus hanging lamps, heating ducts in quasi-sculptured columns and ribbons of wood trim help to move the eye rhythmically from space to space.

A walk west on Chicago from Forest to Marion passes two **"bootleg" Wright houses**, at 1019 and 1027 Chicago. These are examples of architectural moonlighting for which Louis Sullivan, who had Wright under contract, fired his young associate in 1892. Nearly identical Queen Anne houses whose octagonal bays thrust out from a rectangular box, they suggest the simplification Wright's work was undergoing. The following year saw the construction of the **Walter H. Gale House** a few doors down at 1031 Chicago, in which Wright moves from straight lines to curved forms within the Queen Anne format, yet introduces decorative complexity in the roof shingles and lead glass windows.

Triangles: Kenilworth Avenue unfolds a pastiche of styles in 14 houses, most built between 1880 and 1910, Queen Anne and Prairie School predominating. The overall effect is harmonious despite the many differences – notably from the Colonial Revival at 312 Kenilworth, sporting Ionian corner capitals and a centered doorway, to 417 Kenilworth, whose third floor is an intersection of steeply pitched isosceles triangles and deep dormer windows

Unity Temple interior.

over a boxy second floor set on a central square rimmed by a colonnaded porch.

At 217 Home Avenue, the **Farson House**, a dramatic example of Prairie School architecture (1897–99) by George Washington Maher, looms at the end of a landscaped approach. The building retains its original furniture and fixtures, designed by the architect, as well as antique toys and memorabilia of Hemingway and Wright. The **Historical Society of Oak Park and River Forest** is based in the building, which is open for touring a couple of afternoons a week.

Forest Avenue from Chicago past Pleasant contains several important buildings beginning with four row houses circa 1888–89 (200–206 Forest) and culminating in the **Arthur Heurtley House** (318 Forest), built by Wright in 1902. Particularly noteworthy are the modified gable roof, like a Chinese coolie hat that caps the upper floor casement windows, and alternating light and dark horizontal bands of brick cut only by ground floor windows and a circular arched entrance behind an open porch. Not much fancied by the public, the Heurtley House drew considerable praise from architects and remained one of Wright's personal favorites years later.

Open interior: The flattened S-curve of **Elizabeth Court** connecting Forest and Kenilworth makes an enjoyable departure from straight streets and avenues. Next to a rather overblown Queen Anne structure, the modest statement of the **Mrs Thomas Gale House** at 6 Elizabeth Court achieves a quiet dignity. Its open interior space permits passersby to look through the front ground floor windows to the green yard in back. The **William G. Fricke House** at 540 Fair Oaks Avenue, at first glance similar, hedges the uncompromising horizontals with handsome vertical masses, and a varied, complex use of abrupt corners and multiple flat gable roofs almost suggest the flaring rooflines of pagoda architecture.

THE SOUTH SIDE

Chicago's South Side was the home of the "Mickey Finn," the doctored drink that Michael Finn, the unscrupulous owner of the long-defunct Lone Star Saloon and Palm Garden, used to serve unwitting patrons in the 1890s so that he could rifle their pockets after they passed out.

Visitors to the South Side today have a considerably better chance of remaining alert, but not if they happen to mention anything at all positive about the North Side. Any true South Sider within earshot will quickly inform the visitor that there isn't *anything* good about the North Side.

Such is the thinking on the South Side. As with any neighborhood rivalry or urban turf war, the roots of this north-south division are tangled in the past. But it comes down to this: South Siders think North Siders are arrogant twits who say "Ciao." Of course, South Siders don't just argue with North Siders; if no North Siders are available, they'll happily squabble among themselves over anything and everything, including the definition of the South Side. Some say it's all of Chicago south of Madison Street, which would include half of the Loop. Others insist it includes Grant Park and its museums, which are more generally (and in this book) regarded as part of downtown and the Loop. South Siders also tend to claim well-known areas such as Little Italy and Maxwell Street that are southwest of the Loop and are treated by the official University of Chicago mapmakers (and, again, this book) as part of the West Side.

It's difficult to explain the North-South friction in Chicago, but it dates back at least to 1839. That's when Chicago's first South Side pioneers settled in what is now downtown Chicago. They did this to be near the safety of Fort Dearborn and the trade of the Chicago River. Most of the early settlement was on the south bank of the river, west of what is now Michigan Avenue – making, for argument's sake – the first settlers South Siders.

Troubled waters: In 1831, the city fathers thought it would be a good idea to put a bridge across the Chicago River. The river runs east to west through the center of present-day downtown Chicago and eventually splits north and south. The bridge was designed to open commerce to the North Side, an idea that the South Siders immediately deemed senseless.

Since the bridge was repeatedly rammed by boats trying to navigate the narrow river, the City Council eventually ordered it dismantled in 1839. Pioneer South Siders were jubilant. So much so, they splintered the bridge with axes before North Siders could organize to save it. That animosity has remained in various forms throughout the city's history, particularly when it comes to important matters. Like baseball.

The Cubs play in a cute little ballpark on the North Side referred to as "the friendly confines" and named for a chewing gum manufacturer. For decades, the White Sox, long regarded as the city's workingman's team, toiled on the South Side in a park named for a first baseman called Comiskey. The park, at 35th and Shields, was built in 1910 and was the oldest in the major leagues until the White Sox built a new one across the street to open the 1991 season. The old stadium was knocked down shortly afterwards to create parking spaces. The new **White Sox Park** is easily reached via CTA, the 35th street station.

In the mid-19th century the South Side was a place where worker and boss lived side by side. It was not unusual to see an early and perhaps sensorily impaired meatpacker build his home right next to the slaughterhouse and its stench. By the late 1800s, however, the captains of Chicago industry had become a little more particular about their neighbors. Still, the very wealthy lived on the South Side, albeit separate from the masses.

Mansion Row: "Millionaires' Row," in the days when a million was really something, was **Prairie Avenue** between 16th and 22nd streets. It was the unofficial home roosting ground for the city's first entrepreneurs to make it big, including George Pullman of the Pullman railroad car, department store magnate Marshall Field, meatpacking mogul Phillip Armour and about 50 others who built mansions there.

There is little here now to attest to the area's former pedigree, but the Prairie Avenue Historic District has preserved some of the old glory. An example is the **Glessner House** at 1800 S. Prairie, a bulky Romanesque mansion – the only remaining H.H. Richardson-designed building in Chicago that is open to public tours. A block away is the city's oldest building, the **Widow Clarke House**, at 1855 S. Indiana Avenue. This Greek revival house was originally built in 1836 about two blocks from where it

A South Side boxing club.

stands now.

Bertha Palmer, a major mover in Chicago society and the wife of Potter Palmer, founder of the Palmer House hotel, helped bring status to the North Side when she convinced her husband to move away from Prairie Avenue. They built a gaudy mansion on North Lake Shore Drive, and the elite of Prairie Avenue eventually followed. With the millionaires moving north, the South Side's animosity toward the North Side grew.

All in the numbers: South Siders then and now believe that their side of town is where "real people" live, the unpretentious folk who still rely on numbered streets – 95th Street is 95 blocks south of the Madison Street north-south dividing line in the Loop, for instance – instead of the named streets on the North Side.

The South Side also has machine shops, steel mills, can factories and, fittingly, the **Museum of Science and Industry** at 57th Street and Lake Shore Drive. Children love this museum for its clear explanations, demonstrations and hands-on exhibits of scientific principles and how they are applied to industrial uses and everyday life. The space center and Omnimax Theatre, with its stunning nature and science films, are also popular attractions.

The cultural center of the South Side is the University of Chicago and the neighborhood known as **Hyde Park**. One local jewel is the **Oriental Institute**, a museum of antiquities at 1155 E. 58th Street. The institute has galleries representing many ancient societies, their art and artifacts: Egyptian, Assyrian, Mesopotamian, Persian and Palestinian. Each gallery is filled with hundreds of exhibits, including a famous 40-ton Assyrian statute of a winged bull.

Within walking distance from the Oriental Institute is the **Robie House**, 5757 S. Woodlawn, a Prairie School architectural masterpiece designed by Frank Lloyd Wright in 1909. Not far

eighborhood
uor store.

away is the country's first black history museum, **DuSable Museum of African American History**, at 740 E. 56th Street. Founded in 1959, the museum has a permanent exhibit entitled "Up From Slavery" that describes the development of US slavery and includes documents and artifacts of slavery. The museum also has traveling exhibits in addition to memorabilia, sculptures, paintings and photos of and by African Americans.

Ghost yards: The **Chicago Union Stock Yard** once employed 40,000 workers scattered over 500 acres to slaughter cattle and pigs to feed the nation. With just a couple of rendering plants still in operation, the old stockyards are all but gone. The stockyards are now commemorated by the limestone gate erected in 1865 and still standing at Exchange Avenue and Peoria Street (about 41st and Halsted). Now, however, the gate is about the only thing to see, and it leads nowhere.

Like the stockyards, the once-mighty Chicago steel mills have also faded away. Wisconsin Steel, on 106th Street on the southeast side, is nothing but a corrugated steel corpse where weeds and rust have replaced its 3,500 workers. A drive by the deserted plant provides an eerie reminder of American industrial muscle gone soft.

US Steel's South Works has also withered. Founded in 1880, the mill still stands, though mostly empty, on Lake Michigan's southwestern shore, starting at about 79th Street. At its height during World War II, the mill employed more than 18,000 workers. Now, fewer than 1,000 people work at the mill that produced the steel framing for many of Chicago's greatest skyscrapers, including the Sears Tower and the John Hancock Center.

For the flavor of the steel-mill neighborhoods – not to mention a good meal and a good time drinking Niksico beer and eating American-Yugoslavian cuisine – seek out the **Golden Shell**, restaurant. The atmosphere is casual

Wall mural on Japanese American Friendship Center.

and festive amid strumming minstrels and waitresses jockeying for position with platters of stuffed peppers, cabbages and *muckalica*, a pork tenderloin sautéed with green peppers and onions. No matter what else is consumed, however, the dessert is a must: *krem pita*, a lighter-than-air pudding between two layers of pastry with a vanilla whipped topping.

Pulled out: Farther south and west is another industrial ghost. The Pullman plant no longer manufactures luxury railroad cars in **Pullman**, a neighborhood once referred to as "the most perfect city in the world." That was over a century ago, when Pullman had 8,000 residents, about a third of whom labored in the plants of George Pullman's Palace Car Company.

Pullman was a model industrial town, where the company owned everything. Workers were housed, according to their position, in tidy company homes on streets that were paved and landscaped by the company. Plant managers had larger houses than foremen; foremen had larger houses than laborers.

The village, located between 111th Street and 115th Street from **Cottage Grove** to **Langley Avenue**, is today a national landmark where even North Siders are known to visit, perhaps for an enjoyable brunch at the historic **Hotel Florence**, 11111 S. Forrestville. Some of the beauty of Pullman's public buildings, fountains and reflecting ponds can still be seen, but restoration is a continuing battle. It's the kind of area that must be walked through, lingeringly, to be appreciated.

Despite the well laid plans of Pullman's corporate order, several years after the town was founded the workers began to feel squeezed. To them, it didn't seem fair that the company set rents and controlled prices at its local stores. In 1894, a precedent-setting strike brought violence and federal intervention to Pullman. Eventually, the Illinois Supreme Court ruled the company couldn't own the town. Employ-

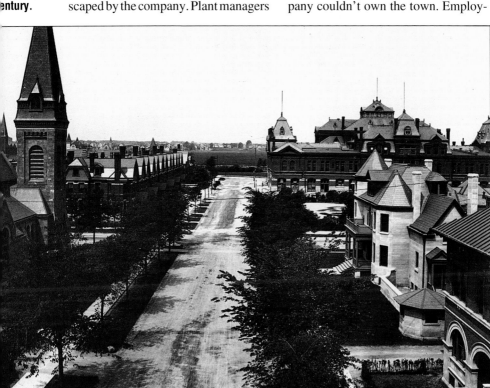

Pullman, the ultimate company town, around the turn of the century.

ees were allowed to buy homes, but company support for the town disappeared. It was never the same. The last Pullman car was manufactured in 1981.

Fair tales: Another bit of South Side history was the World's Columbian Exposition of 1893, a giant fair that included: the first Ferris wheel (250 feet in diameter with a capacity of 1,400 passengers, designed by George W. G. Ferris); "Little Egypt," a belly dancer who became a national sex icon of the Gay Nineties; the **Midway Plaisance**, a strip one mile long and 300 feet wide that was lined with examples of the architecture of the world (now a wide grassway on 59th Street that runs through the University of Chicago); and grounds laid out and landscaped by Frederick Law Olmsted, who also designed New York City's Central Park.

Other legacies of the exposition include **Jackson Park**, the Museum of Science and Industry (originally the fair's Fine Arts building), and the name "Windy City," bestowed by the East Coast press because Chicago had been so loud and strident – also well-known South Side traits – in lobbying to host the fair. In the end the event was a roaring success, claiming 27 million admissions.

Just as the 1893 Columbian Exposition celebrated humankind's past, the next big fair in Chicago, the Century of Progress World's Fair of 1933, looked to the future. This expo, built amid manmade islands and lagoons along the South Side lakefront, used new building materials and modernistic designs to project a bold future despite the bleakness of the Great Depression. Meigs Field was later built on Northerly Island, which was part of the fair's site of 598 acres built into the lakefront with sand and fill. The 1933 fair unleashed another sex-bomb to titillate the American public – Sally Rand, the fan dancer who became famous for her glimpse-of-flesh routines in the fair's Italian village, especially popular among the high-rolling hoodlums of the day.

The university: Along the majestic Midway Plaisance sits another South Side landmark, the **University of Chicago's Rockefeller Chapel**. Built in the mid-1920s, its modified Gothic design was intended "to remove the mind of the student from the busy mercantile condition of Chicago and surround him with the peculiar air of quiet dignity." The university today strives to maintain this theme of quiet dignity. Modeled after England's Oxford University, the gray stone buildings and the quadrangles they form can make for serene strolls with stops at some of the university's other sights such as the **Smart Museum**, 5550 S. Greenwood Avenue, where exhibits feature quality art from ancient to contemporary. For fans of the very latest in art, there's the **Renaissance Society** on the fourth floor of the university's **Cobb Hall** at 5811 S. Ellis. This nearly 80-year-old museum has no permanent collection, but it is famous for helping to launch the careers of many contemporary artists by giving

Buddy Guy, blues guitarist *extraordinaire* hanging out outside the Checkerboard

them their first shows.

The University of Chicago also played a large role in the dawning of the atomic era. Beneath the stands of an athletic field at the University of Chicago, the first sustained and controlled production of atomic energy took place on December 2, 1942. A group of scientists, headed by Enrico Fermi, created the first nuclear reactor, and with it the technology that led to the dropping of two atomic bombs on Japan in 1945 to hasten the end of World War II and, ultimately, usher in the four-decade-long Cold War. The Chicago experiments are commemorated by a **Henry Moore sculpture**, *Nuclear Energy*, on the site of old Stagg Field at 57th Street and Ellis Avenue.

Beverly's hill: The nation's largest urban historic district, containing 3,000 buildings with national register status, is also on the South Side. The **Beverly** neighborhood is situated on a ridge 30 to 40 feet above the rest of the city. Its residential architecture includes two homes designed by Frank Lloyd Wright and 17 houses designed by his student, Walter Burley Griffin, who designed Canberra, the capital of Australia, and who created the standard for the classic Chicago bungalow. **Walter Burley Griffin Place** (10432 South from 1600 West to 1756 West) in Beverly contains several examples of his houses, marked with signs.

The homes of Beverly run the architectural gamut, from Queen Anne to Prairie School to bungalow to modern suburban ranch. There's even the **Irish Castle**, 103rd Street and Longwood Drive, built in 1886 by a Chicago real estate developer who modeled it after one he had seen on the River Dee. North and south of the castle, mansions preside over the neighborhood from atop a glacial ridge.

To get a bit of local South Side flavor, stop in Top Notch Beefburger, 2116 W. 95th Street, for 1950s-style cheeseburgers and fries with thick chocolate shakes served in stainless steel. Reser-

�ᴍiskey ᴀrk, opening ᴀy of the ʜite Sox ᴀseball ᴀson, April ɪ74.

vations are required, but good New Orleans-style cuisine is available at the Maple Tree Inn, 10730 S. Western Avenue. The restaurant is housed in a converted apartment building, part sports bar and part outdoor beer garden. At night the top floor is a wonderfully dark and mellow jazz club.

Chinatown: One of the South Side's most distinctly ethnic neighborhoods is **Chinatown**, a meandering gaggle of oriental architecture, restaurants and shops that was first settled by Chinese immigrants around 1912. **Cermak Road** and **Wentworth Avenue** is the main intersection of Chinatown. The neighborhood continues to serve as a Midwestern receiving area for immigrants from mainland China and Taiwan. Beneath the cheerful, crowded streets lined with many good restaurants, Chinatown sometimes seethes with crime and gang tensions. Even the On Leong building, considered the **Chinese City Hall**, has been raided for gambling in recent years by federal agents. Of course, this is not all that unusual for the South Side – the home of Al Capone in his heydey.

Not far from Chinatown is Capone's one-time headquarters at the old **Lexington Hotel** at Michigan Avenue and Cermak Road (2200 South). Capone had a suite on the corner, where he could keep an eye on the intersection below from his turret-like office. If and when the decrepit hotel opens to the public – which is scheduled for sometime in the 1990s, when developers are finished – inside there are reputedly a secret "escape" stairway and a long narrow room used by Capone's hoods as a tommy gun target range as if they didn't get enough practice on the streets.

Bridge to City Hall: Since 1933, there has only been one mayor from the North Side. Richard J. Daley was almost canonized as "Hizzoner da Mare" for his 21 years (1955 to 1976) in office. During the Daley era, Chicago saw the building of O'Hare Airport and the **Dan Ryan Expressway**, the vehicular spine of the

University of Chicago.

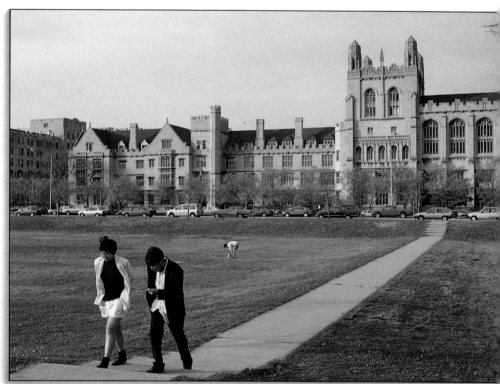

South Side that was named for one of Daley's longtime political cronies.

Another South Sider, Harold Washington, who was elected in 1983 and died in office in 1987, enjoyed nearly Daley-like status in the black community when he became the city's first black mayor after an election scarred by race baiting.

Daley's son, Richard M. Daley, became mayor in 1989 and, like his father, continued to live in the old neighborhood: **Bridgeport**. While typical of the South Side's working-class roots, Bridgeport is not so typical politically. This small and otherwise insignificant neighborhood has produced five mayors, including three of the last six. A favorite watering hole of Bridgeport and its movers and shakers of the 11th Ward is **Schaller's Pump**, 3714 S. Halsted Street. Over a century old, this tavern is nothing fancy but it's full of the local color of the neighborhood, right down to Frank Sinatra singing "Chicago" on the juke box.

Bridgeport, which is north of Pershing Road and outlined by the south branch of the Chicago River, was originally settled by German and Irish immigrants working on the **Illinois and Michigan Canal**. The I&M was a federal public works project designed to link Lake Michigan to the Mississippi River via local rivers connected to the canal. Bridgeport, named for the low bridge near Ashland Avenue that caused barges to unload and have their cargo portaged, became a boomtown by the time the canalworks were finished in 1848.

Later, Bridgeporters labored in the Union Stock Yard, as did the residents of neighboring Back of the Yards, named for its proximity to the stockyards. Here thousands of immigrants came to work, often in appalling conditions. Upton Sinclair's 1906 exposé *The Jungle* told of spoiled meats and miserable working conditions that caused a national uproar and brought about eventual reforms. The Back of the Yards

Cooling off at the university's Laredo Taft sculpture.

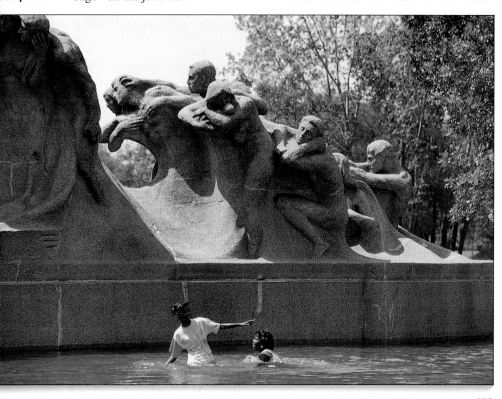

Council, incorporated in 1939, is the country's oldest community council.

Racial tensions: These South Side working-class neighborhoods also figure in a problem that has plagued Chicago for decades: racial unrest. When strikes occurred in places like the stockyards, blacks were often hired from southern states such as Alabama, Georgia and Mississippi to work as strike breakers or scabs. The two world wars also encouraged black migration to Chicago for jobs and in the end the economic competition led to friction and distrust between the blacks and white immigrant workers.

On July 27, 1919, a stone-throwing incident at the 29th Street beach led to the drowning of a black youth and the worst race riot in the city's history. It left 38 people dead and 537 injured. It is also part of a legacy of racism with which the city still struggles.

The South Side has had a black population of varying sizes since the mid-1800s. That black population grew within the city as a separate Chicago, creating over the years a separate economy and a separate society. It was a kind of second city within the second city, a black metropolis, and as off limits to whites as some parts of New York's Harlem.

The separateness of the city can best be seen through the lives of people such as Jesse Binga, a black man who came to Chicago with $5 in his pocket to look for opportunity at the 1893 Columbian Exposition. By the early 1900s he owned a bank and more than 1,000 feet of frontage on South State Street around 34th Street. He became a millionaire philanthropist, respected in the black community. But when he moved into a white neighborhood to fulfill the American dream of a spacious home, his house was repeatedly bombed. The Great Depression ransacked his fortune and his future. He was indicted for actions he took to save his bank and spent some time in jail. He died impoverished, working as a church janitor.

Black spokesmen: Nonetheless, Jesse Binga was representative of a long line of black South Side millionaires who because of their race were often unknown to the white public. He was also one of a long line of South Siders who have offered strong and sometimes controversial leadership to the black community. Notable contemporary examples of spokesmen include Jesse Jackson and Louis Farrakhan, the separatist Black Muslim.

When Jackson resigned as national director of Operation Breadbasket, an aid group for the mainstream civil-rights movement, he was quoted as saying, "I need air. I've got to grow." With those words he founded People United to Save Humanity, commonly known to Chicagoans and throughout the nation as Operation PUSH.

PUSH was Jackson's launching pad. From the stage and pulpit of a converted temple at PUSH **headquarters**, 930 E. 50th Street, Jackson and just about every other major American black

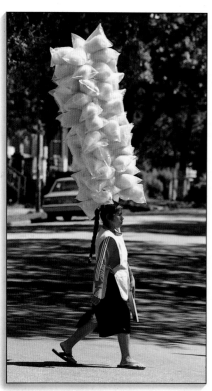

Selling cotton candy on the South Side.

leader of the past quarter century has spoken to enthusiastic audiences. They are often accompanied by swaying, hand-clapping choirs and peppery percussion sections. Whites are welcome to visit and Saturday morning programs are perhaps the best time, particularly if Jackson is making one of his occasional visits from his new headquarters in Washington DC.

Black leadership has been especially important on the South Side because of the racial divisions in a city called the most segregated in America. The South Side has often been portrayed as the base of the black political movement. It has been portrayed just as often as the poor side of town.

The projects: Certainly Chicago has its share of poverty. Driving south on the Dan Ryan Expressway past 35th Street, visitors see row after row of high-rises looming to the east – the Chicago Housing Authority developments, known locally as "the projects."

This, the so-called **State Street Cor-**

ridor, is one of the poorest neighborhoods in the entire United States. These developments house some 37,000 residents, most of whom are black and 75 percent of whom are on welfare. It is a neighborhood of relentless poverty where drug abuse, violence and teenage pregnancy are commonplace. It is not a place to stop and sightsee.

But only 50 blocks south is perhaps one of the largest black middle-class enclaves in the nation. **Chatham**, which runs east of the Dan Ryan around 87th Street, is a neighborhood of perfectly landscaped lawns and houses so neat and orderly they look as though they've been audited. Here, the black residents themselves joke that Chatham would seem like a typical middle-class white neighborhood – if the homeowners would stay indoors. Chatham is worth a visit for what many consider to be one of the finest soul food restaurants in America: Army's and Lou's, at 422 E. 7th Street. The ribs, chitlins and grits just don't get any better than here.

hinatown.

DAY TRIPS

A lifelong New Yorker on his first trip to the Midwest had several meetings that took him to small towns outside Chicago. He returned home with the idea of someday moving to one of those towns himself. "I just couldn't believe the relaxed lifestyles, and the way people were so nice to each other," he said. "Sure, they were the type that said 'Have a nice day' to everyone. But you know what? They really meant it. They were friendly and helpful, especially to strangers."

Many travelers, particularly those from abroad whose image of America has been shaped by films, television programs, books and magazines focusing on the big US cities, are pleasantly surprised by their forays beyond the well-beaten concrete paths of the major urban centers. Chicagoans themselves are devoted to what they call day trips, and joining them for a day out is a fine way to rub shoulders. The Loop shows how Chicagoans work; a day trip shows how they play.

Any Chicagoan's list of favorite day trips is likely to include the **Chicago Botanic Garden**. Even the most frenetic commodities trader will be calmed by the 300 peaceful acres of landscaped hills, lakes, wooded areas and many, many gardens.

Romantics may choose the spacious **Rose Garden**, which exhibits some 5,000 rosebushes representing 100 varieties, including All American Rose Selections. Depending on the season, there are rose-growing demonstrations and gardening tips. For those who seek solitude, there is the **Japanese Garden**, set on three serene islands.

Prairie strolls: For the strollers interested in Illinois, there's the **Naturalistic Garden** exhibiting native plants and landscaping, presented in woodland and bird gardens illustrating how the Prairie State used to look.

Children will enjoy the **Natural Trail**, a scenic one-mile path that winds through the oak-hickory forest. There are wild flowers in the spring, brilliant foliage in the fall and frozen beauty in the winter.

From May through September, musicians come from all over the world to play the **Theodore C. Butz Memorial Carillon**. During the concerts, visitors spread blankets on the lawn south of the greenhouses and enjoy a rare treat. A carillon is a musical instrument made up of at least two octaves of cast-bronze bells. The carillonneur plays the bells with his or her hands and feet from a console. The Butz carillon is one of only about 150 true carillons – those played without electrical assistance or amplification – in North America.

For lunch, the Botanic Garden has the Food for Thought Café on the premises, which features healthy snacks such as a fresh seasonal fruit plate and a vegetable-garden submarine sandwich. Those who would rather sit than walk can take

Preceding pages: suburban church. Left, Grant Wood's American Gothic. Right, beads and braids.

the **tram tour**, perfect for first-time guests. The 45-minute narrated tour encompasses most of the Botanic Garden. In the winter, the trams are enclosed and heated. There are also bicycle paths throughout the area.

Despite its name, the Chicago Botanic Garden is located 25 miles north of the city in suburban **Glencoe**, a half-mile east of the Edens Expressway on Lake-Cook Road. It picked up its Windy City tag because the park is managed by the Chicago Horticultural Society.

Brookfield: More than 30 years later, a middle-aged Londoner still regales his children – and anyone else who might happen to mention either America or zoos – with stories of his first visit as a boy to Chicago and the big zoo in the suburbs. Particularly vivid are his tales of the giant Kodiak bears, standing on their hind legs to a height of 9 feet and roaring. Several teenagers were tossing slices of bread across the rocky ravine setting off the bear's "natural habitat" enclosure. The boy opened his brown paper bag and handed one of the teenagers a peanut-butter sandwich that promptly went sailing towards a Kodiak. The bear stretched its massive neck a foot or so, snagged the sandwich in its sharp teeth and swallowed the boy's lunch in one gulp. "It was worth missing a meal to see that," the man still says today.

Only 16 miles west of the Magnificent Mile, **Brookfield Zoo** is one of the most respected in the United States. More than 2,000 animals reside on 200 acres. Habitats include the **Small Mammal House** with more than 375 bats and the **Lion House**, one of the original buildings unveiled to the public when the zoo opened in 1934.

Among the most popular exhibits are the **Seven Seas Panorama** and Tropic World. Dolphins perform daily at the Seven Seas complex, a 2,000-seat indoor "dolphinarium" that features tropical plants and interconnected pools holding more than a million gallons of **Chicago Botanic Garden.**

240

saltwater. Outside the arena, strollers can explore the naturalistic rocky shores created to resemble the Pacific Northwest. There, seals and sea lions provide more aquatic entertainment.

Although it's always pleasurable, winter may be the best time to take in **Tropic World** because of the warm indoor temperatures. It is located in a huge building, the size of one-and-a-half football fields. Within are three separate exhibits, each representing rain forests in Asia, South America or Africa, complete with rocks, cliffs and waterfalls. Tropic World was completed in the summer of 1984 at a cost of $11 million. Unlike many zoos, where visitors walk up to the animal cages and then walk away, Tropic World strives for a total environment. Here more than 100 mammals and three dozen birds interact with one another – and with the visitors. Zoological purists may argue that it is not perfectly authentic because there aren't any mosquitos, but few visitors complain.

A recently opened exhibit is the **Fragile Kingdom**. Again, the idea behind the two-acre setting of desert, rain forest and rocky grottos is to create realistic exhibits. These, in turn, aim to help viewers appreciate the African and Asian environments and the animals that inhabit these delicate ecosystems, depending on their surroundings and on one another for survival. Here are the black-backed jackal, the Burmese python and the Siberian tiger, among many other residents.

The size of the Brookfield Zoo is apparent in some of the background statistics. For example, Zoo veterinarians see more than 1,000 patients a year and still make house calls – or rather, cage and cave calls. More than 20,400 bales of hay are used each year – which, if placed end to end, would stretch almost 12 miles. Brookfield visitors consume half a million hamburgers and hot dogs and sip 850,000 soft drinks a year. The gift shops sell more than 50,000 stuffed toy animals

ce
ishermen.

annually for those who want a cuddly memory of the wilds. Brookfield Zoo is located at **1st Avenue** and **31st Street** in west suburban Brookfield and open every day of the year. By car, take either Interstate 55 or Interstate 290 and watch for exit signs for the zoo. By train, take the **Burlington/Metra** to the Zoo Stop at Hollywood Station.

ARLINGTON: Race tracks have never been regarded as the ideal place for children – until the new **Arlington International Racecourse** opened a few years ago. The grand plan has been to make racing a sporting event that brings excitement to sophisticated couples and entire families rather than a gathering place for down-and-outs scuffing their way dejectedly through discarded betting stubs. Richard L. Duchossois, chairman of Arlington since 1983, has not only dedicated himself to rebuilding the racing and breeding industry in Illinois, but to making his racecourse a center for international racing.

Arlington opened in 1927 and had its first full season the following year. For several decades, it stayed ahead of its time with new designs and electronic equipment. By 1941, the course was packing them in and set a one-day attendance record of 50,638 that remains unbroken to this day. Eddie Arcaro became the first American jockey to win 3,000 races with a victory in 1953. And in 1980, Spectacular Bid helped the racecourse set a single-day betting record of $3.5 million.

Tragedy struck on July 31, 1985, when Arlington was destroyed by fire. But out of the ashes came hope and fierce determination and, like Chicago itself, Arlington was rebuilt bigger and better. Duchossois borrowed from Arlington's history of innovations, including air-conditioning and the photo-finish camera. He sent architects touring other international racecourses to determine what was best about them. The result is the present Arlington, reopened in 1989 as an attractive blend of convenience and style. By the end of its first week, the racing industry was already calling it the best in the world.

The racecourse offers free parking and valet parking. There's a great grandstand area, where there's still plenty of room for anxious bettors to press up against the rail on the finishing straight. The green marble floors lead to plushly-appointed private suites and orderly, fast-moving queues for the betting windows. There's warm popcorn and cold beer, plus hot grilled steaks and chilled champagne. Tidiness is ensured by uniformed attendants who scurry around scooping up discarded betting tickets and other litter.

The main theme of the racepark is convenience, as evidenced by 750 television monitors. These are scattered around the grounds and in the stands where visitors cannot see the finishing post. Even the post call is the best around – trumpet player Joe Kelly, who for years led the famous house band at the old Gaslight Club mansion in Chicago, makes the call.

Thrills at Six Flags Great America.

Newcomers feel welcome due to racing exhibits and video programs which help them learn the basics of betting. Duchossois has also created a sense of involvement with special events such as the International Festival of Racing. The biggest races are the Arlington Million, the first Sunday in September, and the Arlington Challenge Cup, in mid-summer.

Arlington International Racecourse is located off Route 53 on **Euclid Avenue**. The season runs from May through early October. Sunday is family day with a petting zoo, puppet shows and pony rides. From downtown Chicago, take Interstate 90 northwest to Route 53. Go north, then exit on Euclid and go east, following the signs. For mass transit, the racetrack can provide information on the special trains and buses operating from downtown Chicago during the racing season.

SIX FLAGS: Among the memories of those Chicago residents over 30 is Riverview Park, a long-time amuse-ment center at Western and Belmont avenues in the heart of the city. In place of those heart-stopping, creaking old wooden roller coasters, which cranked up for the last time in 1967, stands a shopping mall.

But nine years after Riverview closed, **Six Flags Great America** opened. The adventures keep getting better every year. Here's the official description for the **Iron Wolf**, the nation's tallest and fastest looping, stand-up roller coaster, inaugurated in 1990: "Riders who accept the standing challenge will travel down a 90-foot drop reaching speeds up to 55 miles per hour entering a hair-raising 360-degree vertical loop, towering 80 feet into the sky. Dashing from the loop, riders spiral through intertwining hairpin curves, culminating in a spine-tingling cork-screw-type single loop that takes riders nearly parallel to the ground."

If that's not enough, there are plenty of other rides that keep fans lined up. The Demon does an 82-foot vertical

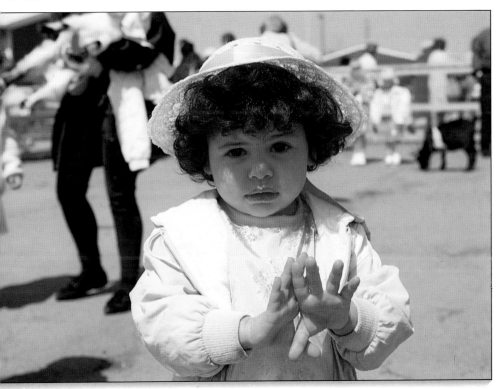

drop, a double corkscrew and several vertical loops. The Tidal Wave accelerates to high speeds, then hits a 76-foot-tall vertical loop, forward and then backward.

There are also rides that are only slightly more sedate, such as the Rue Le Dodge bumper cars, or the White Water Rampage rubber boats – great for cooling off in hot weather. For the little ones, there are attractions such as **Bugs Bunny Land** and the grand double-deck carousel with more than 100 gaily-colored animals.

The park is divided into regional theme areas such as **Hometown Square**, **Yankee Harbor** and **Orleans Place**. The colors of the various attractions are vibrant against the bright blue sky, and people watchers will have a great time. For more structured, non-riding entertainment, Great America features the **Pictorium Theatre**, one of the world's largest screens, showing fast-paced action movies of rushing rapids or men in flight. Several theaters around the park offer singing and dancing cartoon characters, high diving acts and Broadway-style reviews.

To get the most out of Great America, a few pointers may prove helpful. Avoid Saturdays and Sundays if at all possible. Get there early. When school's in session, hundreds of children seem to be on field trips. Pick up a map and note the rides and attractions that are most appealing. The park is circular in design, so go in one direction instead of back and forth. Even on what seem to be mild days, bring sun block and a light jacket: the weather can change quickly.

Finally, pack a lunch or pick up some food on the way and leave it in the car for a picnic in the parking lot. The park – and the parking lot – have many food stands, but the prices are high and the quality is probably not as good as whatever you might bring. However, Great America does offer one taste treat, for those who don't mind waiting in lines: the **Funnel Cake Foundry**, located in

Rural Illinois barn.

the County Fair area. Fried dough is funneled into a circle and covered with chocolate, strawberry, cherry, hot caramel or – the favorite – powdered sugar.

Six Flags Great America is located in **Gurnee**, halfway between Chicago and Milwaukee, just off Interstate 94 at Route 132 (Grand Avenue). The season runs from late April through early October. Pets are not allowed at Six Flags, but the park has a boarding facility for a nominal fee. Strollers and wheelchairs are also available on a first-come, first-serve basis for a nominal fee. Cameras can be borrowed with a security deposit.

MILWAUKEE: It's another city and another state, but it's worth a trip of a couple hours into another world: **Milwaukee, Wisconsin**. If driving, take Interstate 94 and just head north. Around **Lincolnshire**, there's an exit sign for **Half Way Road**. It got its name because during the horse-and-buggy days the road marked the half-way point between Chicago and Milwaukee. Drivers today can just follow the signs;

downtown to downtown, the journey is only about 90 miles. There's also the train. Amtrak schedules several trains back and forth each day.

Milwaukee is a compact city of 640,000 people. Short walks and cab rides open up a city of old-world charm, uncrowded streets, great German food and beer. For a glimpse of a bygone era, stop off at the **Milwaukee Public Museum**. The Streets of Old Milwaukee exhibit and the European Village offer a respectful sense of the spirit that built this northern city of immigrants. Outside the museum, check out Third Street, between State Street and Highland Avenue, for the **Old World section** of town with its vivid 19th-century architecture.

Across the street from Usinger's Sausage store sits **Mader's**, a Milwaukee classic for more than 90 years. Visited by presidents and presidential candidates, Mader's ranks as one of the most famous German restaurants in North America and has won scores of dining

he
Milwaukee
orticulture
omes.

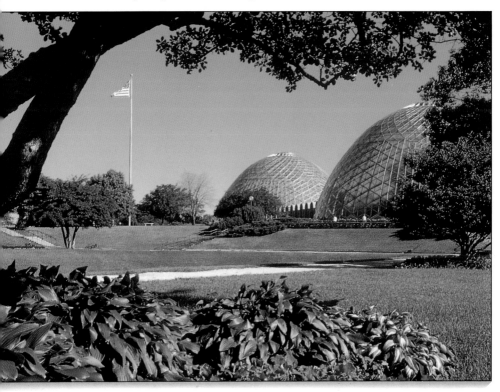

awards. Complete dinners are no longer 20 cents with tip, as they were in 1902, but they remain high in quality and are good value for money. There are several brewery tours in Milwaukee, but if you'd rather hoist a stein, Mader's has a large selection.

Another good place to eat is **Karl Ratzsch's Old World Restaurant**, which provides even more hearty German fare, as well as continental cuisine. From here, head west on Mason to **Water Street**. At 779 N. Front Street, an alley west of Water, between Mason and Wells, there's a tiny office marked "International Exports Limited." Go into the office, follow the instructions and a bookcase will slide open to reveal a secret passage that takes you to the Safe House, a nightclub shrine to Agent 007, spies and espionage. Each area of this unusual bar has a different decor, such as the Mata Hari booth and the Checkpoint Charlie room.

Sports fans can check out the action with the Milwaukee Brewers (baseball) and the Green Bay Packers (football) at **County Stadium**. The Milwaukee Bucks (basketball) and the Milwaukee Admirals (ice hockey) are at the **Milwaukee Exposition, Convention Center and Arena**. Locals tend to call it "the Mecca."

The **Performing Arts Center** showcases theater, ballet and several other cultural events. For outdoor activities, **Summerfest** in early July is an 11-day outdoor party on the lakeshore with plenty of Wisconsin foods, such as roast corn on the cob and grilled bratwursts, and a impressive lineup of well-known entertainers at its jazz, rock, country and main stages.

The **Mitchell Park Horticultural Conservatory** features three massive glass domes, each seven stories high. Inside are tropic, arid and seasonal displays, great for taking pictures. The **Milwaukee County Zoo** rates among the finest zoological parks in the world with some 4,500 animals on exhibit. The **Annunciation Greek Orthodox Church** was the last major building to come off Frank Lloyd Wright's drawing board, and is the scene of an annual July Greekfest.

LAKE GENEVA: One section of Wisconsin, northwest of Chicago on the Illinois-Wisconsin state line, is a walker's dream come true. A gorgeous 26-mile footpath completely circles the glistening waters of **Lake Geneva**. Many hikers choose the sweet-smelling springtime to follow the old trail, tramped out by the original Indian inhabitants; others opt for the season of winter snows to crunch along the icy, but still walkable path.

The trail occasionally cuts through private property, though the courts have ruled that common law over generations has made the path a public right of way. Legally, however, entrance to the footpath itself must come through public property. Veterans suggest **Big Foot Beach Park**, **Lake Geneva Library Park**, **Williams Bay** and **Fontana Beaches** as good entry points.

Left, farmyard art. Right, retired farmer.

246

INSIGHT GUIDES
Travel Tips

FOR THOSE
WITH MORE THAN
A PASSING INTEREST
IN TIME...

Before you put your name down for a Patek Philippe watch *fig. 1*, there are a few basic things you might like to know, without knowing exactly whom to ask. In addressing such issues as accuracy, reliability and value for money, we would like to demonstrate why the watch we will make for you will be quite unlike any other watch currently produced.

"Punctuality", Louis XVIII was fond of saying, "is the politeness of kings."

We believe that in the matter of punctuality, we can rise to the occasion by making you a mechanical timepiece that will keep its rendezvous with the Gregorian calendar at the end of every century, omitting the leap-years in 2100, 2200 and 2300 and recording them in 2000 and 2400 *fig. 2*. Nevertheless, such a watch does need the occasional adjustment. Every 3333 years and 122 days you should remember to set it forward one day to the true time of the celestial clock. We suspect, however, that you are simply content to observe the politeness of kings. Be assured, therefore, that when you order your watch, we will be exploring for you the physical—if not the metaphysical— limits of precision.

Does everything have to depend on how much?

Consider, if you will, the motives of collectors who set record prices at auction to acquire a Patek Philippe. They may be paying for rarity, for looks or for micromechanical ingenuity. But we believe that behind each $500,000-plus

bid is the conviction that a Patek Philippe, even if 50 years old or older, can be expected to work perfectly for future generations.

In case your ambitions to own a Patek Philippe are somewhat discouraged by the scale of the sacrifice involved, may we hasten to point out that the watch we will make for you today will certainly be a technical improvement on the Pateks bought at auction? In keeping with our tradition of inventing new mechanical solutions for greater reliability and better time-keeping, we will bring to your watch innovations *fig. 3* inconceivable to our watchmakers who created the supreme wristwatches of 50 years ago *fig. 4*. At the same time, we will of course do our utmost to avoid placing undue strain on your financial resources.

Can it really be mine?

May we turn your thoughts to the day you take delivery of your watch? Sealed within its case is your watchmaker's tribute to the mysterious process of time. He has decorated each wheel with a chamfer carved into its hub and polished into a shining circle. Delicate ribbing flows over the plates and bridges of gold and rare alloys. Millimetric surfaces are bevelled and burnished to exactitudes measured in microns. Rubies are transformed into jewels that triumph over friction. And after many months—or even years—of work, your watchmaker stamps a small badge into the mainbridge of your watch. The Geneva Seal—the highest possible attestation of fine watchmaking *fig. 5*.

Looks that speak of inner grace *fig. 6*.

When you order your watch, you will no doubt like its outward appearance to reflect the harmony and elegance of the movement within. You may therefore find it helpful to know that we are uniquely able to cater for any special decorative needs you might like to express. For example, our engravers will delight in conjuring a subtle play of light and shadow on the gold case-back of one of our rare pocket-watches *fig. 7*. If you bring us your favourite picture, our enamellers will reproduce it in a brilliant miniature of hair-breadth detail *fig. 8*. The perfect execution of a double hobnail pattern on the bezel of a wristwatch is the pride of our casemakers and the satisfaction of our designers, while our chainsmiths will weave for you a rich brocade in gold *figs. 9 & 10*. May we also recommend the artistry of our goldsmiths and the experience of our lapidaries in the selection and setting of the finest gemstones? *figs. 11 & 12*.

How to enjoy your watch before you own it.

As you will appreciate, the very nature of our watches imposes a limit on the number we can make available. (The four Calibre 89 time-pieces we are now making will take up to nine years to complete). We cannot therefore promise instant gratification, but while you look forward to the day on which you take delivery of your Patek Philippe *fig. 13*, you will have the pleasure of reflecting that time is a universal and everlasting commodity freely available to be enjoyed by all.

Should you require information on any particular Patek Philippe watch, or even on watchmaking in general, we would be delighted to reply to your letter of enquiry. And if you send fig. 1: The classic face of Patek Philippe.

fig. 4: Complicated wristwatches circa 1930 (left) and 1990. The golden age of watchmaking will always be with us.

fig. 2: One of the 33 complications of the Calibre 89 astronomical clock-watch is a satellite wheel that completes one revolution every 400 years.

fig. 5: The Geneva Seal is awarded only to watches which achieve the standards of horological purity laid down in the laws of Geneva. These rules define the supreme quality of watchmaking.

fig. 3: Recognized as the most advanced mechanical regulating device to date, Patek Philippe's Gyromax balance wheel demonstrates the equivalence of simplicity and precision.

fig. 6: Your pleasure in owning a Patek Philippe is the purpose of those who made it for you.

fig. 7: Arabesques come to life on a gold case-back.

fig. 8: An artist working six hours a day takes about four months to complete a miniature in enamel on the case of a pocket-watch.

fig. 9: Harmony of design is executed in a work of simplicity and perfection in a lady's Calatrava wristwatch.

fig. 10: The chainsmith's hands impart strength and delicacy to a tracery of gold.

fig. 11: Circles in gold: symbols of perfection in the making.

fig. 12: The test of a master lapidary is his ability to express the splendour of precious gemstones.

PATEK PHILIPPE
GENEVE

fig. 13: The discreet sign of those who value their time.

your card marked "book catalogue" we shall post you a catalogue of our publications. Patek Philippe, 41 rue du Rhône, 1204 Geneva, Switzerland, Tel. +41 22/310 03 66.

A Wise Man Never Thinks How Far He's Come. He Thinks How Far He Can Still Travel.

REMY XO BECAUSE LIFE IS WHAT YOU MAKE IT

TRAVEL TIPS

GETTING THERE

Unless otherwise stated, all telephone numbers are preceded by the area code (312). The number (800) indicates a toll free call.

BY AIR

Chicago, served by many major American and foreign air carriers, is the home of the world's busiest airport. **O'Hare International Airport** is located about 18 miles from downtown on the Kennedy Expressway (Interstates 90 and 94) at Mannheim Road. It has an international terminal and three domestic terminals. There are information booths on the upper level of each terminal and outside the "Meeter-Greeter" area of the international terminal. There is a foreign currency exchange in the international terminal. Tel: 686-2200 for general airport information. It's ordinarily a 20-minute trip by car between the airport and downtown but traffic is so unpredictable, especially during rush hour, that it's advisable to allow an hour for travel time.

    Continental Air Transport, tel: 454-7800, provides bus service between the airport baggage claim area and about 35 downtown hotels. Many hotels provide their own shuttle service, so inquire when making reservations. Taxis are available on the lower level of each terminal. Limousine service or car rentals can be arranged in advance or at the booths near the baggage claim area. Probably the cheapest way to get downtown, and the surest way to avoid traffic jams, is the **Chicago Transit Authority** (CTA) Rapid Transit line which is located under Terminal 4. The trains run frequently to and from the Dearborn Street station downtown.

    Midway Airport, 5700 S. Cicero Avenue, a smaller, less crowded alternative to O'Hare for domestic flights, is located about 7 miles southwest of downtown. Its one building is divided into three terminals. Information is

available at tel: 767-0500. Continental Air Transport provides bus service between this airport and about a dozen downtown hotels. Tel: 454-7800 to find out times. The reservation booth is in Concourse A, while boarding is at the main terminal. Taxis are available in front of the main (middle) terminal. Limos and car rentals are available near the baggage claim area. Some hotels provide their own shuttle service. There is no direct CTA line.

BY BUS

Greyhound/Trailways has nationwide service to its main terminal in the Loop (downtown), at Clark and Randolph streets. It also has two neighborhood stations: the 95th Street and Dan Ryan Expressway CTA station on the south side; and the Cumberland CTA station at 5800 N. Cumberland Avenue on the northwest side near **O'Hare Airport.** Tel: 781-2900 for fares and schedule information.

BY RAIL

Chicago is serviced by **Amtrak**, a passenger line offering nationwide service. Tel: (800)-USA-RAIL. Amtrak comes in to Chicago's **Union Station** at Jackson and Canal streets, tel: 558-1075.

BY CAR

The major east–west route across northern Illinois is **Interstate 80**, which passes near Chicago from Indiana to the east or Iowa to the west. Coming from the north, the main **interstates** are **90** and **94**, which merge about 10 miles north of downtown to form the **Kennedy Expressway** (I-90/94), a direct route into downtown. **I-57** runs across the state from the south, and connects with the **Dan Ryan Expressway** (I-90/94) for the downtown area.

Swatch. The others just watch.

seahorse/fall winter 94-95

shockproof
splashproof
priceproof
boreproof
swiss made

swatch✛
SCUBA 200

American Express offers Travelers Cheques built for two.

Cheques *for Two*[SM] from American Express are the Travelers Cheques that allow either of you to use them because both of you have signed them. And only one of you needs to be present to purchase them.

Cheques *for Two* are accepted anywhere regular American Express Travelers Cheques are, which is just about everywhere. So stop by your bank, AAA* or any American Express Travel Service Office and ask for Cheques *for Two*.

AMERICAN EXPRESS **Travelers Cheques**
®

TRAVEL ESSENTIALS

VISAS & PASSPORTS

To enter the United States, travelers must have a valid passport. Before departing from their own countries, foreign visitors should contact the nearest United States Embassy or Consulate for information on whether a visa is necessary.

HEALTH TIPS

Chicago can be extremely hot and humid in summer, and extremely cold and snowy in winter. The weather can change dramatically within minutes in any season, so it's best to be prepared for anything. During the summer months insects, and particularly pesky mosquitos, can be a problem, especially in areas of woods or ponds. There is no national health service in the United States and some hospitals or clinics will not provide treatment without assurances of payment, so foreigners may want to purchase private medical insurance in advance.

MONEY MATTERS

Bureaux de change are relatively rare in America. To obtain US dollars at **O'Hare Airport**, there is a foreign currency exchange in the International Terminal that is open from 10am–8pm daily and exchanges about 40 of the major currencies. Tel: 686-7965.

Another source for exchanging currency is **American Express**, which has a number of offices in Chicago, including one at 625 N. Michigan Avenue, tel: 435-2570. Some large banks also have currency exchange windows. Take along your passport if cashing travelers checks.

CUSTOMS

After picking up their baggage, visitors need to present customs documents which are usually passed out on planes but can be picked up at the customs desks. The time it takes to clear customs can be anywhere from a few minutes to an hour, depending on how many travelers are arriving at the same time and how many agents are on duty.

Narcotics and many foods cannot be brought into the United States. Other items might not be permitted depending on the traveler's origin. Pets are allowed, though they must have proof that their inoculations are current. Personal possessions are not normally liable for duty for US visitors, provided they intend to take them out of the country with them. There are limits, however, on tobacco, alcohol and certain foreign products; Cuban cigars are banned, for example, because of a US trade embargo. Visitors who are not sure should check with their travel agents or US consulates before leaving home.

WHAT TO WEAR

It's pretty much "anything goes" for clothing in Chicago. For daytime sightseeing and casual meals, shorts and a T-shirt in summer or jeans and a sweatshirt in winter are acceptable. Comfortable walking shoes are an absolute must.

Somewhat dressier clothes are recommended for some dinner and nighttime activities. For the smarter restaurants or theaters, men should wear jackets and ties, and women dresses.

In summer, bring a bathing suit to enjoy the beaches along Lake Michigan, and be prepared for hot, humid weather. Because it's cooler in the evening, especially near the lake, a light jacket is recommended. In winter, everyone needs a warm coat, hat, gloves, and, in case of snow, a pair of boots.

PORTER SERVICES

Porter services are available in most airports and other transportation centers, as well as in most hotels. The fee is usually entirely up to the traveler, but most range from $1–$3 a bag, depending on distance and difficulty for the porter. In addition, most airports and transportation centers have self-push baggage carts, sometimes free and sometimes for a rental fee ranging from 25 cents to $1.

RESERVATIONS

Chicago is generally an informal town, but it's also the kind of place where people go out a lot. That means reservations are recommended – sometimes well in advance – for the most popular theaters, restaurants and special events with limited seating.

ON DEPARTURE

Remember to check with the airline or the airport before departure to confirm flight numbers and times, and to make seat reservations in advance if possible. Also check the terminal and the time you should check in. Most airlines now require international travelers to check in two hours before scheduled departure, and checking in late can mean losing even confirmed or assigned seats.

GETTING ACQUAINTED

GOVERNMENT & ECONOMY

Chicago has a city council form of government. The city council is headed by the mayor. The city is divided into 50 wards, based on the population, each with about 60,000 residents. Each ward is represented by an elected alderman, who is part of the council. In theory, this is a "strong council, weak mayor" system. In reality, the mayor of Chicago wields a great deal of power.

The entire city of Chicago is located in **Cook County**. Cook County is governed by the Cook County Board, which is made up of 17 members; 10 from Chicago, and 7 from the suburbs. The board is headed by a president, who is one of the 17 members.

Both Chicago and Cook County have "home rule," which allows them to decide many local issues, such as taxation, without approval from the state Legislature in Springfield, Illinois.

Although the southern part of Illinois has a lot of agriculture, Chicago's economy is based on big business. **The Loop** is generally regarded as the business and commercial district. LaSalle Street is the financial district, regarded as the "Wall Street" of the Midwest and the home of the commodities exchanges that influence world production and prices of agricultural and other products.

Besides white-collar industries such as insurance, accounting, publishing and state-government administration, Chicago is also one of the retail capitals of America, which is demonstrated vividly along shopping streets such as Michigan Avenue's "**Magnificent Mile**."

As in most large cities, there is a wide gap between the richest and the poorest people in Chicago, though the overall standard of living is quite high. Much of Chicago depends on a service economy, and good, prompt service is regarded as the norm rather than something out of the ordinary.

GEOGRAPHY & POPULATION

Chicago is located in the northeast corner of Illinois in the section of the United States referred to as the Midwest. It's situated on the Great Lakes, at the southwest tip of **Lake Michigan**, which makes up the city's entire eastern border. The city's other large waterway is the Chicago River. About 100 years ago a decision was made to reverse the flow of the river, so now water flows to the Illinois River, instead of into the lake. (On St Patrick's Day, part of the annual celebration is to dye the river green, though some say they can't tell any difference).

Most of the land in and around Chicago is flat, as is much of the Midwest. Perhaps it was the lack of hills that contributed to the desire for tall buildings, and eventually led to the much-recognized skyline of Chicago.

Although Chicago is the best-known city in Illinois, it is not the capital. That honor goes to **Springfield**, located 200 miles to the south in the middle of the state. Of approximately 11.5 million people in Illinois, 7.5 million live in the Chicago area. The population of Chicago alone is almost 3 million.

For inhabitants of a big city, Chicagoans are often surprisingly friendly; many people are quick to get into conversations with anyone and everyone, and an encounter with a foreign visitor is almost always reason enough to stop and have a chat. The makeup of the city is a reflection of its many neighborhoods. The most recent available analysis breaks the population down as follows: whites 38 percent, African-Americans 39 percent, Hispanics 20 percent, Asians and others 4 percent. The Hispanics represent the fastest-growing ethnic group.

TIME ZONES

Chicago is in the **Central Time Zone**, which is one hour behind New York, two hours ahead of California and six hours behind Greenwich Mean Time. On the last Sunday in April the clock is moved ahead an hour for daylight savings time, and on the last Sunday in October it's moved back an hour to return to standard time.

When it's noon in Chicago (Standard Time) it is:

8am in Hawaii
10am in California
1pm in New York and Montreal
6pm in London
10pm in Moscow
2am (the next day) in Singapore and Hong Kong
3am (the next day) in Tokyo

CLIMATE

Chicago is a great place to experience all four seasons. Summers get quite hot and humid, but it's usually cooler near the lake (as mentioned in almost every weather forecast) because of cooling breezes coming off Lake Michigan. Winter in Chicago means cold temperatures, often with snow. Spring brings its share of rain, but the temperatures are usually moderate, as in the autumn.

Average daily Fahrenheit high temperatures in Chicago:

Month	Temp
January	29°F
February	34°F
March	44°F
April	59°F
May	70°F
June	79°F
July	85°F
August	82°F
September	75°F
October	64°F
November	48°F
December	35°F

Updated recorded weather reports can be heard by calling 976-1212.

To convert Fahrenheit to Centigrade temperatures, deduct 32, multiply by 5, divide by 9. To convert Centigrade to Fahrenheit, multiply by 9, divide by 5, and add 32.

Centigrade	Fahrenheit
0	32 (Freezing)
15	59
20	68
25	77
30	86
37	99
100	212 (Boiling)

CULTURE & CUSTOMS

Chicagoans are often friendly, but their forwardness sometimes puts off foreigners, and even visitors from other parts of America, who regard them as brash or harsh in speech and manner. Courtesy is appreciated, but so is bluntness – getting to the point, saying what you mean and meaning what you say. Conversations with strangers can sometimes take surprisingly personal turns.

Good service is expected and received throughout Chicago, and visitors should never hesitate to ask for assistance, even if it is for something out of the ordinary. Unusual requests may deserve a tip or gratuity of some sort. Even if "something extra" is declined, Chicagoans won't take offense that it has been offered.

TIPPING

The actual amount of the tip should depend on satisfaction with the service received. The following can be used as a guideline:

Waiter/Waitress, 15–20 percent.
Bartender, 10–15 percent.
Hotel Doorman, $1–$3 for carrying bags; 50¢–$1 for calling taxi.
Hotel Porter/Bellman, $1–$3 per bag; $1–$2 for opening room.
Room-Service Waiter, 15 percent.

Hotel Chambermaid, $1–$2 per night.
Taxi Driver, 15 percent.

LANGUAGE

Some hotels can provide translators, and
many employ a concierge or other staff who
may be multilingual.
The following firms can provide translation
services or an interpreter:
Advance Language, 333 N. Michigan
Avenue, tel: 782-8123.
Berlitz Translation Services, 845 N. Michigan Avenue, tel: 943-5178.
International Language and Communications Center, Inc., 79 W. Monroe Street,
tel: 236-3366.

WEIGHTS & MEASURES

The United States, unlike most of the world,
uses the imperial system for measurements.
Although the metric system is slowly working its way into usage, it's still not widespread.
Therefore, some basic conversions might
prove helpful:
  1 ounce = 28.5 grams
  1 pound (16 ounces) = 453 grams
  1 pint = 0.568 liter
  1 quart = 1.137 liters
  1 gallon = 4.5 liters
  1 inch = 2.54 centimeters
  1 foot (12 inches) = 0.3048 meters (30.48
    centimeters)
  1 yard (3 feet) = 0.9144 meters
  1 mile (1,760 yards) = 1.609 kilometers
  1 gram = 0.035 ounce
  1 kilogram = 2.205 pounds
  1 millimeter = 0.039 inch
  1 centimeter = 0.393 inch
  1 meter = 3.28 feet
  1 kilometer = 0.62 mile
  1 liter = 1.056 quarts

ELECTRICITY

The standard for the United States is 110
volts DC. Electrical plugs have two flat pins.
European appliances may need converters,
but some hotels supply them. Guests staying
in hotels that supply hair dryers can leave
theirs at home.

BUSINESS HOURS

Businesses and government offices in Chicago are generally open from 9am–5pm
Monday–Friday. Because many people from
the suburbs and outlying areas commute to
work in the city, the hour before 9am and the
hour after 5pm are the busiest times on the
roads, as everyone hurries to or from jobs at
approximately the same time. If plans permit,
try to avoid driving during these times.
  Banking hours are generally 8.30 or 9am–
3pm. Some banks have longer hours; some
are open a half-day on Saturday and closed
on Wednesday.

HOLIDAYS

Many government agencies, local banks and
businesses close during the holidays listed:
  January 1: New Year's Day
  January 15: Martin Luther King's
    Birthday
  February 12: Abraham Lincoln's
    Birthday
  3rd Monday in February: George
    Washington's Birthday
  Last Monday in May: Memorial Day
  July 4: Independence Day
  1st Monday in September: Labor Day
  2nd Monday in October: Columbus Day
  1st Tuesday in November: Election Day
  November 11: Veterans' Day
  4th Thursday in November: Thanksgiving
  December 25: Christmas

FESTIVALS

Chicago has many annual festivals, often
with an ethnic flavor that combines food,
music, the arts and culture.

JANUARY

Chinese New Year Parade, Wentworth
Avenue and Cermak Road, tel: 326-5320.

MARCH

St Patrick's Day, Parade starts at Dearborn
Street and Wacker Drive, tel: 263-6612.
South Side Irish Parade, 103rd Street and
Western Avenue, tel: 238-1969. Celebrated
the weekend before St Patrick's Day.

JUNE

International Theater Festival of Chicago, various theaters, tel: 644-3370.
Chicago Gospel Festival, Petrillo Band Shell, Grant Park, tel: 744-3315.
Chicago Blues Festival, Petrillo Band Shell, Grant Park, tel: 744-3315.
Water Tower Arts and Crafts Festival, Chicago Avenue between Michigan Avenue and Lake Shore Drive, tel: 991-4748.
Taste of Chicago, Grant Park, tel: 744-3315. June 27–July 4. A very popular event, featuring lots of food from a variety of Chicago restaurants. Music, too.

JULY

Taste of Chicago, continues in Grant Park, tel: 744-3315. This festival culminates with a spectacular fireworks display over Lake Michigan, accompanied by the Grant Park Symphony Orchestra performing Tchaikovsky's *1812 Overture*.
Fourth of July, fireworks on the lakefront and in almost every Chicago neighborhood.
Air and Water Show, North Avenue Beach, tel: 294-2200.
Taste of Lincoln Avenue, food fair between Fullerton and Wrightwood Avenues, tel: 472-9046.
Old St Patrick's World's Largest Block Party, Adams and Des Plaines streets, tel: 782-6171.

AUGUST

Venetian Night Boat Parade, Monroe Harbor, tel: 744-3315.
Antique Show, O'Hare Expo Center, tel: (708) 692-2220.
Chicago Jazz Festival, Petrillo Band Shell, Grant Park, tel: 744-3315.
Illinois State Fair, Springfield (not Chicago), tel: (217) 782-6661.

SEPTEMBER

Viva Chicago, Grant Park, tel: 744-3315.
Ribfest, Grant Park, tel: 222-3232. Backyard chefs compete for the title of best barbecue artist in town.
Berghoff Oktoberfest, Adams Street, from State Street to Dearborn Street, tel: 427-3170.

OCTOBER

Columbus Day Parade, Dearborn Street and Wacker Drive, tel: 828-0010.
Chicago International Film Festival, international films shown at various theaters, tel: 644-3400.
History Mystery Bicycle Tour and Festival, 96th Street and Longwood Drive, tel: 233-3100. A puzzle-solving bicycle tour, followed by food, music and games.

NOVEMBER

Christmas Around the World, Museum of Science and Industry, tel: 684-1414. A popular display of Christmas trees as decorated in various countries.
Lighting of the City's Christmas Tree, Daley Center Plaza, tel: 744-3315.
Christmas Parade, Michigan Avenue from Balbo Avenue to Wacker Drive, tel: 935-8747.

DECEMBER

Caroling to the Animals, Lincoln Park Zoo, tel: 294-4662.
Christmas Flower Show, Lincoln Park Conservatory, tel: 294-4770.

RELIGIOUS SERVICES

For help in locating specific services to attend, try the Chicago Church Federation, tel: 977-9929. The following is a list of churches and synagogues in the downtown and near north area:
Annunciation Greek Orthodox Cathedral, Greek Orthodox, 1017 N. LaSalle Street, tel: 664-5485.
Assumption Church Servite Fathers, Roman Catholic, 323 W. Illinois Street, tel: 644-0036.
Cathedral Church of St James, Episcopal, 65 E. Huron Street, tel: 787-7360.
Central Church of Chicago, Non-denominational, 18 S. Michigan Avenue, 9th Floor, tel: 332-4840.
Central Synagogue of the Southside Hebrew Congregation, Conservative, 30 E. Cedar Street, tel: 787-0450.
Chicago Loop Synagogue, Traditional, 16 S. Clark Street, tel: 346-7370.
Chicago Temple, First United Methodist Church, 77 W. Washington Street, tel: 236-4548.

Christ the King, Lutheran in America, 637 S. Dearborn Street, tel: 939-3720.
Church of the Ascension, Episcopal, 1133 N. LaSalle Street, tel: 664-1271.
Congregation Kol Ami, Reform, 150 E. Huron Street, tel: 664-4775.
First St Paul's Evangelical Lutheran Church, Lutheran, 1301 N. LaSalle Street, tel: 642-7172.
Fourth Presbyterian Church, Presbyterian, 126 E. Chestnut Street, tel: 787-4570.
Grace Episcopal Church, Episcopal, 637 S. Dearborn Street, tel: 922-1426.
Holy Name Cathedral, Roman Catholic, 735 N. State Street, tel: 787-8040.
Lake Shore Drive Synagogue, Traditional, 70 E. Elm Street, tel: 337-6811.
Lubavitch Chabad of the Loop, Orthodox, 401 S. LaSalle Street, Suite 9-770, tel: 427-7770.
Old St Mary's Church, Roman Catholic, 21 E. Van Buren Street, tel: 922-3444.
Second Presbyterian Church, Presbyterian, 1936 S. Michigan Avenue, tel: 225-4951.
Seventeenth Church of Christ, Christian Scientist, 55 E. Wacker Drive, tel: 236-4671.
St Patrick's Church, Roman Catholic, 718 W. Adams Street, tel: 782-6171.
St Peter's Church, Roman Catholic, 110 W. Madison Street, tel: 375-5111.

COMMUNICATIONS

NEWSPAPERS

There are two major daily newspapers in Chicago, the *Chicago Tribune* and the *Chicago Sun-Times*. Both are morning papers and are available everywhere: hotels, paper boxes on the street, stores, etc. The papers carry local, national and international news. They also have weekend sections (check Friday editions) with up-to-the minute information on entertainment events in Chicago. *Chicago Tribune*, 435 N. Michigan Avenue, tel: 222-3232.

Chicago Sun-Times, 401 N. Wabash Avenue, tel: 321-3000.

The *Chicago Defender* is another daily paper with emphasis on the black community, 2400 S. Michigan Avenue, tel: 225-2400.

The Reader is a liberal free weekly, available on Thursday primarily on the north side. 11 E. Illinois Street, tel: 828-0350.

Crain's Chicago Business is a weekly paper for Chicago's business news and other issues. 740 N. Rush Street, tel: 649-5200.

Streetwise is a paper sold by, and benefiting, the homeless of Chicago. It can be bought from individuals throughout the Loop 62 E.13th, tel: 554-0060.

MAGAZINES

Chicago is a monthly magazine that contains a good guide to restaurants and events in addition to its feature articles. 414 N. Orleans, tel: 222-8999.

NEWSSTANDS

Chicago Main Newsstand, Main Street and Chicago Avenue, Evanston, tel: 864-2727. A large selection of local, national and international papers can be obtained from: **Krochs & Brentanos**, 29 S. Wabash Avenue, tel: 332-7500. Some out of town and foreign newspapers.

RADIO

Radios pick up two frequencies, AM and FM. The most popular stations include:

AM

670	WMAQ	News
720	WGN	Variety, Talk
780	WBBM	News
820	WSCR	Sports Talk
890	WLS	Talk
1000	WMVP	Sports

FM

93.1	WXRT	Progressive Rock
93.9	WLIT	Light Favorites
94.7	WLS	News, Talk
95.5	WNUA	Smooth Jazz
96.3	WBBM	Top 40
97.9	WLUP	Personality/ Entertainment
98.7	WFMT	Classical, Fine Arts
99.5	WUSN	Country

INSIGHT *pocket* GUIDES

North America
Atlanta
Boston
British Coumbia
Florida
Florida Keys
Hawaii
Miami
Montreal
New York City
North California
Quebec
San Francisco
South California
Toronto

Latin America and The Caribbean
Bahamas
Baja
Belize
Bermuda
Jamaica
Mexico City
Puerto Rico
US· Virgin Islands
Yucatan Peninsula

Europe
Aegean Islands
Algarve
Alsace
Athens
Barcelona
Bavaria
Berlin
Brittany
Brussels
Budapest

Corsica
Costa Blanca
Costa Brava
Cote d'Azur
Crete
Denmark
Florence
Gran Canaria
Hungary
Ibiza
Ireland
Lisbon
Loire Valley
London
Madrid
Mallorca
Malta
Marbella
Milan
Moscow
Munich
Oslo/Bergen
Paris
Prague
Provence
Rhodes
Rome
Sardinia
Scotland
Seville
Sicily
Southeast England
St Petersburg
Tenerife
Tuscany
Venice
Vienna

Middle East and Africa
Istanbul
Kenya
Maldives
Morocco
Seychelles
Tunisia
Turkish Coast

Asia/Pacific
Bali
Bali Birdwalks
Bangkok
Beijing
Bhutan
Canton
Chiang Mai
Fiji
Hong Kong
Jakarta
Kathmandu,
   Bikes & Hikes
Kuala Lumpur
Macau
Malacca
Nepal
New Delhi
New Zealand
Penang
Phuket
Sabah
Sikkim
Singapore
Sri Lanka
Sydney
Thailand
Tibet
Yogyakarta

● ● ● ● ● ● ● ● ● ● ● ● ● ● ● ● ● ● ● ●

United States: Houghton Mifflin Company, Boston MA 02108
Tel: (800) 2253362 Fax: (800) 4589501

Canada: Thomas Allen & Son, 390 Steelcase Road East
Markham, Ontario L3R 1G2
Tel: (416) 4759126 Fax: (416) 4756747

Great Britain: GeoCenter UK, Hampshire RG22 4BJ
Tel: (256) 817987 Fax: (256) 817988

Worldwide: Höfer Communications Singapore 2262
Tel: (65) 8612755 Fax: (65) 8616438

" I was first drawn to the Insight Guides by the excellent "Nepal" volume. I can think of no book which so effectively captures the essence of a country. Out of these pages leaped the Nepal I know – the captivating charm of a people and their culture. I've since discovered and enjoyed the entire Insight Guide Series. Each volume deals with a country or city in the same sensitive depth, which is nowhere more evident than in the superb photography. "

Sir Edmund Hillary

Don't be overcharged for overseas calls.

Save up to 70% on calls back to the U.S. with WorldPhone.®*

While traveling abroad, the last thing you need to worry about is being overcharged for international phone calls. Plan ahead and look into WorldPhone – the easy and affordable way for you to call the U.S. and country to country from a growing list of international locations.

Just dial 1-800-955-0925 to receive your free, handy, wallet-size WorldPhone Access Guide – your guide to saving as much as 70% on phone calls home.

When calling internationally, your WorldPhone Access Guide will allow you to:

- Avoid hotel surcharges and currency confusion
- Choose from four convenient billing options
- Talk with operators who speak your language
- Call from more than 90 countries
- Just dial and save – regardless of your long distance carrier back home

WorldPhone is easy. And there's nothing to join. So avoid overcharges when you're traveling overseas. Call for your free WorldPhone Access Guide today – before you travel.

Call 1-800-955-0925.

THE TOP 25 WORLDPHONE COUNTRY CODES.		
COUNTRY / WORLDPHONE TOLL-FREE ACCESS #		**COUNTRY** / WORLDPHONE TOLL-FREE ACCESS #
Australia (CC)◆		**Japan** (cont'd.)
To call using		To call anywhere other
OPTUS■	008-5511-11	than the U.S.	0055
To call using		**Korea** (CC)
TELSTRA■	1-800-881-100	To call using KT■	009-14
Belgium (CC)◆	0800-10012	To call using DACOM■	0039-12
China (CC)	108-12	Phone Booths+	Red button 03,
(Available from most major cities)			then press*
For a Mandarin-speaking		Military Bases	550-2255
Operator	108-17	**Mexico** ▲	95-800-674-7000
Dominican Republic	1-800-751-6624	**Netherlands** (CC)◆	06-022-91-22
El Salvador◆	195	**Panama**	108
France (CC)◆	19▼-00-19	Military Bases	2810-108
Germany (CC)	0130-0012	**Philippines** (CC)◆	
(Limited availability in eastern Germany.)		To call using PLDT■	105-14
		To call PHILCOM■	1026-12
Greece (CC)◆	00-800-1211	For a Tagalog-speaking	
Guatemala◆	189	Operator	108-15
Haiti (CC)+	001-800-444-1234	**Saudi Arabia** (CC)+	1-800-11
Hong Kong (CC)	800-1121	**Singapore**	8000-112-112
India (CC)	000-127	**Spain** (CC)	900-99-0014
(Available from most major cities)		**Switzerland** (CC)◆	155-0222
Israel (CC)	177-150-2727	**United Kingdom** (CC)	
Italy (CC)◆	172-1022	To call using BT ■	0800-89-0222
Japan◆		To call using	
To call to the U.S. using KDD■	0039-121	MERCURY■	0500-89-0222
To call to the U.S. using IDC■	0066-55-121		

(CC) Country-to-country calling available. May not be available to/from all international locations. Certain restrictions apply.	+ Limited availability. ▼ Wait for second dial tone. ▲ Rate depends on call origin in Mexico.	■ International communications carrier. ◆ Public phones may require deposit of coin or phone card for dial tone.

WORLDPHONE℠
From MCI

Let it take you around the world.

100.3	WPNT	Rock/Contemporary
101.9	WTMX	70s, 80s & 90s
103.5	WFYR	Soft Hits
104.3	WJMK	Oldies
105.9	WCKG	Classic Rock
107.5	WGCI	Black Contemporary

TELEVISION

The main channels available on all television sets are:

Channel 2	WBBM	CBS
Channel 5	WMAQ	NBC
Channel 7	WLS	ABC
Channel 9	WGN	Independent
Channel 11	WTTW	PBS
Channel 32	WFLD	Fox

In hotels that offer cable (and most of them do), a listing will likely be provided showing what programming is available on each channel. Some specialty channels include:

ESPN	National sports
CNN	News
TMC	Movies
HBO	Movies
Showtime	Movies
Disney	Family fare
Max	Movies
Nickelodeon	Children's
Sportschannel	Local sports
VH-1	Music Videos
MTV	Music Videos
HLN	News
TWC	Weather

POSTAL SERVICES

The main post office is located at 433 W. Van Buren Street, tel: 765-4357. It is open from 7am-9pm Monday-Friday, 8am-5pm Saturday. There's also an O'Hare Airport post office that is open 24 hours.

The post office has 67 full service branches in or around Chicago. Most are open from 8.30am–5pm, Monday–Friday, and 8.30am–1pm Saturday. Check the phone book for the nearest location. The post office offers a postal answer line with different recordings depending on the information that is required. Tel: 427-5960.

TELEPHONES

Public telephones are located everywhere, both on the street and in major buildings. The city of Chicago is in area code **312**, the suburbs in **708**. When calling within the same area code, dial only the seven-digit phone number; when calling the other area code, dial 1-three digit area code-seven digit phone number. Calls between these two area codes are charged as local calls. (If unsure about the area code, go ahead and dial without it and a recording will advise on the proper area code.)

To find out local phone numbers call information at 411. For US long distance numbers the area code can be obtained from the operator (dial 0), then dial 1-(area code)-555-1212. Most overseas cities can be dialed direct. If you require assistance, dial 00 for a long-distance operator.

TELEX & FAX

Most hotels and many copy or printing shops and other businesses have fax machines that visitors can use for a fee. Telexes can also be sent through most hotels, and telegrams can be sent through Western Union or the telephone companies.

EMERGENCIES

SECURITY & CRIME

Gangsters no longer roam the streets of Chicago with their tommyguns, but there are some very real security risks in the city today – especially in some of the poorer neighborhoods, or in the less populated downtown areas late at night.

Visitors who stick to the main hotel, shopping and tourist areas have little cause for concern. The more adventurous who set off to explore Chicago's neighborhoods should first seek the advice of locals. Most areas are safe and friendly but a few, particularly in the public housing areas of the West Side and South Side, are not.

Hotel rooms and cars should be locked when not in use, of course. Don't leave valuables in hotel rooms; use the hotel safe instead. Joggers should stick to daytime routes in well-populated areas.

As in other big cities everywhere, pickpockets are drawn to large crowds, such as those at festivals, concerts and sporting events. Don't carry large amounts of cash or credit cards. Wallets should be carried in inside pockets, and women should keep a hand on their purses. Similarly, purses should not be hung off the backs of chairs in restaurants. If there is a theft or attack, dail 911. The police are prompt and courteous.

MEDICAL SERVICES

In an emergency, dial 911.
For **Ambulance Dispatch** (24-hour), tel: (708) AMT-9898.
For a **non-emergency**, call the Medical Referral Service, tel: 670-2550.
For **dental care**, the Chicago Dental Society emergency service can help 24 hours a day. Monday–Friday 9am–5pm, tel: 836-7300; all other hours, tel: 726-4321.
Poison control is handled at Rush-Presbyterian – St Luke's, tel: 942-5969. Can also be called toll free on 1-800-942-5969.

AREA HOSPITALS

Loop: Rush-Presbyterian–St Luke's Hospital, 1753 W. Congress Parkway, tel: 942-5000. Cook County Hospital, 1835 W. Harrison, tel: 633-6000.
North: Northwestern Memorial, Superior Street and Franklin Court, tel: 908-2000.
South: Michael Reese, 31st and Lake Shore Drive, tel: 791-2000.

Some pharmacies with long hours are:
Walgreens, 757 N. Michigan Avenue, tel; 664-8686;
Perry Drugs, 990 W. Fullerton, tel; 975-0339;
Cosmopolitan Drugs, 754 N. Clark Street, tel; 787-2152.

LEFT LUGGAGE

Most airports, train and bus terminals have left-luggage rooms or coin-operated lockers. Most hotels also have a left-luggage room for that last day of stay when visitors must check out but have a few hours to kill before leaving town.

GETTING AROUND

ORIENTATION

The numbering system in Chicago makes it easy to find your way around. The city is laid out in a grid pattern. The corner of **State and Madison streets** (downtown) is the center point. Any address N., S., E., or W., is north, south, east, or west of that point. Each block is equal to 100 address numbers, so 800 N. State Street, is a point eight blocks north of Madison. Keep in mind that Lake Michigan is to the east.

The lakefront in Chicago has been developed for public use. Starting from the lake, the first area of land is the parkland, consisting of beaches, recreational lands, gardens and some of the popular museums. Heading west away from the lake, the next area is the downtown, with its many stores, businesses and hotels. Here are the skyscrapers and interesting buildings that make up Chicago's famous skyline.

To the north, west, and south of the downtown are residential areas. Chicago is a city of diverse neighborhoods: Beverly, Bridgeport, Hyde Park, Lincoln Park, Rogers Park and so on – each a part of the same city, yet with its own name and identity, and often its own ethnic or racial flavor.

Surrounding Chicago in an ever-widening band are the suburbs. Primarily residential areas, they usually have a street or two (strips), a specific area (district) or malls for business and shopping. There are often excellent family restaurants in the suburbs.

Each suburb may use its own numbering system for streets and addresses, but many follow the pattern begun in the city.

RECOMMENDED MAPS

Rand McNally has a number of good maps of Chicago, and most bookstores and souvenir shops offer a variety. Especially recommended is *Chicago, Illinois: Visitors Guide and Birds-Eye View.*

The CTA publishes a transit map that can also serve as a good guide to the streets in the city. It can be requested from CTA (Chicago Transit Authority), Merchandise Mart, Chicago, Illinois 60654.

AIRPORT/CITY

It's ordinarily a 20-minute trip by car between O'Hare Airport and downtown but traffic is so unpredictable, especially during rush hour, that it's advisable to allow an hour for travel time. Taxis are readily available, but are fairly expensive.

Continental Air Transport, tel: 454-7800, provides bus services between the airport baggage claim area and about 35 downtown hotels. Many hotels provide their own shuttle service, so inquire when making reservations. Taxis are available on the lower level of each terminal. Limousine service or car rentals can be arranged in advance or at the booths near the baggage claim area.

Probably the cheapest way to get downtown, and the surest way to avoid traffic jams, is the **Chicago Transit Authority** (CTA) Rapid Transit line under Terminal 4. The trains run frequently to and from the Dearborn Street station downtown.

Midway Airport, 5700 S. Cicero, is a smaller, less crowded alternative to **O'Hare**, located about seven miles southwest of downtown. Its one building is divided into three terminals. For information, tel: 767-0500.

DOMESTIC TRAVEL

O'Hare Airport, besides its international terminal, has three domestic terminals with flights and connections to all parts of the United States. Call 686-2200. Midway Airport, 5700 S. Cicero Avenue, has three domestic terminals, call 767-0500.

In addition to O'Hare and Midway airports (*see* Traveling to Chicago), **Meigs Field**, just south of downtown at 12th Street and the lakefront, provides commuter flights to downstate Illinois and Wisconsin. Call 744-4787 for information.

Some budget travelers prefer to see America by bus, "riding the dog" with passes that allow unlimited trips during a certain period of weeks. **Greyhound/Trailways** has nationwide services from its main terminal in the Loop (downtown), at Clark and Randolph streets. Call 781-2900 for fare and schedule information.

America's rail network has been dramatically reduced in recent decades, and the prices are often not much better than airfare. Nonetheless, long-haul **Amtrak** passes for travelers can still be a bargain, and many still prefer the romance of the rails. General information on Amtrak trains and fares for the entire country is available toll-free at (800) USA-RAIL. Amtrak's main Chicago terminal is Chicago's **Union Station** at Jackson and Canal streets, tel: 558-1075.

PUBLIC TRANSPORTATION

Chicago's public transportation network includes buses and rapid transit trains, both subway and elevated (or the "El," as everyone will call it). An excellent transit system map can be requested free from CTA (Chicago Transit Authority), Merchandise Mart, Chicago, IL 60654.

Bus stops are marked with signs which indicate the bus routes they serve. Buses run about every 15 minutes during the day, less often at night.

The RTA (Regional Transportation Authority), tel: 836-7000, will provide travel information 24 hours a day except on major holidays. The RTA service provides commuter trains to the suburbs and exurbs via the Metra lines that leave the city from four central stations.

TAXIS

Taxis in Chicago are metered. Fares begin at under $1.50 for the first one-fifth of a mile (or fraction of that). It also costs extra for each additional one-sixth of a mile or 60 seconds of waiting time. There's a charge for each additional passenger between the ages of 12 and 65. A 15 percent tip is standard for the driver. A taxi ride to or from O'Hare Airport will cost between $25 and $30; the ride to or from Midway Airport costs between $18 and $22. A shared ride program is available for a flat rate of $15 (O'Hare) or $10 (Midway) for each person with a maximum of four people.

Here are some of the taxi services in Chicago (Check the *Yellow Pages* of the phone book under taxicabs for many more):
Yellow Cab Co, tel: 829-4222.
Checker Taxi Co, tel: 243-2537.
Flash Cab Co, tel: 561-1444.

CAR RENTALS

Visitors concentrating on the downtown area probably don't need a car. Between public transportation and a little walking, the usual tourist areas are all accessible. Also, taxis are plentiful. There are quite a few parking lots, including underground parking at Grant Park, but these can be expensive. Cheaper on-street parking is difficult to find.

Here is a small sample of rental agencies (Check the *Yellow Pages* of the phone book under Automobile Rentals for more). Reservations are advised:
Alamo, tel: (800) 327-9633.
Budget, tel: (800) 527-0700.
Hertz, tel: (800) 654-3131.
Avis, tel: (800) 331-1212.
Dollar, tel: (800) 800-4000.
Enterprise, tel: (800) 325-8007.

WALKING & CYCLING

Chicago is a great walking town for those who are fit, but like most American cities it is much more spread out than most European cities. Visitors who aren't used to extensive walking shouldn't try to hit all of Chicago's downtown landmarks on foot.

Besides using bicycles for cruising along the lakefront, some visitors find that – if they can brave the traffic – cycling is an efficient and cheap way to see a lot of the city very quickly. Bicycle rentals are available at:
Lincoln Park, Fullerton Avenue west of Lake Shore Drive.
Village Cycle Shop, 1337 N. Wells Street, tel: 751-2488.

HITCHHIKING

Besides being dangerous, hitchhiking is strictly illegal in and around Chicago, as it is over most of the United States. The practice is regarded as too risky by both drivers and travelers, particularly in urban areas.

COMPLAINTS

For help with a problem, or to file a complaint, some contacts are:
Better Business Bureau, tel: 346-3313. 10am–2.30pm.
City of Chicago Consumer Information and Complaints: tel: 744-9400.
Governor's Office of Consumer Affairs: tel: (800) 814-2754.

If the complaint is serious enough to require legal assistance, the following service will make referrals to lawyers who are registered with the service.
Illinois Lawyer Referral Service: tel: (800) 252-8916.

WHERE TO STAY

Chicago can be a fairly expensive city for accommodation, but there is also a wide variety of hotels and motels in different price ranges. Most hotels – and all the better ones – have restaurants and bars. Seasonal bargains and packages with both overseas and domestic flights are often available, along with "weekender" rates offered by hotels that cater to expense-account business travelers during the week. Tourists trying to save money may find the best bargains a few blocks away from downtown, but still within an easy bus or taxi ride. Here are some of the recommended hotels in Chicago:

LUXURY

The Barclay Chicago, 166 E. Superior Street, 60611, tel: 787-6000 or toll free (800)

621-8004. All suites, multilingual concierge, and in a good location.

The Drake Hotel, 140 E. Walton Place, 60611, tel: 787-2200 or toll free (800) 527-4727. Lavish lobby, worth a visit even if not staying at the hotel. Shopping arcade on first floor. Three restaurants including the Cape Cod Room.

Fairmont, 200 N. Columbus Drive, 60601, tel: 565-8000 or toll free (800) 332-3442. Located at the Illinois Center. Complete business services. High tea served.

Four Seasons Hotel, 120 E. Delaware Place, 60611, tel: 280-8800 or toll free (800) 332-3442. Located above Bloomingdales. Indoor pool and health center.

Hotel Nikko, 321 Dearborn Street, 60610, tel: 744-1900 or toll free (800) NIKKO-US. Fitness center. Business services.

Hyatt Regency Chicago, 151 E. Wacker Drive, 60601, tel: 565-1234 or toll free (800) 233-1234. At Illinois Center. Over 2,000 rooms. Atrium Lobby, comedy club nightly, shuttle buses to airports.

Le Meridien Chicago, 21 E. Bellevue Place, 60611, tel: 266-2100 or toll free (800) 443-2100. Penthouse suites available. Jazz pianist. Business services.

Omni Ambassador East, 1301 N. State Street, 60610, tel: 787-7200 or toll free (800) THE-OMNI. Old fashioned elegance. Home of the Pump Room and Byfields.

Park Hyatt, 800 N. Michigan Avenue, 60611, tel: 280-2222 or toll free (800) 233-1234. Lavish contemporary style. Multilingual concierge and staff. Home of La Tour Restaurant.

The Ritz-Carlton Chicago, 160 E. Pearson Street, 60611, tel: 266-1000 or toll free (800) 332-3442. Located above Water Tower Place. Grand lobby. Nightly entertainment and dancing in the "The Bar."

Swissôtel Chicago, 323 E. Wacker Drive, 60601, tel: 565-0565 or toll free (800) 65-GRAND. At Illinois Center. Aims for quiet European ambience. Health spa with indoor lap pool. Also offers jazz and classical music.

EXPENSIVE

Blackstone, 636 S. Michigan Avenue, 60605, tel: 427-4300 or toll free (800) 622-6330. Plenty of gangster history and ambience of bygone days.

Chicago Hilton and Towers, 720 S. Michigan Avenue, 60605, tel: 922-4400 or toll free (800)-HILTONS.

Chicago Marriott Downtown, 540 N. Michigan Avenue, 60611, tel: 836-0100 or toll free (800) 228-9290.

Executive Plaza, A Clarion Hotel, 71 E. Wacker Drive, 60601, tel: 346-7100 or toll free (800) 621-4005.

Holiday Inn Chicago City Centre, 300 E. Ohio Street, 60611, tel: 787-6100 or toll free (800) 465-4329.

Holiday Inn Mart Plaza, 350 N. Orleans Street, 60654, tel: 836-5000 or toll free (800) 465-4329.

Hotel Inter-Continental, 505 N. Michigan Avenue, 60611, tel: 944-4100 or toll free (800) 628-2112.

The Knickerbocker Chicago, 163 E. Walton Place, 60611, tel: 751-8100 or toll free (800) 621-8140.

Lenox House Suites, 616 N. Rush Street, 60611, tel: 337-1000 or toll free (800) 44-LENOX.

The Mayfair Regent, 181 E. Lake Shore Drive, 60611, tel: 787-8500 or toll free (800) 545-4000.

The Palmer House Hilton, 17 E. Monroe Street, 60603, tel: 726-7500 or toll free (800) HIL-TONS.

The Radisson Plaza Ambassador West, 1300 N. State Parkway, 60610, tel: 787-7900 or toll free (800) 333-3333.

Sheraton Chicago Hotel & Towers, 301 East North Water Street, 60611, tel: 464-1000 or toll free (800) 325-3535.

Sheraton Plaza, 160 E. Huron Street, 60611, tel: 787-2900 or toll free (800) 325-3535.

Tremont, 100 E. Chestnut Street, 60611, tel: 751-1900 or toll free (800) 621-8133.

The Westin Hotel, 909 N. Michigan Avenue, 60611, tel: 943-7200 or toll free (800) 228-3000. At north end of Magnificent Mile. Health club.

Whitehall, 105 E. Delaware Place, 60611, tel: 944-6300 or toll free (800) 621-8295.

MODERATE TO EXPENSIVE

Ascot House, 1100 S. Michigan Avenue, 60605, tel: 922-2900 or toll free (800) 272-4220.

Avenue Hotel, 1154 S. Michigan Avenue, 60605, tel: 427-8200 or toll free (800) 621-4196.

Congress Hotel, 520 S. Michigan Avenue, 60605, tel: 427-3800 or toll free (800) 635-1666.

Claridge Hotel, 1244 N. Dearborn Street, 60610, tel: 787-4980 or toll free (800) 245-1258.

Gold Coast Group (small hotels in renovated older buildings). Toll free (800) 621-8506. Group includes: The Talbott, 20 E. Delaware Place, tel: 944-4970. The Delaware Towers, 25 E. Delaware Place, tel: 944-4245. The Elms, 18 E. Elm Street, tel: 787-4740.

Midland, 172 W. Adams Street, 60603, tel: 332-1200 or toll free (800) 621-2360.

The Raphael, 201 E. Delaware Place, 60611, tel: 943-5000 or toll free (800) 821-5343.

River North Hotel, 125 W. Ohio Street, 60610, tel: 467-0800 or toll free (800) 528-1234.

BED & BREAKFAST

Bed and Breakfast Chicago is a clearing-house of available bed and breakfast facilities in the Chicago area. Rather than a European-style inn that includes breakfast as part of the payment, a B&B in Chicago is more likely a family which opens its home to guests. Reservations must be made. Contact Bed & Breakfast Chicago, PO Box 14088, Chicago, IL 60614, tel: 951-0085.

YOUTH HOSTELS

There is only one hostel in the Chicago area, and it is located well away from the downtown area: Chicago International Hostel, 6318 N. Winthrop Avenue, tel: 262-1011.

FOOD DIGEST

WHAT TO EAT

As the major city in America's heartland, Chicago boasts a wide variety of regional, ethnic and foreign cuisine. The city is known, however, for several specific types of food. Beef of all kinds, particularly prime rib and steaks, have been a specialty of the city since its days as the nation's stockyards, the US butchering capital. An influence from the southern black migration has been "barbecue ribs," the large meaty spare ribs slathered in tangy sauce. Chicago claims to have invented the deep-dish pizza – one of the few items of native fare that vegetarians can enjoy, too – and to have refined the form of Vienna sausage known as the Chicago hot dog. But whatever the style of food, diners in Chicago can almost always be assured that the portions will be large – even by American standards.

WHERE TO EAT

The following restaurants, grouped by style of food, are recommended:

AMERICAN

Barney's Market Club, 741 W. Randolph Street, tel: 372-6466. One of Chicago's oldest restaurants, specializing in prime rib, steak and lobster.

Mr Beef on Orleans, 666 N. Orleans Street, tel: 337-8500. Offers the best beef sandwich in Chicago. Very casual. Celebrity photos on the wall.

Bigsby's Bar and Grill, 1750 N. Clark Street, tel: 642-5200. Lincoln Park location. Part-owner Michael Jordan, the basketball star, is frequently in the restaurant.

Billy Goat Tavern & Grill, 430 N. Michigan Avenue, tel: 222-1525. Lower level Michigan Avenue. Hangout for the city's press corps. Cheeseburgers are a must.

Binyon's Restaurant, 327 S. Plymouth Court, tel: 341-1155. A popular spot for bankers, attorneys, traders. Famous for its turtle soup.

Blackhawk Lodge, 41 E. Superior Street, tel: 280-4080. American cooking with an emphasis toward healthy choices.

Blackie's, 755 S. Clark Street, tel: 786-1161. Traditional family fare – soups, salads, chili. Specialty is cheeseburgers.

Bub City Crabshack & Bar-B-Q, 901 W. Weed Street, tel: 266-1200. Fun-filled, spacious eatery decorated as a Texas honky-tonk. Plenty of seafood and barbecue selections. Great for garlic lovers.

Butch McGuire's, 20 W. Division, tel: 337-9080. Lunch, dinner and weekend brunch in a lively saloon atmosphere.

City Tavern, 33 W. Monroe Street, tel: 280-2740. Cherrywood paneling and soft lights, across from the Shubert Theatre. Features include homemade sandwiches, omelettes and grilled steaks.

Demon Dogs, 944 N. Fullerton Avenue, tel: 281-2001. Best hot dog stand in the city. Among the best fries.

The Eccentric, 159 W. Erie Street, tel: 787-8390. House specialties: Prime Rib and Rice Crusted Tuna. Homemade desserts.

Ed Debevic's, 640 N. Wells Street, tel: 664-1707. A campy, upbeat '50s diner known for its homestyle food and sassy service.

Entre Nous, 200 N. Columbus Avenue (Fairmont Hotel), tel: 565-8000. An intimate restaurant with "classique" cuisine.

The Fireplace Inn, 1448 N. Wells Street, tel: 664-5264. Ski lodge atmosphere. Barbecued ribs, steaks, seafood, sandwiches. Outdoor dining available.

Gold Coast Dogs, 418 N. State Street, tel: 527-1222; 804 N. Rush Street, tel: 951-5141; 2100 N. Clark, tel: 327-8887. Chicago hot dogs, also burgers and sandwiches.

Gordon, 500 N. Clark Street, tel: 467-9780. Seasonal New American menu highlighting fresh seafood. Brunch on Sundays.

Hamburger Hamlet, 44 E. Walton Street, tel: 649-6601. A Gold Coast institution offering a variety of made to order hamburgers, chili *fajitas*, salads and more.

Hard Rock Café, 63 W. Ontario Street, tel: 943-2252. Mick Jagger's guitar, George Harrison's Beatles suit, Michael Jackson's platinum records and yes, even food, especially hamburgers.

Harry Caray's Restaurant, 33 W. Kinzie Street, tel: 465-9269. Baseball memorabilia decorate the walls while steaks and chops dominate the menu.

Houston's Restaurant, 616 N. Rush Street, tel: 649-1121. Something for everyone here, fish, ribs, soups, steaks, etc, served in a convenient location.

Jim's Hot Dog Stand, 1320 S. Halsted Street. The local police eat here, so it must be filling.

Michael Jordon's Restaurant, 500 N. LaSalle Street, tel: 644-3865. Michael Jordon, the world-famous basketball player, opened this restaurant featuring his favorite foods with a bit of sport thrown in, in the form of a multimedia lounge and memorabilia.

Planet Hollywood, 633 N. Wells, tel: 266-7827. Restaurant and entertainment complex owned and frequented by celebrities.

Red Kerr's, 138 S. Clinton Street, tel: 733-5377. Sports celebrity restaurant owned by Bulls announcer, Johnny "Red" Kerr. Try a barbecue, and maybe see a Chicago sports personality.

Maple Tree Inn, 10730 S. Western Avenue. New Orleans cajun food in a neighborhood Beverly restaurant with a jazz club and an outdoor garden.

Prairie, 500 S. Dearborn Street, tel: 663-1143. Open for breakfast, lunch and dinner. Modernized basic recipes.

The Pump Room, 1301 N. State Parkway, tel: 266-0360. A famous restaurant, known since the 1930s for its "Booth One," which is reserved for celebrities.

Signature Room at the 95th, 875 N. Michigan Avenue, tel: 787-9596. Enjoy elegant dining and a great view of the city from the 95th floor of the John Hancock Building. The menu changes with the seasons.

That Steak Joynt, 1610 N. Wells Street, tel: 943-5091. Steaks and ribs. Offers a Second City dinner/theatre package.

Top Notch Beefburger, 2116 W. 95th Street, tel: 445-7218. 1950s-style burgers and milk shakes in a classic diner in the classic neighborhood of Beverly.

ARAB

Old Jerusalem, 1411 N. Wells, tel: 944-0459.

ARMENIAN

Sayat Nova, 157 E. Ohio Street, tel: 644-9159. Romantic restaurant with a reputation for good food. Authentic Armenian-Middle Eastern dishes include mezzas, kebabs and vegetarian specialties.

BARBECUED RIBS

Army's and Lou's, 422 E. 7th Street, tel: 483-6550. Many consider this to be one of the finest soul food restaurants in America. The ribs, chitlins and grits just don't get any better than here.

Carson's Ribs, 612 N. Wells Street, tel: 280-9200. Won a *Chicago* magazine contest for the best ribs in town. Meaty ribs in a tangy sweet sauce. Other entrées also available.

Fireplace Bar & Grill, 1960 N. Racine, tel: 528-4300. Ribs, pizza and more. TVs for sporting events.

Miller's Pub, 134 S. Adams, tel: 263-4988. Popular spot for sports and theatergoers. Casual atmosphere. Possible celebrity sightings.
Twin-Anchors Restaurant and Tavern, 1655 N. Sedgwick Street, tel: 266-1616. Among the best ribs in Chicago. Great burgers too. Pleasant neighborhood watering hole.

CHINESE

House of Hunan, 535 N. Michigan, tel: 329-9494.
Haylemon Restaurant, 2201 S. Wentworth Avenue, tel: 225-0891.
Jade East Restaurant, 218 W. Cermak Road, tel: 362-4224.
King Wah Restaurant, 2225 S. Wentworth Avenue, tel: 842-1404.
Mandar-Inn Restaurant, 2249 S. Wentworth Avenue, tel: 842-4014.
65 Seafood Restaurant, 2414 S. Wentworth Avenue, tel: 225-7060.
Szechwan House, 600 N. Michigan Avenue, tel: 642-3900. Good location and food, from the spicy foods of Szechwan Province to the delicately flavored dishes of Taiwan.
Three Happiness Restaurant, 209 W. Cermak Road, tel: 842-1964. This is a tiny storefront with limited seating. Serves very good Cantonese and Szechuan food.
Triple Crown Seafood, 211 W. 22nd Place, tel: 790-1788.

CONTINENTAL

Arnie's, 1030 N. State Street, tel: 266-4800. Gold Coast glitz. This award-winning restaurant has an a la carte menu featuring rack of lamb, Sicilian veal chop and prime steaks. Has a great Sunday brunch.
Crickets, 100 E. Chestnut Street, tel: 280-2100. Varied menu featuring international and American dishes. A place to "see and be seen" for many.
The Rafael, 201 E. Delaware Place (Raphael Hotel), tel: 943-5000. Intimate setting, reasonable prices.

DELICATESSEN

The Bagel Restaurant, 3107 N. Broadway, tel: 477-0300. North Side. Traditional deli, serves bulging sandwiches and award-winning soups.

D.B. Kaplan's Delicatessen, 845 N. Michigan Avenue (Water Tower Place, 7th Floor), tel: 280-2700. More than 150 creative deli options. Carryout and delivery available. A mural of celebrity caricatures throughout the restaurant.
Manny's Coffee Shop & Deli, 1141 S. Jefferson Street, tel: 939-2855. Near south. Dine in or carry out, a complete breakfast menu, plus sandwiches, homemade soups and salads for lunch. The specialty is corned beef.
Moe's Deli & Pub, 611 N. Rush Street, tel: 828-0110. Near North. Triple decker sandwich creations, homemade soups and desserts, daily specialties. Delivery and carryout services are available.

ETHIOPIAN

Mama Desta's Red Sea Restaurant, 3216 N. Clark Street, tel: 935-7561. Ethiopian cooking. Diners eat with their hands. Bring several friends.

FRENCH

Ambria, 2300 N. Lincoln Park West, tel: 472-5959. Serving Chef Gabino Sotelino's cuisine LeGere.
Bistro 110, 110 E. Pearson Street, tel: 266-3110. Hospitable and comfortable, specialties include angel-hair pasta, oven-roasted chicken and crème brûlée for dessert. Extensive French-American wine list.
Café Bernard, 2100 N. Halsted Street tel: 871-2100. Country French cuisine. Located in the heart of Lincoln Park.
Charlie Trotter's, 816 W. Armitage, tel: 248-6228. Contemporary multi-cultural cuisine.
Chez Paul, 660 N. Rush Street, tel: 944-6680. Quiet elegance in the McCormick Mansion.
The Dining Room, 160 E. Pearson Street (Ritz-Carlton), tel: 227-5866. Beautiful setting, daily specials, foie gras salad is a specialty.
Everest Room, 410 S. LaSalle Street, tel: 663-8920. One of the top restaurants in the country, with a view to match.
Le Francais, 269 S. Milwaukee Avenue, Wheeling, tel: (708) 541-7470. Although not located in Chicago, this suburban restaurant is world famous. Contemporary French cuisine in a provincial atmosphere.
Un Grand Café, 2300 N. Lincoln Park West, tel: 348-8886. Authentic Parisian Bistro overlooking Lincoln Park. You can dine on the patio in warm weather.

Yvette Wintergarden, 311 S. Wacker Drive, tel: 408-1242. Art deco Loop bistro located in a tropical atrium. Serves light French-American cuisine.

GERMAN

The Berghoff Restaurant, 17 W. Adams Street, tel: 427-3170. Wide selection of meat, poultry and fish items. German fare among the best in the city. They make their own beer and root beer.

Golden Ox, 1578–82 Clybourn Avenue, tel: 664-0780. "Old World" atmosphere, strolling musicians, good German food and a good beer garden.

Zum Deutschen Eck, 2924 N. Southport Avenue, tel: 525-8121. A cozy German restaurant featuring Schnitzel Dijon and sauerbraten. Live entertainment.

GREEK

Denis' Den, 2941 N. Clark Street, tel: 348-8888. A mini-trip to Greece. Live music, dancing encouraged. Homemade Greek food.

Greek Islands, 200 S. Halsted Street, tel: 782-9855. Festive, with room to dance. An exposed steam table showcases many of the house offerings.

Papagus, 600 N. State Street, tel: 642-8450. Features regional Greek cuisine and a variety of *Mezedes*.

The Parthenon, 314 S. Halsted Street, tel: 726-2407. Big and bustling. *Saganaki*, lamb, Greek sausage, suckling pig.

HUNGARIAN

Kenessey's, 403 W. Belmont Avenue, tel: 929-7500. Elegant Hungarian cooking and live gypsy music. Best-priced wine selection in Chicago. Homemade pastries.

INDIAN

Bukhara Restaurant & Bar, 2 E. Ontario Street, tel: 943-0188. Authentic cuisine from the Northwest Territory of India. Tandoori dishes. Glass walled kitchen to view preparations.

Daavat Restaurant, 211 E. Walton Street, tel: 335-1001. Casual atmosphere, curries and tandoori dishes.

Gaylord India, 678 N. Clark Street, tel: 664-1700. Traditional tandoori specialties.

Kanval Palace Restaurant, 70 E. Walton Street, tel: 787-0400. Intimate and elegant.

Klay Oven Restaurant, 414 N. Orleans Street, tel: 527-3999. Traditional tandoori and Karhai dishes.

ITALIAN

Al's No 1 Italian Beef, 169 W. Ontario, tel: 943-3222. Rated Chicago's No 1 Italian beef restaurant by *Chicago* magazine.

Avanzare, 161 E. Huron Street, tel: 337-8056. Focuses on the delicately flavored cuisine of Northern Italy. Tempting seafood and pasta dishes, especially among the daily specials.

Bice Ristorante, 158 E. Ontario Street, tel: 664-1474. Northern Italian cuisine. Homemade pastas. Signature carpaccio, risottos, mussels, vongole, and veal Milanese style. Elegant dining room or outdoor garden.

Bravissimo, 508 N. Clark Street, tel: 644-1427. Inspired Italian cuisine in a relaxed, sophisticated setting. Dishes add creative flair to Northern and Southern classics. The best calamari in Chicago.

Carlucci Restaurant, 2215 N. Halsted Street, tel: 281-1220. Regional Italian cuisine. Elegant dining room or outdoor garden.

Centro, 710 N. Wells Street, tel: 988-7775. A serious place for pasta, prime steaks, chops and broiled seafood in the art district.

Coco Pazzo, 300 W. Hubbard, tel: 836-0900. Chef from Bergame, Italy. Elegant loft space.

Como Inn Restaurant, 546 Milwaukee Avenue, tel: 421-5222. Serving Chicago since 1924. Complimentary parking.

Gennaro's Restaurant, 1352 W. Taylor Street, tel: 243-1035. Family business specializing in gnocchi, ravioli, stuffed eggplant, fried calamari.

Gene & Georgetti, 500 N. Franklin Street, tel: 527-3718. For over 50 years this restaurant has offered Italian specialties, steaks and other dishes.

Italian Village, 71 W. Monroe Street, tel: 332-7005. Three restaurants featuring Italian American dishes. Extensive wine list.

Lino's, 222 W. Ontario Street, tel: 266-0616. Casual but elegant dining in a club-like setting featuring Northern Italian cuisine.

Maggiano's Little Italy, 516 N. Clark, tel: 644-7700. A classic recreation of a New York City pre-war "Little Italy" dinner house. Family-style dining available.

Rico's Restaurant, 626 S. Racine Avenue, tel: 421-7262. Located in the "Little Italy" neighborhood, with home cooking specialties.

The Rosebud Café, 1500 W. Taylor Street, tel: 942-1117. Also located in "Little Italy."

Scoozi, 410 W. Huron Street, tel: 943-5900. The neoclassic atmosphere of a 15th-century artist's studio recreated in the River North gallery district. Italian countryside cuisine.

Spiaggia, 980 N. Michigan Avenue, tel: 280-2754. Main dining room on the 2nd floor offers a view of Lake Michigan; northern Italian cuisine, including homemade pastas and brick-oven pizza. Next door is **Café Spiaggia** (tel: 280-2764), a casual European café with some of the same items and an extensive antipasto bar.

Stefani's, 1418 W. Fullerton Parkway, tel: 348-0111. Northern Italian cuisine. Host restaurant for politicians of note from Italy.

Trattoria No. 10, 10 N. Dearborn Street, tel: 984-1718. Charming and warm, featuring a variety of Italian dishes.

Tuscany, 1041 W. Taylor Street, tel: 829-1990. In Little Italy. Open kitchen, woodburning oven and grill remind you of a Tuscan eatery.

JAPANESE

Benihana of Tokyo, 166 E. Superior Street, tel: 664-9643. One of a US-wide chain, featuring Hibachi-style cooking – the chef prepares dinner at the table.

Benkay, 320 N. Dearborn Street (Hotel Nikko), tel: 744-1900. Authentic Japanese cuisine in an elegant setting. A Sushi Room, a Tatami Room, Teppan-Yaki tables, or Western-style dining rooms.

Hatsuhana, 160 E. Ontario Street, tel: 280-8287. A very large sushi bar, with many varieties of ocean fish flown in daily.

LEBANESE

Beirut, 5204 N. Clark Street. Known for its great kebabs.

MEXICAN

Frontera Grill, 445 N. Clark Street, tel: 661-1434. Wonderful Mexican cooking in a Southwestern setting. Menu changes weekly and represents several regions. Reservations an absolute must.

El Jardin, 3335 N. Clark Street, tel: 528-6775. Mexican cuisine, two outdoor gardens, Sunday brunch.

Hat Dance, 325 W. Huron Street, tel: 649-0066. Good service and value, appealing to upscale young professionals.

Su Casa, 49 E. Ontario Street, tel: 943-4041. In an 18th-century hacienda setting, specialties include chicken fajitas and red snapper.

PIZZA

Bacino's, 75 E. Wacker Drive, tel: 263-0070. One of the best pizza joints around. Spinach pizza is a specialty.

California Pizza Kitchen, 414 N. Orleans, tel: 222-9030 and Water Tower Place, 7th level, tel: 787-7300. 26 varieties of wood-fired pizzas. Also pastas, salads, soup. Children's menu available.

Edwardo's, 1212 N. Dearborn Street, tel: 337-4490 or 521 S. Dearborn Street, tel: 939-3366. Chicago style stuffed pizza. Dining in, carry out or delivery.

Father and Son Pizza and Italian Restaurant, 645 W. North Avenue, tel: 654-2564. Family-run business with gourmet bakery. Home delivery available.

Gino's East, 160 E. Superior Street, tel: 943-1124. Often a wait to get in.

Pizzeria Uno, 29 E. Ohio Street, tel: 321-1000.

Pizzeria Due, 619 N. Wabash Avenue, tel: 943-2400. Chicago-style, deep-dish pizza was created at Pizzeria Uno in 1943. Pizzeria Due opened in 1955 to handle the overflow. A must-try for pizza lovers.

POLISH

Busy Bee, 1500 N. Damen, tel: 772-4433. The last remaining gourmet Polish restaurant in old Polish downtown.

Orbit, 2940 N. Milwaukee Avenue, tel: 276-1355. A popular and boisterous restaurant in the Jackowo (Polish downtown area), known for *pirogi*.

Przybylo's White Eagle Banquet Hall, 6845 N. Milwaukee, tel: (708) 647-0660. The largest Polish restaurant in all the Midwest, it can handle seven wedding receptions at one time.

SEAFOOD

Cape Cod Room, 140 E. Walton Place (Drake Hotel), tel: 787-2200. A famous dining spot with an extensive seafood menu. Specialties include the Bookbinder red snapper soup.

Catch 35, 35 W. Wacker, tel: 346-3500. More than 30 fresh seafood specialties. Oyster bar and display kitchen. There's also live entertainment.

Nick's Fishmarket, One First National Plaza, tel: 621-0200. Sophisticated atmosphere, good service and wide range of fresh fish and seafood.

Shaw's Crab House and **Shaw's Blue Crab Lounge & Oyster Bar**, 21 E. Hubbard Street, tel: 527-2722. Some of the freshest seafood in the city. The oyster bar has a wide selection. 1930s decor.

SPANISH

Café Baba Reeba, 2024 N. Halsted Street, tel: 935-5000. Features a variety of hot and cold tapas. Regional specialties, including paella. Outdoor café.

STEAK

Barney's Market Club Steakhouse, 741 W. Randolph Street, tel: 372-6466. Double cut prime rib of beef, daily specials. Casual dining in historic Haymarket Square.

Chicago Chop House, 60 W. Ontario Street, tel: 787-7100. Meat and potato place. Specialties include prime rib and a 64 oz. T-bone. Piano bar nightly.

Eli's The Place for Steak, 215 E. Chicago Avenue, tel: 642-1393. Prime aged steaks are the specialty. As famous for its cheesecake as for its steaks and excellent service.

Gibson's Bar & Steakhouse, 1028 N. Rush Street, tel: 266-8999. 1940s style, with supersized steaks. Piano bar with the late night food.

Kinzie Street Chop House, 400 N. Wells Street, tel: 822-0191. Clubby and sophisticated, featuring local art. Serves prime dry-aged steaks, chops, seafood and pasta dishes.

Lawry's the Prime Rib, 100 E. Ontario Street, tel: 787-5000. Roast prime rib carved tableside from a rolling cart, in one of three thicknesses. Huge salad bowls.

Morton's of Chicago, 1050 N. State Street, tel: 266-4820. Clubby atmosphere. "Menu"

consists of prime cuts on a platter. Strictly for meat eaters.

Palm Restaurant, 17 E. Monroe Street, tel: 944-0135. Specializing in steak and lobster since 1926.

Ruth's Chris Steak House, 431 N. Dearborn, tel: 321-2725. American prime steaks, lamb veal, pork chops. Fresh fish and select Creole dishes.

The Saloon, 200 E. Chestnut, tel: 280-5454. Comfortable, club-like setting. Its specialties include prime dry-aged steaks, chops, prime rib and seafood.

SWEDISH

Svea, 3258 W. Foster Avenue, tel: 539-8021. An Andersonville landmark well-known for its authentic Swedish pancakes and excellent boysenberry pie.

THAI

Star of Siam, 11 E. Illinois, tel: 670-0100.
Thai Classic, 3332 N. Clark Street, tel: 404-2000. Spicy Thai fish and other seafood, along with saté and other standards.

TURKISH

Konak, 5150 N. Clark Street, tel: 271-6688. Kebab and eggplant salad are specialties.

VEGETARIAN

Reza Restaurant, 432 W. Ontario, tel: 664-4500. *Also* 5255 N. Clark, tel: 561-1898. Persian cuisine served with raw veggies, lentil soup, rice and pita bread.

VIETNAMESE

Pasteur, 4759 N. Sheridan Road, tel: 271-6673. A critically-acclaimed café situated in Chinatown.

Lao Vien, 1129 W. Argyle Street, tel: 275-1112. A long and narrow storefront restaurant which offers diners good street views through the windows while they dine.

DRINKING NOTES

Bar, tavern, saloon, pub – in Chicago, all these terms mean someplace to get an alcoholic beverage. Some places serve food, but not all. At most bars, mixed drinks and bottled beer are available, as well as the beers "on tap" or "draft." Beer can often be bought by the pitcher. Soft drinks are always available. Soft drinks and mixed drinks will typically be served with generous amounts of ice, unless otherwise requested.

Some bars allow customers to run a tab; the waitress or bartender keeps track and presents the bill upon departure. Don't forget the tip for the waitress (15–20 percent) or bartender (10–15 percent).

Drinking and driving is dangerous, and the laws on drunk driving are extremely rigid in Illinois.

There are many different types of drinking establishments in Chicago. The neighborhood bar is usually a simple, friendly place, often with a regular crowd, where it might be easy to strike up a conversation. Theme bars have become very popular, and in Chicago the theme is sports. Hotel bars or lounges have traditionally been rather quiet and elegant, sometimes with piano music. But some of the newer ones offer more variety, such as bands or comedy.

Many Chicago bars are open late, until 1am or 2am, and some places that feature entertainment are allowed to remain open until 5am. Many downtown bars are open by midday, although neighborhood taverns are sometimes open at breakfast time.

SPORTS BARS

Sports bars represent a distinctly American concept that has been raised to an art form in Chicago. Some are owned by sports figures, some are near sports stadiums, others have a sports theme and frequently a big screen TV for watching games.

Some of the well known sports bars are:
Cubby Bear, 1059 W. Addison Street, tel: 327-1662. Across from Wrigley Field, a popular spot for Cubs games. Three 10-foot TV screens and 15 smaller monitors.

Harry Caray's, 33 W. Kinzie Street, tel: 465-9269. This bar and dining room, owned by the Cubs' announcer, is decorated with baseball photos and memorabilia.

Ranalli's Sports Bar and Grill, 1925 N. Lincoln Avenue, tel: 642-9500. Satellite sports TV on an 8-foot screen as well as 10 smaller screens. Popular with famous American athletes, fans and sports personalities.

Sluggers, 3540 N. Clark Street, tel: 248-0055. Located across from Wrigley Field, this place is packed after Cubs games. Try the batting cages for baseball practice.

THINGS TO DO

CITY

Besides its museums, festivals, sports and special events, Chicago has many attractions and tours. Here are some of the most popular in town:

Battletech Center, 435 E. Illinois Street, tel: 836-5977. Experience virtual reality when you slide into a cockpit and battle others on a computer-generated playing field.

Buckingham Fountain, Grant Park and Lakefront (Congress Parkway and Lake Shore Drive), tel: 294-2200. A wonderful, large fountain modeled on the Latona Fountain at Versailles. It operates from May 1–Oct 31 with a multi-colored light display every night from 9–11pm.

Capone's Chicago, 605 N. Clark Street, tel: 654-1919. Witness the pivotal events and personalities that created Chicago's most dangerous era, the Roaring Twenties.

Chicago Board of Trade, 141 W. Jackson Blvd, tel: 435-3590, group tours 435-3625. The largest commodity futures exchange in the world. A viewing gallery, and exhibits are on the fifth floor. Open: Monday–Friday 8am–2pm. Admission: free.

Chicago Board Options Exchange, 440 S. LaSalle Street, tel: 786-5600. Visitor's gallery open: Monday–Friday 8.30am–3.15pm.

Chicago Cultural Center, 78 E. Washington Street, tel: 744-6300. This complex features theaters, concert halls, museums, films, etc. It also offers daily free programs and exhibits covering a wide range of performing, visual and literary arts. For a listing of events dial FINE-ARTS (346-3278). Open: Monday–Thursday 9am–7pm, Friday 9am–6pm, Saturday 9am–5pm. Closed: Sunday and holidays.

Chicago Fire Academy, 558 W. De Koven Street, tel: 744-4728. Located on the site where the Chicago Fire of 1871 is believed to have started. One-hour guided tours of the facilities for training firefighters are offered. Open: Monday–Friday twice a day. Visits by appointment only. Admission: free.

Chicago Mercantile Exchange, 30 S. Wacker Drive, tel: 939-8249. Visitor's gallery open: Monday–Friday 7.30am–3.15pm. Admission: free.

Citygolf Chicago, 435 E. Illinois Street, tel: 836-5936. Two miniature golf courses depicting Chicago landmarks. For kids and adults of all ages.

Cruises. Wacky Pirate Cruise, Mercury Cruiselines, a one-hour cruise departing from the south side of the Chicago River at Michigan Avenue Friday–Sunday at 10am. Also Thursday 10am in July. Reservations are required, tel: 332-1366. Children under 12 must be accompanied by an adult.

Richard J. Daley Center Plaza, 50 W. Washington Street, tel: 346-3278. Site of Chicago's famous Picasso sculpture. There are frequent outdoor concerts during the summer, and a Christmas tree that will delight young and old in December.

Eating Out. Rock & Roll McDonald's, 600 N. Clark Street, tel: 644-7940. Eat a Big Mac in a pop-music motif.

Garfield Park Conservatory, 300 N. Central Park Boulevard, tel: 533-1281. Acres of horticultural exhibits featuring four major shows annually. Open: daily 9am–5pm. Admission: free.

John Hancock Center, 875 N. Michigan Avenue, tel: 751-3681. Visit the Observatory to view the area from one of the world's tallest buildings. Open: daily 9am–midnight.

Kids' Movies. Children's Film Festival, 1517 W. Fullerton Avenue, tel: 929-KIDS. Weekend films for younger and older children.

Kids' Theater. Beverly Art Center, 2153 W. 111th Street, tel: 445-3838. A children's theater series on Saturday afternoons for children aged three and older. Varied performances by touring companies include fairy tales and puppet shows.

Lifeline Theatre, 6912 N. Glenwood Avenue, tel: 761-4477. This theater is geared toward 5–12 year olds.

Lincoln Park Conservatory, 2400 N. Stockton Drive, tel: 294-4770. Exhibit areas include a palm house and fernery. Features four major flower shows annually. Open: daily 9am–5pm.

Lincoln Park Zoo, 2200 N. Cannon Drive, tel: 935-6700. Highlights include the Koala Exhibit, Great Ape House, Polar Bear Pool with underwater viewing window, and Birds of Prey Exhibit. Be sure to take the kids to the Children's Zoo with Discovery Center and Zoo Nursery, and the Farm in the Zoo. Open: daily 9am–5pm. Admission: free.

Midwest Stock Exchange, 440 S. LaSalle Street, tel: 663-2980. Visitor's gallery open: Monday–Friday 8.30am–3pm.

McCormick Place, 230 S. Lake Shore Drive, tel: 791-7000. The largest indoor exhibit area in the country for trade shows or conventions. **Arie Crown Theatre** is located here, tel: 791-6000. Tours are available.

Merchandise Mart, Wells Street at Chicago River, tel: 527-7600. Home to some of the most beautiful furniture and furnishings. Tours available Monday-Friday at noon. Call 644-4664 for tour information. Admission: free.

Puppet Parlor, 1922 W. Montrose Avenue, tel: 774-2919. Weekend performances including children's classics.

Puppet Shows. Animart Puppet Theatre, 3901 N. Kedzie Street, tel: 267-1209. Weekend performances featuring puppets, marionettes and audience participation.

Sears Tower, 233 S. Wacker Drive (enter on Jackson Street), tel: 875-9696. The world's tallest building. The 103rd floor skydeck at 1,353 feet above ground is reached by express elevator in just over a minute. The skydeck is open daily March-September 9am-11pm; October-February 9am-10pm.

Shopping. Saturday's Child, 2465 N. Lincoln Avenue, tel: 248-2665. FAO Schwarz, 835 N. Michigan Avenue (Watertower Place), tel: 787-8894.

The Children's Bookstore, 2465 N. Lincoln Avenue, tel: 248-2665. Books for sale, plus activities such as story hours and plays.

United Skates of America, 4836 N. Clark Street, tel: 271-5668. Two roller skating floors. Game room. Food available.

Harold Washington Public Library, 400 S. State Street, tel: 747-4310. One of the world's largest public libraries. Information services, cultural programs, exhibits, art and, of course, books. Closed on Sunday and holidays.

Water Tower Pumping Station, Pearson and Michigan streets, tel: 467-7114. Survived the Chicago Fire of 1871. Currently houses "Here's Chicago," a 45-minute sound and sight show about Chicago. Doors open daily at 9.30am with continuous shows.

Oprah Winfrey, HARPO Studios, 110 N. Carpenter Street, tel: 591-9444. Ring at least a week in advance for reservations for seats in the audience of one of America's most popular daytime television talk shows. Free.

SUBURBS

Baha'i Temple, Linden Avenue and Sheridan Road, Wilmette, tel: (708) 256-4400. This house of worship is listed in the National Register of Historic Places. There's a visitors' center with displays and presentations. Telephone for tours. Admission: free. Open: October–May 10am–5pm, May–October 10am–10pm. Service daily at 12.15pm and Sunday 3pm.

Brookfield Zoo, First Avenue and 31st Street, Brookfield, tel: (708) 242-2630. A great place to spend a day. See animals in naturalistic settings. Visit Tropic World and see the animals in tropical forest storms three times a day. There are dolphin shows in the new Seven Seas Panorama, and a children's zoo. Open: daily 10am-5pm. Admission: free Tuesday and Thursday.

Chicago Botanic Garden, Lake Cook Road, half a mile off the Edens Expressway, Glencoe, tel: (708) 835-5440. Three hundred acres of gardens, lakes, trails, greenhouses, an education center, museum, library and restaurant. Open: daily 7am–sunset, except Christmas. Admission free, but parking fee.

Drury Lane Children's Theatre, 2500 W. 95th Street, Evergreen Park, tel: (708) 779-4000. Four children's productions a year performed in the round.

Frank Lloyd Wright Home Studio, 951 Chicago Avenue, Oak Park, tel: (708) 848-1978. A walking tour is offered. The area has over 30 buildings designed by Frank Lloyd Wright. Open: daily 10am–5pm.

Kohls Children's Museum, 165 Green Bay Road, Wilmette, tel: (708) 256-6056. A hands-on museum geared toward children aged 1–10. They call themselves "a place to pretend, invent, touch explore, discover, learn." Open: Tuesday–Saturday 10am–4pm, Sunday noon–4pm.

The Lambs, Interstate 94 and Route 176, Libertyville, tel: (708) 362-4636. A community for the developmentally disabled, there's a restaurant, bakery, ice cream parlor, country store, farmyard, petting zoo, miniature golf, picnic area and special events. Open: daily 9am–5pm, except major holidays.

Marriott's Lincolnshire Theatre for Young Audiences, Lincolnshire, tel: (708) 634-0200. Sometimes includes audience participation.

Medieval Times Dinner and Tournament, 2001 N. Roselle Rd, Schaumburg, tel: (708) 843-3900. Knights on horseback compete in games of skill, combat and jousting while you enjoy a medieval feast at an 11th-century castle. Reservations required. Wednesday–Sunday.

Morton Arboretum, Route 53, Lisle, tel: (708) 719-2400. Has 1,500 acres of plants, gardens, and woodlands. Tours and special programs most Sundays. Restaurant.

Oak Park Conservatory, 617 Garfield Street, Oak Park. Exhibits of desert and tropical flora, collections of Illinois plants and displays on the specialized biology of ferns.

Riverboat Casinos. Empress River Casino, Joliet, tel: (708) 345-6789. **Harrah's Casino**, Joliet, tel: (800) 342-7724. **Hollywood Casino**, Aurora, tel: (800) 888-7777.

Santa's Village, Routes 25 and 72, Dundee, tel: (708) 426-6571. See Santa everyday. Amusement rides, shows, waterpark, picnic groves. Young children especially seem to enjoy this. Open: May–September, Monday–Friday 10am–6pm, Saturday and Sunday 11am–7pm.

Show Biz Pizza, in various suburban locations, has video games, preschool rides, skee ball and a stage with a mechanical band singing and entertaining. The kids love it. The pizza is passable.

Six Flags Great America, Interstate 94 at Route 132, Gurnee, tel: (708) 249-1776. Amusement park with over 130 rides and attractions. Don't miss the Rolling Thunder Roller Coaster. Open: May–September 10am–9pm.

BUS & WALKING TOURS

Double Decker Bus Tours, Sears Tower, Water Tower and other stops, tel: 922-8919. Narrated tours of Chicago landmarks by Chicago Motor Coach Co. Tours: daily 10am–5pm.

Culture Bus Tours (CTA), Art Institute, Michigan Avenue and Adams Street, tel: 836-7000. Guided bus tours of Chicago neighborhoods and attractions. Three routes, every half hour, 10.30am–5pm, Sunday and holidays (May–September).

Chicago Architectural Tours, 224 S. Michigan Avenue, tel: 922-8687. Walking, bus and boat tours of Chicago's world-famous architecture. There are also exhibitions, lectures, books, gifts and memorabilia dedicated to the art of design.

Chicago Supernatural Tours, PO Box 29054, tel: (708) 499-0300. Ghost tours.

Untouchable Tours, PO Box 43185, tel: 881-1195. Visit Prohibition-era gangster sites. Reservations suggested.

BOAT TOURS

Chicago From The Lake, North Pier Terminal, 509 E. Illinois Street, tel: 527-1977. Reservations required. 90-minute architectural tour. Also a children's tour.

Mercury, Chicago's Skyline Cruiseline, departs from the South Side of Chicago River at Michigan Avenue, tel: 332-1353. Also a children's cruise, tel: 332-1366.

Shoreline Marine Cruises, tel: (708) 673-3399. 30-minute cruises from north of Shedd Aquarium during the day, from dock just east of Buckingham Fountain in the evening, or Adler Planetarium day and evening.

Spirit of Chicago, South Side of Navy Pier, tel: 321-1241. Reservations required. Lunch, dinner, and moonlight cruises with entertainment. Brunch cruise on Sundays.

Star of Chicago, North Side of Navy Pier, tel: 644-5914. Reservations required. Lunch, dinner, cocktail and moonlight cruises with entertainment. Brunch cruises at weekends.

Wendella Sightseeing Boats, North Side of Chicago River at Michigan Avenue, tel: 337-1446. One to two-hour cruises.

HORSE-DRAWN CARRIAGES

Chicago Horse & Carriage Ltd, Pearson Street and Michigan Avenue, south of Water Tower Place, tel: 944-6773.

J.C. Cutters, Michigan and Chicago avenues, tel: 664-6014.

The Noble Horse, a block west of Michigan Avenue at Old Water Tower, tel: 266-7878.

MULTILINGUAL TOURS

Chicago Europe Language Center, 180 N. LaSalle Street, Suite 2510, tel: 276-6683.

Chicago Adventures Inc., 2953 W. Devon Avenue, tel: 338-7310.

On The Scene Tours, 505 N. LaSalle Street, tel: 661-1440.

CULTURE PLUS

MUSEUMS

Adler Planetarium, 1300 S. Lake Shore Drive, 322-0304. Three floors of exhibits. Multi-media sky show for all over the age of 5. Open: daily 9am–5pm, Friday 9am–9pm. Admission: free Tuesday.

Art Institute of Chicago, S. Michigan Avenue at Adams street, tel: 443-3600. World-famous collection of American and European paintings, sculptures, prints, drawings, etc. A junior museum for children. Open: Monday–Friday 10.30am–4.30pm, Tuesday 10.30am–8pm, Saturday 10am–5pm, Sunday and holidays 12pm–5pm. Admission: free Tuesday.

Chicago Academy of Sciences, 2001 N. Clark Street, tel: 871-2668. Visit life-size wildlife scenes of the Great Lakes area, a walk-through prehistoric coal forest and the dinosaur exhibit. A hands-on children's gallery. Many workshops and programs. Open: 10am–5pm daily. Admission: free Monday.

Chicago Children's Museum, 435 E. Illinois Street (North Pier Building), tel: 527-1000. Hands-on exhibits, workships and events. Open: Tuesday–Friday 12.30pm–4.30pm, Saturday and Sunday 10am–4.30pm. Preschool section only opens Wednesday, Thursday, and Friday at 10am.

Chicago Historical Society, 1601 N. Clark Street, tel: 642-4600. Museum and research center for Chicago and American history, includes a diorama room depicting scenes from Chicago history. Open: 9.30am–4.30pm

Monday–Saturday, noon–5pm Sunday. Admission: free Monday.

Chicago Maritime Museum, North Pier Chicago, tel: 836-4343. Exhibits of Midwestern and Great Lakes maritime history.

DuSable Museum of African-American History, 740 E. 56th Place, tel: 947-0600. History and culture of Africans and Americans of African descent. Open: Monday–Friday 9am–5pm, Saturday and Sunday noon–5pm.

Field Museum of Natural History, Roosevelt Road and S. Lake Shore Drive, tel: 922-9410. Visit an Egyptian tomb including burial chambers, see mummies on display, and explore Egyptian life. There's plenty of hands-on experience in "Place of Wonder" and "Sizes" to make it fun for kids. Open: 9am–5pm daily. Admission: free Wednesday.

Hull House, 800 S. Halsted Street, tel: 413-5353. A museum dedicated to the settlement house movement and its founder, Jane Addams. Open: Monday–Friday 10am–4pm, Sunday noon–5pm.

International Museum of Surgical Science, 1516 N. Lake Shore Drive, tel: 642-6502. An insight to the history of surgery, with lurid graphics on tumors, amputations and Napoleon's death mask.

Museum of Broadcast Communications, Chicago Cultural Center, 78 E. Washington, tel: 629-6000. Tapes of old TV and radio shows are available. Exhibits include the original Charlie McCarthy and Mortimer Snerd Puppets. Open: Monday–Saturday 10am–4.30pm, Sunday noon–5pm.

Museum of Contemporary Art, 237 E. Ontario Street, tel: 280-5161. Emphasis on 20th-century painting and performance art. Changing exhibits. Open: Tuesday–Saturday 10am–5pm, Sunday noon–5pm. Admission: free Tuesday.

Museum of Contemporary Photography, 600 S. Michigan Avenue, tel: 663-5554. Traces the development of photography, with both special exhibits and a permanent collection.

Museum of Holography, 1134 W. Washington Boulevard, tel: 226-1007. Holographic art from around the world including moving and computer generated holograms. Special exhibits. Open: Wednesday–Sunday 12.30pm–5pm.

Museum of Science and Industry, 57th at Lake Shore Drive, tel: 684-1414. More than 2,000 exhibits, most designed for visitor participation. See the full scale replica of an underground coal mine, a World War II German submarine and hatching chicks. Visit the **Henry Crown Space Center and Omnimax Theater**. Open: Monday–Friday 9.30am–4pm, Saturday, Sunday and holidays 9.30am–5.30pm, Memorial Day–Labor Day 9.30am–5.30pm daily. Admission: free Thursday (except Omnimax).

Oriental Institute, 1155 E. 58th Street, tel: 702-9520. Part of University of Chicago. Five galleries display artifacts of ancient Near East. Open: Tuesday–Saturday 10am–4pm, Sunday noon–4pm. Admission: free.

Peace Museum, 350 W. Ontario, tel: 440-1860. Exhibits and programs related to war and peace. Open: Tuesday-Saturday 11am-5pm.

Polish Museum of America, 984 N. Milwaukee Avenue, tel: 384-3352. Ethnic museum of Polish art and dress. Special events on weekends. Open: daily noon-5pm.

Printing Museum, 731 S. Plymouth Court, tel: 987-1059. A Printer's Row museum with exhibits on the history and development of printing processes.

Shedd Aquarium, 1200 S. Lake Shore Drive, tel: 939-2426. World's largest indoor aquarium with fresh and saltwater fish. Watch the divers hand-feed the sharks, turtles and other fish in the coral reef in the aquarium. Visit Beluga whales and dolphins in the oceanarium. Open: 9am–6pm daily. Admission: free Thursday to aquarium only. Admission tickets can be pre-purchased through Ticketmaster, tel: 559-1212.

Smart Museum, 5550 S. Greenwood Avenue, tel: 702-0200. On the University of Chicago campus: ancient to contemporary art.

Maurice Spertus Museum of Judaica, 618 S. Michigan Avenue, tel: 922-9012. A celebration of Jewish culture through art, along with exhibits recalling the Holocaust.

Swedish American Museum, 5211 N. Clark Sreett. Features pictures and artifacts of Swedish immigrants' contributions to the growth of Chicago. Open: Tuesday–Friday 11am–4pm, Saturday and Sunday 11am–3pm.

Terra Museum of American Art, 666 N. Michigan Avenue, tel: 664-3939. American art from 17th–20th century. Open: Tuesday noon–8pm, Wednesday–Saturday 10am–5pm, Sunday noon–5pm.

CONCERTS

Classical

Chicago Symphony Orchestra, Orchestra Hall (September–May), 220 S. Michigan Avenue, tel: 435-8111 for tickets, 435-8122 for schedule. In summer, at Ravina, Highland Park, tel: 728-4642.

Grant Park Symphony Orchestra, Free concerts through the Chicago Park District at Petrillo Band Shell, Grant Park, tel: 294-2420.

Orchestra of Illinois, 506 S. Wabash, tel: 341-1975.

Popular Music

Park West, 322 W. Armitage Avenue, tel: 929-5959.

Alpine Valley Music Theater, East Troy, Wisconsin, tel: 899-SHOW.

Poplar Creek Music Theatre, 4777 W. Higgins Road, Hoffman Estates, tel: (708) 559-1212. Outdoor concerts.

Rosemont Horizon, 6920 N. Mannhein Road, Rosemont, tel: 559-1212.

Ravinia, Highland Park, tel: RAV-INIA, features varied music acts (including jazz, classical, R&B, dance) that can be heard and seen from the pavilion, or from the grassy picnic area.

World Music Theatre, 183rd Street and Oak Park Avenue, Tinley Park, tel: 559-1212. Nice suburban location but public transportation is not available.

BALLET

Ballet Chicago, 222 S. Riverside Plaza, tel: 993-7575. Studio at 1016 N. Dearborn Street, tel: 664-6888.

Hubbard Street Dance Co., 218 Wabash Avenue, tel: 663-1642.

OPERA

Lyric Opera of Chicago, 20 N. Wacker Drive, tel; 332-2244. (September–February) Hard to get tickets for these popular performances.

Chicago Opera Theatre, 20 E. Jackson Boulevard, tel: 663-0555.

The Light Opera Works, 927 Noyes, Evanston, tel: (708) 869-6300. (June–December). Specializes in Gilbert and Sullivan.

THEATERS

For a current listing, phone Curtain Call, 977-1755. Tickets are generally available at the box office, sometimes by mail, and through Ticketron, tel: TIC-KETS or Ticketmaster, tel: 559-1212. Another ticket source is Hot Tix which sells half-price (plus service charge) tickets for same-day performances, and full-price advance tickets. Call 977-1755 for locations and availability.

DOWNTOWN

Arie Crown Theater, 2300 S. Lake Shore Drive, tel: 791-6000. In McCormick Place, primarily road companies of Broadway shows. The place to see *The Nutcracker* at Christmas.

Auditorium Theater, 70 E. Congress Parkway, tel: 922-2110. Great acoustics.

Goodman Theater, 200 S. Columbus Drive, tel: 443-3800. Specializes in contemporary work with many well-known actors.

Kuumba Theatre, 1900 W. Van Buren Street, tel: 461-9000.

Shubert Theatre, 22 W. Monroe Street, tel: 977-1700.

OFF LOOP

Beverly Art Center, 2153 W. 111th Street, tel: 445-3838. An active art center with a Saturday afternoon children's series performed by traveling groups.

Body Politic Theatre, 2261 N. Lincoln Avenue, tel: 871-3000. Comedies and satires.

Court Theatre, 5535 S. Ellis Street (on campus of the University of Chicago), tel: 753-4472. Classics.

Organic Theater Co., 3319 N. Clark Street, tel: 327-5588. Performance art.

Steppenwolf Theater, 2851 N. Halsted Street, tel: 335-1650. National reputation for method acting. Alumni include John Malkovich.

Theatre on the Lake, Fullerton Parkway and the Lakefront. Strictly community theater performing well-known Broadway shows at 8pm Tuesday through Saturday during the summer.

Victory Gardens Theater, 2257 N. Lincoln Avenue, tel: 871-3000. Serious plays. Very professional.

Wisdom Bridge Theatre, 1559 W. Howard Street, tel: 743-6442.

SUBURBAN

Candlelight Dinner Playhouse, 5620 S. Harlem Avenue, Summit, tel: (708) 496-3000.
Drury Lane/Oakbrook Terrace, 100 Drury Lane, Oakbrook Tce, tel: (708) 530-8300.
Marriott's Lincolnshire Theatre, Route 21 and Milwaukee Road, Lincolnshire, tel: (708) 634-0200.
Pheasant Run Theatre, Route 64, St Charles, tel: (708) 584-6300.
Village Players, shared by the suburbs of Oak Park and River Forest, a small theater with locals taking roles in many of the famous Broadway shows.

MOVIES

Cinemas are plentiful in the suburbs. Their numbers have shrunk in the downtown area. Here are the main ones:
Watertower, 845 N. Michigan Avenue, tel: 649-5790.
McClurg Court, 330 E. Ohio Street, tel: 642-0723.
Biograph, 2433 N. Lincoln Avenue, tel: 348-4123 (Note: this is where Dillinger was gunned down by the FBI).
Chestnut Station, Clark and Chestnut streets, tel: 337-7301.
Burnham Plaza, 826 S. Wabash Avenue, tel: 922-1090; 900 N. Michigan Ave, tel: 787-1988.
All of the above, except the Biograph, are wheelchair accessible; all except the Watertower have sound systems for the hearing impaired. Often children under six are not admitted, so check in advance. For additional theaters, or to check what's currently playing, check a local newspaper.

FOREIGN FILMS

Fine Arts Theatre, 418 S. Michigan Avenue, tel: 939-3700. A good selection of foreign and domestic independent films.
Music Box Theatre, 3733 N. Southport Avenue, tel: 871-6604. Beautiful old-fashioned movie house with premieres, previews and classic American and foreign films.

DIARY OF EVENTS

There's almost always something going on in Chicago. For the latest information on entertainment and events, turn to the local newspapers, especially on Friday when comprehensive weekend listings are printed. Here are some annual events:

JANUARY

Chicago Boat, Sports and RV Show, McCormick Place, tel: 836-4740.
Chicago Sport Fishing, Travel and Outdoor Show, O'Hare Expo Center, Rosemont, tel: (708) 692-2220.
Chinese New Year Parade, Wentworth Avenue and Cermak Road, tel: 326-5320.

FEBRUARY

Chicago Auto Show, McCormick Place, tel: 791-7000.
Azalea and Camellia Show, Lincoln Park Conservatory, tel: 294-4770. Garfield Park Conservatory, tel: 533-1281.

MARCH

Medinah Shrine Circus, Medinah Temple, 600 N. Wabash Avenue, tel: 266-5050.
Ice Capades, Rosemont Horizon, Rosemont, tel: (708) 635-6601.
St Patrick's Day, parade starts at Dearborn Street and Wacker Drive, tel: 263-6612.
South Side Irish Parade, 103rd Street and Western Avenue, tel: 238-1969. A similar celebration which takes place the weekend before St Patrick's Day.

APRIL

Antique Show, O'Hare Expo Center, tel: (708) 692-2220.
Spring and Easter Flower Show, Lincoln Park Conservatory, tel: 294-4770.

MAY

Chicago International Art Expo, Navy Pier, tel: 787-6858.
Buckingham Fountain Re-Opens, Grant Park, tel: 294-2493.

JUNE

Western Open, Butler Golf Course, Oakbrook, tel: (800) 458-5535.
International Theater Festival of Chicago,

includes various theaters, tel: 644-3370.

Chicago Gospel Festival, Petrillo Band Shell, Grant Park, tel: 744-3315.

Chicago Blues Festival, Petrillo Band Shell, Grant Park, tel: 744-3315.

Old Town Art Fair, 1900 N. Lincoln Avenue, tel: 337-1938.

Chicago International Boat Show, Navy Pier, tel: 787-6858.

Water Tower Arts and Crafts Festival, Chicago Avenue between Michigan Avenue and Lake Shore Drive, tel: 991-4748.

Taste of Chicago, Grant Park, tel: 744-3315. June 27–July 4. A very popular event, featuring lots of food from a variety of Chicago restaurants. Music, too.

Printers Row Book Fair, Dearborn and Harrison streets, tel: 987-1980.

Beverly Art Fair, Beverly Art Center, 2153 W. 111th St, tel: 445-3838.

Ravinia, opens for a summer full of outdoor concerts, Highland Park, tel: RAV-INIA.

Grant Park Concerts, Petrillo Band Shell, Grant Park, tel: 294-2420. Free concerts by the Grant Park Symphony Orchestra.

JULY

Taste of Chicago, continues in Grant Park, tel: 744-3315. The festival culminates with a spectacular fireworks display over Lake Michigan, accompanied by the Grant Park Symphony Orchestra performing Tchaikovsky's *1812 Overture*.

Fourth of July, fireworks on the lakefront and in almost every Chicago neighborhood.

Air and Water Show, North Avenue Beach, tel: 294-2200.

Taste of Lincoln Avenue, food fair between Fullerton and Wrightwood avenues, tel: 472-9046.

Old St Patrick's World's Largest Block Party, Adams and Des Plaines Streets, tel: 782-6171.

Chicago to Mackinac Yacht Races, sailing from Monroe Street Harbor, tel: 861-7777.

AUGUST

Gold Coast Art Fair, River North, Wells and Ontario streets, tel: 280-5740.

Bud Billiken Parade, 35th Street and South King Drive, tel: 225-2400.

Chicago International Sky Nights, Lakefront, tel: 744-3315.

Venetian Night Boat Parade, Monroe Harbor, tel: 744-3315.

Antique Show, O'Hare Expo Center, tel: (708) 692-2220.

Chicago Jazz Festival, Petrillo Band Shell, Grant Park, tel: 744-3315.

Illinois State Fair, Springfield (not Chicago), tel: (217) 782-6661.

SEPTEMBER

Viva Chicago, Grant Park, tel: 744-3315.

Ribfest, Grant Park, tel: 222–3232. Backyard chefs compete for the title of best barbecue artist in town.

Berghoff Oktoberfest, Adams Street, from State to Dearborn streets, tel: 427-3170.

Chicago Bears, season-opening games, Soldier Field, tel: 295-6600.

Lyric Opera, season-opening concerts, Civic Center for Performing Arts, tel: 346-0270.

Chicago Symphony Orchestra, season-opening concerts, Orchestra Hall, tel: 435-6666.

OCTOBER

Columbus Day Parade, Dearborn Street and Wacker Drive, tel: 828-0010.

Chicago International Film Festival, various theaters, tel: 644-3400.

History Mystery Bicycle Tour and Festival, 96th Street and Longwood Drive, tel: 233-3100. A puzzle-solving bicycle tour, followed by food, music and games.

NOVEMBER

Antique Show, O'Hare Expo Center, tel: (708) 692-2220.

Craft Show, O'Hare Expo Center, tel: (708) 692-2220.

Christmas Around the World, Museum of Science and Industry, tel: 684-1414. Christmas trees as decorated in various countries.

Lighting of the City's Christmas Tree, Daley Center Plaza, tel: 744-3315.

Christmas Parade, Michigan Avenue from Balbo to Wacker drives, tel: 935-8747.

DECEMBER

A Christmas Carol, Goodman Theater, tel: 443-3800.

The Nutcracker, Arie Crown Theater, tel: 791-6000.

Caroling to the Animals, Lincoln Park Zoo, tel: 294-4662.
Christmas Flower Show, Lincoln Park Conservatory, tel: 294-4770.

NIGHTLIFE

There is plenty of nightlife in Chicago. Most hotels have one or more lounges, many of which are popular spots. The local newspapers and listings magazines have descriptions. Many places never have cover charges, while some do only on weekends.

NIGHT SPOTS

America's Bar, 219 W. Erie St, tel: 915-5986. A mainstream dance bar.
Baja Beach Club, North Pier, 401 E. Illinois St, tel: 222-1992. Disco, cabaret, restaurant. Often a wait to get in.
Cabaret Metro, 3730 N. Clark St, tel: 549-0203. Dance to rock music.
Excalibur, 632 N. Dearborn St, tel: 266-1944. Another popular spot, again with long lines. Three floors.
Gamekeepers Tavern and Grill, 1971 N. Lincoln Ave, tel: 549-0400. Young professionals.
Ginger Man, 3740 N. Clark St, tel: 787-8141. Exotic beers, big pool tables.
Goose Island Brewing Co., 1800 N. Clybourne Ave, tel: 915-0071. Serves home-brewed beer.
Ka-Boom, 747 N. Green St, tel: 243-4800. River West location. Six different environments from hot dance to cool jazz.
Pyramid Room of Cairo, 720 N. Wells St, tel: 266-6620. River North location. Ambiance of an Egyptian desert oasis.
Sheffields, 3258 N. Sheffield Ave, tel: 281-4989. An easy-going corner bar, with many brands of beer and a summer beer garden.
Smart Bar, 3730 N. Clark St, tel: 549-4140. Haven for Chicago's black-clad hipsters.
Whiskey River, 1997 N. Clybourn Ave, tel: 528-3400. Country nightclub with free dance lessons every night. Live music Wed-Sat.

SINGLES BARS

The Rush Street area has traditionally been considered the place for singles bars. Caters to the under-40 crowd, and a good number of tourists. Parking is hard to find. Among the most popular bars are:
Bamboo Bernie's, 2247 N. Lincoln Ave, tel: 549-3900. Tropical drinks. Indoor beach volleyball.
Bootleggers, 13 W. Division, tel: 266-0944.
Butch McGuires, 20 W. Division St, tel: 337-9080.
Mother's, 26 W. Division St, tel: 642-7251.
She-Nannigans, 16 W. Division St, tel: 642-2344.
Snuggery, 15 W. Division St, tel: 337-4349.

BLUES CLUBS

As the home of Chicago blues, the guitar-driven music form that evolved from the downhome Mississippi Delta folk music and then had so much influence on modern rock, the city still has a number of clubs and bars devoted almost exclusively to the form, and often featuring many of the legendary bluesmen. They include:
Biddy Mulligan's, 7644 N. Sheridan Road, tel: 761-6532.
Blue Chicago on Clark, 536 N. Clark St, tel: 661-0100. 1940s-style bar.
BLUES, 2519 N. Halsted St, tel: 528-1012.
Blues Chicago, 937 N. State St, tel: 642-6261.
BLUES Etcetera, 1124 West Belmont Ave, tel: 525-8989.
Kingston Mines, 2548 N. Halsted St, tel: 477-4646.
Legends, 754 S. Wabash Ave (owned by guitar great, Buddy Guy), tel: 427-0333.
Lilly's, 2513 N. Lincoln Ave, tel: 525-2422.
New Checkerboard Lounge, 423 E. 43rd St, tel: 624-3240. (Considered a rough area. Home of the Blues Hall of Fame.)
Wise Fool's Pub, 2270 N. Lincoln Ave, tel: 929-1510.

JAZZ CLUBS

Andy's, 11 E. Hubbard St, tel: 642-6805.
The Bulls, 1916 N. Lincoln Park West, tel: 337-3000.

Cotton Club, 1710 S. Michigan Ave, tel: 341-9787.
Gold Star Sardine Bar, 680 N. Lake Shore Drive, tel: 664-4215.
Green Mill, 4802 N. Broadway, tel: 878-5552. A legendary jazz club once owned and frequented by gangsters. Now there's good music every night except Monday, when local would-be poets recite their material for praise or heckling in the "Poetry Slam."
Jazz Showcase, 636 S. Michigan Ave, tel: 427-4300.
Kiku's, 754 W. Wellington St, tel: 281-7878.
Milt Trenier's Nite Club, 610 N. Fairbanks Ct, tel: 266-6226. Live jazz/blues nightly.
The Other Place, 7600 S. King Drive, tel: 874-5476.
Oz, 2917 N. Sheffield Ave, tel: 957-8100.
Pop's for Champagne, 2934 N. Sheffield, tel: 472-1000. Nightly live jazz in champagne bar. Sunday brunch.

LOCAL BARS

Chicago also claims to have invented the American sports bar, though most places now calling themselves such are not the old shot-and-a-beer neighborhood joints, but rather trendy spots popular among both men and women, including some who aren't necessarily interested in the latest scores. See "Drinking Notes" for details.

CABARET & COMEDY CLUBS

Funny Firm, 318 W. Grand St, tel: 321-9500. River North location. Up and coming local talent and national standup comedians.
The Improv, 504 N. Wells St, tel: 527-3286. Largest club in Chicago. Nationally recognized standup comics. Children's variety show on Saturday afternoons.
Second City, 1616 N. Wells St, tel: 337-3992. Improvisation. This famous spot was a springboard for Jim and John Belushi, Bill Murray, Dan Akroyd and John Candy, to name a few.
Zanies, 1548 N. Wells St, tel: 337-4027. First full-time comedy club in Chicago. Local and national talent.

SHOPPING

SHOPPING HOURS

Most stores and shops open at 9 or 10am and stay open until at least 6pm; many often remain open until 8 or 9pm.

SHOPPING AREAS

Downtown has its share of boutiques, fashion shops and galleries, along with several of America's best department stores and a myriad of cheaper chain stores, discount houses and manufacturers' outlets. Chicago has enthusiastically embraced the concept of the shopping center, and now the shopping mall. A number of shopping centers and districts can be recommended for the quality and variety of their shops, and for the exciting innovation of their design.

WHERE TO SHOP

Chicago Place Mall, 700 N. Michigan Ave, tel: 642-4811. Fifty specialty shops including Saks Fifth Avenue and Louis Vuitton. Eighth floor food court in a tropical garden. European gourmet supermarket.
Gurnee Mills Outlet Mall, Interstate 94 and Route 132, Gurnee, tel (800) YES-SHOP. Over 200 stores, manufacturers' and retail outlets offering savings on top-name brands.
Magnificent Mile, Michigan Avenue from Chicago River to Oak Street. Glamorous shopping area including Tiffany, Cartier, Chanel, Ralph Lauren, Saks Fifth Avenue, I. Magnin and Bonwit Teller.
Nike Town Chicago, 669 N. Michigan Ave, tel: 642-6363. Nike shoes, clothes, hats, posters and displays. A one-of-a-kind sport store.
Northbrook Court, in suburban Northbrook, is an enclosed, upscale mall whose 144 shops are aimed at the country-club set.
900 North Michigan Shops, 900 N. Michigan Ave. This is home to the Chicago branch

of Bloomingdales, plus dozens of boutiques and specialty shops, including Gucci. Also restaurants and theaters.

North Pier, 435 E. Illinois St, tel: 836-4300. A relatively new area offering restaurants, shopping, night clubs, and museums. **Oak Street** consists of renovated brownstones, and its outstanding specialty shops emphasize diversity and quality. A fun place to window shop.

Old Orchard, in suburban Skokie, is a large, well-designed mall aimed at providing a pleasing, everyday shopping experience.

State Street, Carson Pirie Scott & Co., at State and Madison Streets, tel: 744-2000, and Marshall Fields, at 111 N. State St, tel: 781-4917, each have department stores here. Open: Mon and Thurs 9.45am–7.30pm; other days: 9.45am–5.45pm; one Sunday a month.

Water Tower Place, 835 N. Michigan Ave, tel: 440-3165. An atrium shopping mall with Marshall Fields, Lord & Taylor and seven floors of specialty shops. Plenty of restaurants and movie theaters too. Open: Mon–Fri 10 am–7pm (Marshall Fields until 8pm, Lord & Taylor until 9pm), Sat 10am–6pm, Sun 12 noon–6pm.

Woodfield Mall, in suburban Schaumburg, tel: (708) 330-0220, has 235 shops and stores and is reputed to be the second-largest mall in the United States. Buses run regularly from downtown and elsewhere.

SOUVENIRS

Accent Chicago, 835 N. Michigan Ave (Water Tower, 7th floor), tel: 944-1354. Complete Chicago themed gift store.
Chicago Tribune Gift Store, 435 N. Michigan Ave, tel: 222-3080. Unique gifts.
Hello Chicago, 700 N. Michigan, tel: 787-0838. Large selection of T-shirts and sweatshirts with Chicago scenes.

SALES TAX

The sales tax in Chicago is 8 percent: 7 percent for the state of Illinois and another 1 percent for the city of Chicago. The sales tax is added to the listed cost of almost everything, including books, food and clothing. Unlike many European countries, where the value-added tax can be deducted when purchases are being exported, there are no provisions for reimbursement of the sales tax.

CLOTHING CHART

Women's Dresses/Suits

American	Continental	British
6	38/34N	8/30
8	40/36N	10/32
10	42/38N	12/34
12	44/40N	14/36
14	46/42N	16/38
16	48/44N	18/40

Women's Shoes

American	Continental	British
4½	36	3
5½	37	4
6½	38	5
7½	39	6
8½	40	7
9½	41	8
10½	42	9

Men's Suits

American	Continental	British
34	44	34
—	46	36
38	48	38
—	50	40
42	52	42
—	54	44
46	56	46

Men's Shirts

American	Continental	British
14	36	14
14½	37	14½
15	38	15
15½	39	15½
16	40	16
16½	41	16½
17	42	17

Men's Shoes

American	Continental	British
6½	—	6
7½	40	7
8½	41	8
9½	42	9
10½	43	10
11½	44	11

SPORTS

SPECTATOR

Baseball: Two major league teams make their homes in Chicago, playing from early April through early October. The Chicago Cubs play in the National League. Their home park is **Wrigley Field**, the oldest park in the major leagues. Located at Clark and Addison Streets (1060 W. Addison St), Wrigley can be reached by the Howard "El" train. Spend an afternoon or an evening (possible since the highly controversial installation of lights in 1988) amid the ivy-covered walls. For tickets, tel: 559-1212; to reach the office, tel: 924-1000.

The Chicago White Sox play in the American League. They can be seen at **Comiskey Park**, just off the Dan Ryan Expressway at 35th and Shields Streets. The park can be reached on the Dan Ryan "El" Line. To get tickets, tel: 559-1212; for any other information, tel: 924-1000.

Basketball: The Chicago Bulls entertain their fans at **United Center**, 1901 W. Madison St, which can be reached on the Madison Street Bus No. 20. Tel: 455-4000.

Football: The Chicago Bears play at **Soldier Field,** at 12th Street and the lakefront. Tel: 663-5100.

Ice Hockey: The Chicago Black Hawks play in **United Center**, 1901 W. Madison St. Tel: 455-7000.

Racetracks: The Chicago area has a number of tracks where horse racing, both thoroughbred and harness, can be enjoyed, including Arlington, which has been completely rebuilt "family style" after burning down a few years ago. **Arlington International Racecourse**, Euclid and Wilke Streets, Arlington Heights, tel: (708) 255-4300. **Balmoral Park Racetrack**, I-394 and the Calumet Expy, Crete, tel: 568-5700. **Hawthorne Downs Racetrack,** 3501 S. Laramie Ave, Cicero, tel: (708) 780-3700. **Maywood Park Race-**track, North Avenue and 5th Street, Maywood, tel: 626-4816. **Sportsman's Park Racetrack**, 3301 S. Laramie Ave, Cicero, tel: 242-1121. **Off-Track Betting Facilities**, 177 N. State St, tel: 419-8787; 233 W. Jackson Blvd, tel: 427-2300.

Auto Racing: Raceway Park, 130th Street and Ashland Ave, Calumet Park, tel: (708) 385-4035. **Santa Fe Speedway**, 9100 S. Wolf Road, Hinsdale, tel: (708) 839-1050.

Polo: Oak Brook Polo Club, 2700 S. York Road, Oak Brook, tel: (708) 571-7657.

PARTICIPANT

The Chicago Park District, tel: 294-2493, is a source of information for most sports.

Bowling: Marina City Bowling Lanes, 300 N. State St, tel: 527-0747.

Bicycling: A 20-mile path runs along the lakefront. Bicycle rentals are available through Bike Chicago at three locations: Oak Street Beach at Division, Buckingham Fountain, and Lincoln Park Zoo at Fullerton. Tel: (800) 915-2453. Tours available, or use a free self-guided Chicago tour map.

Canoeing: Chicagoland Canoe Base, 4019 N. Narragansett Ave, is a source for rentals and information, tel: 779-1489. American Youth Hostels (tel: 327-8114) and the Field Museum (tel: 922-9410) arrange trips.

Cross-Country Skiing: Chicago's flat lands are ideal, especially in the parks or in the forest preserves, tel: 261-8400.

Fishing: A license is required to fish in Illinois. It can be obtained at City Hall, 121 N. LaSalle Street, the State of Illinois Center, 100 W. Randolph Street, or some tackle shops or currency exchanges. For information on fishing spots call: Chicago Sportfishing Association, Burnham Park Harbor, tel: 922-1100; the Forest Preserve District, tel: 261-8400; or the Illinois Dept. of Conservation, tel: 814-2070.

Golf: The Chicago Park District, tel: 294-2200, has a number of nine-hole courses and one 18-hole course: Jackson Park, 63rd Street and Stony Island (18 holes); Robert A. Black, 2045 W. Pratt Blvd; Columbus Park, 5700 W. Jackson Blvd; Marquette Park, 6700 S. Kedzie St; South Shore Country Club, 71st Street and South Shore Drive; Waveland, 3600 N. Lake Shore Drive.

In addition, many of the surrounding suburbs have courses open to the public. They may be a bit more expensive, but they're generally nicer courses.

Ice Skating: McFetridge Sports Complex, 3845 N. California Ave, has indoor skating, tel: 478-0210. Outdoor skating is available when the weather is suitably cold at Daley Centennial Plaza, 337 E. Randolph St, tel: 294-4790.

Jogging: The path along the lakefront is shared by bicyclists and joggers. Avoid jogging in deserted areas after dark. For additional information, contact the Chicago Area Runners Association, tel: 666-9836.

Racquetball: Park District and McFetridge Sports Complex, tel: 478-0210.

Swimming: The Chicago Park District has 31 beaches along Lake Michigan. The beaches are open from June 15 to Labor Day, from 9am–9.30pm. Lifeguards are on duty, and no alcohol is allowed. For information, tel: 294-2333.

Tennis: Tennis courts are available throughout the city, generally without charge. The Chicago Park District can advise on the nearest courts, tel: 294-2493.

Tobogganing: A number of toboggan slides are located in the Cook County Forest Preserves, tel: 261-8400. Toboggans can be rented at each location.

SPECIAL INFORMATION

DOING BUSINESS

If you're interested in doing business in Chicago, or starting a business in Chicago, there are many sources of information:

Illinois Department of Commerce and Community Affairs, International Business Division, tel: (312) 814-7164.

Chicagoland Chamber of Commerce, tel: (312) 580-6900.

International Visitors' Center, tel: (312) 645-1836. Resources and contacts at all levels in business. They can also help you set up itineraries, especially for groups.

CHILDREN

Chicago is a great place to bring kids. Many hotels let children stay in their parents' room for a small charge or for free; ask when making reservations. Many restaurants can provide a special children's menu – usually for children under 12, with smaller portions and lower prices.

Pick up a copy of *Chicago Parents*, a free monthly magazine usually available in libraries or children's bookstores, which lists events of interest to children and their families. Copies or annual subscriptions are available from: Wednesday Journal, Inc., 141 S. Oak Park Ave, Oak Park, IL 60302, tel: (708) 386-5555.

RECOMMENDED FOR CHILDREN

A dozen things to do with children:

Art Institute's Junior Museum, South Michigan Avenue at Adams Street, tel: 443-3600. The Junior Museum offers an assortment of absorbing activities for children of all ages. There are workshops, tours and demonstrations, including such things as puppet making and calligraphy. Some games send children throughout the museum in search of clues.

Brookfield Zoo, First Avenue and 31st Street, Brookfield, tel: (708) 485-0263. Children especially enjoy the Children's Zoo, where they can touch the animals, watch the cows being milked and just get close. Brookfield has an annual "Teddy Bear Picnic" in June, and an annual Halloween party with a costume parade.

Chicago Children's Museum, 435 E. Illinois St (North Pier), tel: 527-1000. This museum is made for inquisitive kids, and even has a preschool section. Everything is hands-on. There are family workshops on weekends, and everyday fun such as enclosing yourself in a giant bubble

Chicago Cultural Center, 78 E. Washington St, tel: 269-2835. The Cultural Center offers a variety of programs for children presented by the Thomas Hughes Children's Library. Call for details.

Field Museum of Natural History, Roosevelt Road and Lake Shore Drive, tel: 922-9410. There are many exhibits for children, like the giant dinosaurs and Egyptian mummies. The Place of Wonder is specifically for kids, and the Sizes exhibit has lots of fun things to try. Workshops are offered on weekends.

Kohl Children's Museum, 165 Green Bay Road, Wilmette, tel: (708) 251-7781. A hands-on museum geared toward kids. Exhibits rotate throughout the year, plus there are story times and puppet shows. The learning store offers a variety of creative toys.

The Lambs, Interstate 94 and Route 176, Libertyville, tel: (708) 362-4636. Something for everyone. Kids will probably like the ice cream parlor and bakery. There's a farmyard to visit, a petting zoo and miniature golf, plus a picnic area and a restaurant. And special events are held throughout the year.

Lincoln Park Zoo, 2200 N. Cannon Drive, tel: 935-6700. A free zoo right in the city. Children will enjoy everything, especially the Children's Zoo, where they can pet some of the animals, and the Farm in the Zoo. Very popular is the underwater viewing window in the Polar Bear Pool. Paddle boats may be rented on the zoo pond.

Museum of Science and Industry, 57th Street at Lake Shore Drive, tel: 684-1414. There's so much to do here. Favorites include Colleen Moore's Fairy Castle, Hatching Chicks and a giant train set. For the younger children, find the Curiosity Place.

Santa's Village, Routes 25 and 72, Dundee, tel: (708) 426-6751. Amusement rides, especially for younger children, shows that the whole family can enjoy, a water park and picnic groves are among the attractions. But best of all, Santa is always there.

Shedd Aquarium, 1200 S. Lake Shore Drive, tel: 939-2426. The world's largest fishbowl. A favorite spot is the Coral Reef at feeding time as the turtles, sharks and other fish are fed by hand.

Six Flags Great America, I-94 at Route 132, Gurnee, tel: (708) 249-1776. The largest amusement park around. Plenty of rides and shows for one admission fee. (It's fairly expensive so plan on spending the whole day.) For some thrill-seekers, the roller coasters alone make the trip worthwhile.

ALTERNATIVE LIFESTYLES

The hub of Chicago's gay community is Lakeview East, or New Town as it's often called. Halsted, Broadway and Clark Streets between Diversey and Addison Streets is the approximate area for many shops owned and supported by gays.

The City of Chicago has a gay liaison officer who can be contacted on 744-4152.

Gay and Lesbian Pride Week is celebrated each year in late June, and culminates with a popular gay and lesbian pride parade.

Gays are very much a part of everyday life in Chicago, but there are also many places, organizations and publications that specialize in gay life.

Gay Publications: *Windy City Times*, 970 W. Montana, tel: 935-1974. *Outlines*, 3059 N. Southport Ave, tel: 871-7610. *Gay Chicago Magazine*, 3121 N. Broadway, tel: 327-7271.

Gay Community Service: Horizons Community Services, Inc., 3225 N. Sheffield Ave, has a gay and lesbian helpline, tel: 929-4357, offering confidential counseling and references.

Howard Brown Memorial Clinic, 945 W. George St, tel: 871-5777, provides confidential diagnosis and treatment.

Gay Politics: Illinois Gay and Lesbian Task Force, 615 W. Wellington Ave, tel: 975-0707, is an organization involved in civil rights issues and educating the public.

Gay Choruses: Chicago Gay Men's Chorus, tel: 275-7295.

Windy City Gay Chorus, tel: 404-9242.

Gay Library: Gerber-Hart Library, 3352 N. Paulina, tel: 883-3003. This is Chicago's premier gay and lesbian library and resource center. Gerber-Hart's circulating collection consists of nearly 6,000 books and periodicals, plus an archive.

Gay Bars: There are many bars in the Lakeview East area. Some are strictly gay or lesbian, others welcome all. Wander through the neighborhood, or pick up one of the publications that lists area bars. Some possibilities:

The Legacy, 3042 W. Irving Park Road, tel: 588-9405. Opened since 1961, formerly the "21 Club."

Lost and Found, 3058 W. Irving Park Road, tel: 463-9617. Opened in 1965, a lesbian bar.

Vortex Nightclub, 3631 N. Halsted, tel: 975-6622. Nightclub and dance bar with light show. Multi-level complex. Theme parties.

PHYSICALLY CHALLENGED

Chicago tries to make itself accessible to the handicapped. Almost all the museums and many restaurants have wheelchair access. The City of Chicago Department on Aging and Disability offers information and referral at tel: 744-4016 (TDD & Voice), or tel: 744-6777 (TDD only). The city also offers a 24-hour information hotline for those with impaired hearing, tel: 744-8599 (TDD).

Door-to-door transportation can be arranged for those with limited mobility through special services, tel: 521-1154. It can be difficult to get rides at certain times, so try to plan ahead. It would be wise to have a statement from a doctor verifying the disability. Access Living, although aimed primarily at residents, will provide assistance with travel for visitors.

Contact Access Living, 851 W. Van Buren St, Suite 525, Chicago, IL 60607, tel: 226-5900. Wheelchair Getaways of Illinois, Inc, PO Box 338, Wilmette, tel: (708) 671-3376 leases vans specially converted for wheelchair users.

USEFUL ADDRESSES

TOURIST INFORMATION

Information on Chicago is readily available by mail, phone, or in person from:
Chicago Convention and Tourism Bureau, McCormick Place on the Lake, 2301 S. Lake Shore Dr, Chicago IL 60611, tel: 567-8500. Groups and conferences only.
Chicago Offfice of Tourism, Chicago Cultural Center, 77 E. Randolph, Chicago, 60602, tel: 744-2400. Handles general questions from the public.
Illinois Office of Tourism, 100 W. Randolf St, Suite 3-400, Chicago, IL 60601, tel: 814-4732 or (800) 223-0121.
International Visitors' Center, 520 N. Michigan Ave, Chicago, IL 60611, tel: (312) 645-1836.
Visitor Information Center, Historic Water Tower, 806 N. Michigan Ave, Chicago IL 60611. Walk-in facility only.
Mayor's Office of Special Events, 121 N. LaSalle St, Chicago, IL 60602, tel: (312) 744-3315.
General Information, tel: (312) 744-3370, 24-Hour Hotline.

CONSULATES

Argentina: 20 N. Clark St, tel: 263-7435.
Australia: 321 N. Clark St, tel: 645-9440.
Austria: 400 N. Michigan Ave, tel: 222-1515.
Belgium: 333 N. Michigan Ave, tel: 263-6624.
Brazil: 401 N. Michigan Ave, tel: 464-0244.
Canada: 310 S. Michigan Ave, tel: 427-1031.
Chile: 333 N. Michigan Ave, Suite 728, tel: 726-7097.
China: People's Republic of, 104 S. Michigan Ave, tel: 346-0287.
Colombia: 122 S. Michigan Ave, tel: 341-0658.
Costa Rica: 8 S. Michigan Ave, tel: 263-2772.
Denmark: 360 N. Michigan Ave, tel: 329-9644.
Ecuador: 612 N. Michigan Ave, tel: 642-8579.
Egypt: 505 N. Lake Shore Drive, tel: 670-2633.
Finland: 35 E. Wacker Drive, tel: 346-1150.
France: 737 N. Michigan Ave, tel: 787-5359.
Germany: 104 S. Michigan Ave, tel: 263-0850.
Greece: 168 N. Michigan Ave, tel: 372-5356.
Guatemala: 333 N. Michigan Ave, tel: 332-1587.
Haiti: 919 N. Michigan Ave, Suite 3311, tel: 337-1603.
Iceland: 221 N. LaSalle St, tel: 236-7600.
India: 150 N. Michigan Ave, tel: 781-6280.
Ireland: 400 N. Michigan Ave, tel: 337-1868.
Israel: 111 E. Wacker Drive, tel: 565-3300.
Italy: 500 N. Michigan Ave, tel: 467-1550.
Jamaica: 188 W. Randolph St, tel: 372-1202.

Japan: 737 N. Michigan Ave, tel: 280-0400.
Korea: 500 N. Michigan Ave, tel: 822-9485.
Liberia: 423 E. 60th St, tel: 643-8635.
Lithuania: 10000 S. Bell St, tel: 233-9122.
Luxembourg: 180 N. LaSalle St, tel: 726-0354.
Mexico: 300 N. Michigan Ave, tel: 855-1380.
Monaco: 1 E. Superior St, tel: 642-1242.
The Netherlands: 303 E. Wacker Drive, tel: 856-0110.
Norway: 503 W. Golf, Arlington Heights, tel: 956-6969.
Panama: 1150 N. State St, tel: 944-5759.
Peru: 180 N. Michigan Ave, Suite 700, tel: 853-6170.
Philippines: 30 N. Michigan Ave, tel: 332-6458.
Poland: 1530 N. Lake Shore Drive, tel: 337-8166.
South Africa: 200 S. Michigan Ave, tel: 939-7929.
Spain: 180 N. Michigan Ave, tel: 782-4588.
Sri Lanka: 11 S. LaSalle St, tel: 236-3306.
Sweden: 150 N. Michigan Ave, Suite 1250, tel: 781-6262.
Switzerland: 757 N. Michigan Ave, tel: 915-0061.
Thailand: 35 E. Wacker Drive, tel: 236-2447.
Turkey: 360 N. Michigan Ave, tel: 263-0644.
United Kingdom: 33 N. Dearborn St, tel: 346-1810.
Uruguay: 79 W. Monroe, tel: 236-3369.
Venezuela: 20 N. Wacker Drive, tel: 236-9655.
Yugoslavia: 307 N. Michigan Ave, tel: 332-0169.

FURTHER READING

American Apocalypse: The Great Fire and The Myth of Chicago, By Ross Miller, University of Chicago Press, 1990. A look at the rebuilding of Chicago following the fire that destroyed most of the city.

Chicago Architecture 1872–1922, Edited by John Zukowsky, Prestel-Verlag, Munich, in association with the Art Institute of Chicago.

Streetwise Chicago, A History of Chicago Street Names, by Don Hayner and Tom McNamee, Loyola University Press, 1988. A fun look at Chicago through the history of its street names.

Sweet Home Chicago: The Real City Guide, by Sherry Kent, Mary Szpur and Tom Horwitz, Chicago Review Press, 1987. A Chicago guide for residents of Chicago.

Something Wonderful Right Away, edited by Jeffrey Sweet, 1978, Avon Books. An oral history of the Second City troupe and the Compass Players.

The Plan of Chicago: 1909–1979, Art Institute of Chicago, 1979, ed. John Zukowsky.

The Chicago School of Architecture, Carl W. Condit, University of Chicago Press, 1964.

Chicago's Famous Buildings, Third Edition, University of Chicago Press, 1980, ed. Ira J. Bach.

Chicago Since the Sears Tower: A Guide to New Downtown Buildings, Mary Alice Molloy, Inland Architect Press, 1988.

Urban Blues, Charles Keil, the University of Chicago Press, 1966. Published by Stel-Verlag, Munich, in association with the Art Institute of Chicago.

OTHER INSIGHT GUIDES

Other Insight Guides which highlight destinations in this region include:

Insight Guide: Crossing America documents three routes by car, vividly portraying the people and places you'll encounter on the way.

ART/PHOTO CREDITS

Photography by

Cover, 14/15, 16/17, 18/19, 20/21, 27, 52/53, 59, 60, 61, 62, 63, 64, 68, 77, 86, 87, 88, 90, 94, 95, 96, 97, 98, 99, 102/103, 104/105, 106/107, 110/111, 113, 114, 119, 120, 130/131, 132/133, 134/135, 140, 142/143, 144, 145, 148, 149, 150, 151, 152, 153, 154, 155, 164/165, 166/167, 169, 170, 171, 172, 173, 176, 178, 182, 192/193, 195, 196, 197, 199, 200, 201, 202, 203, 204/205, 206, 207, 212, 213, 222/223, 224, 225, 226, 227, 232, 233, 234, 236/237, 239, 243, 247	**Chuck Berman**
240	**Chicago Botanic Garden**
26, 28, 29, 30, 31, 33, 34, 35, 36, 37L, 37R, 38, 40/41, 42, 46, 47, 65, 160, 161, 163, 229	**Chicago Historical Society**
32, 43, 44, 45, 49, 50, 51, 65, 70, 71, 78, 80R, 81, 156/157, 159, 162, 230, 231	*Chicago Sun-Times*
54/55, 74/75, 117, 124/125	**Eddy Posthuma de Boer**
121	**Field Museum of Natural History**
3	**Wolfgang Fritz**
24/25, 84/85, 116, 184L, 188, 208, 209, 211, 213, 214/215, 216, 220, 241, 244, 246, 248	**Luke Golobitsh**
39	**Raymond W. and Martha Hilpert Gruner**
185R	**Fernando Jones**
139	**Cathy Kleiman, Lincoln Park Zoo Society**
245	**Milwaukee Visitors and Convention Bureau**
122	**NASA**
9, 22/23, 56/57, 89, 100/101, 177, 194	**Marc PoKempner**
76, 79, 83, 91, 92/93, 118, 147, 172R, 184R, 186, 187, 221	**James Quinn**
242	**Six Flags Great America**
48, 66/67	**Topham Picture Source**
58, 138, 174, 175, 179, 183, 185L, 210, 228, 235L, 235R	**Harry Walker**
112, 115, 126, 127, 128L, 128R, 137, 146, 151, 198, 218, 219	**Margaret Wright**

Maps	**Berndtson & Berndtson**
Illustrations	**Klaus Geisler**
Visual Consultant	**V. Barl**

INDEX

R

S

T

U

V

W

X – Z

A
B
C
D
E
G
H
I
J
a
b
d
e
f
g
h
i
j
k
l